CHANGING WOMAN CHANGING WORK

CHANGING WOMAN CHANGING WORK

Nina Boyd Krebs Ed.D.

MACMURRAY & BECK

Aspen, Colorado

Printed and Bound in the United States of America
Library of Congress Catalog Card Number: 93-077399

Publisher's Cataloging in Publication
(Prepared by Quality Books Inc.)

Krebs, Nina.
    Changing woman, changing work / by Nina Boyd Krebs.
    p.   cm.
    Includes bibliographical references and index.
    ISBN 1-878448-56-0 (hard.)

    1. Vocational guidance for women.   2. Women—Psychology.   I.
    Title.

HD6057.9.K74 1993   650.1'4'024042
                                                    QBI93–659

The passages from Ruth Gendler's *The Book of Qualities* on pages 12-13, and 188, are reprinted by permission from Ruth Gendler, *The Book of Qualities* (San Francisco: HarperCollins, 1988).

Stephanie Ganic Braunstein's "Apology", which appears on pages 210-211, is reprinted by permission of the author.

"Changing Woman Said It So", which appears on page 21 is reprinted from *Meditations with the Navajo*, by Gerald Hausman, Copyright 1987, Bear and Company, Inc., P.O. Drawer 2860, Santa Fe, NM 87504.

THIS BOOK IS DEDICATED TO

ERICA SCHAFER • KAREN FLEMING

DAVID KREBS

who
ground my energy,
touch my feelings,
fire my heart,
and inspire my love.

Contents

FIRE

PASSION
AT WORK

AIR

SPIRIT:
A NEW VISION

Preface

September 1987. With our friends Elsa and Rich, my husband Dave and I dipped and swayed along a northern California Highway—the back way to Mendocino—to celebrate their marriage. A few persistent sunbeams penetrated the redwoods' darkness with their mystical optimism. We were all excited. I felt cradled in a rare opportunity to talk about my summer's experience—the intensity of a women's spirituality camp in June and then the Creativity and Madness Seminar in Aspen in August. And the deepening of my commitment to write this book.

I knew the time had come. For several years I had wanted to write another book. I had reflected, strategized, puzzled about ways to capture my profound experience working as an external consultant for a burgeoning family-owned business. I couldn't formulate that experience honestly and still safeguard the trust my client had granted me.

I'd worked over twenty years as a psychotherapist and nearly that long as a consultant. As well as the ever present home/work balancing act all of us do, I constantly wrestled with another—trying to balance my interest in working deeply with individuals with a passion for understanding and having an impact on the organizational systems in which we live our lives. I've heard thousands of stories and dealt with buckets of pain. Much of the pain has been about women struggling to live their lives fully—to honor personal connections and to thrive in workplaces that impose formidable constraints. I wanted to give something back—to share some of what I had learned about life from these women and from my own efforts as well.

In 1986, I was invited to be on a panel with economist Sylvia Hewlett, whose book *A Lesser Life: The Myth of Women's Liberation in America*, had just been released. The panel never happened, but reading the book affected me more than I wanted it to. I practically worship Gloria Steinem and the Women's Movement, but I could see that Hewlett—who takes the women's movement to task—hit the mark in some ways that resonated with my experience. The ordinary, middle-of-the-road woman—who forms a large segment of today's work force—doesn't have a voice or model for feeling powerful in her own right. Outspoken women tend to polarize the feminine by rejecting or minimizing relationships with men on one side or capitulating to the patriarchy on the other. As individuals, we gravitate toward one of these limited models and live it as if it were our own. Or, we muddle around in the middle and feel like we're nowhere in our identities as women.

I began to think about writing a book that would support today's working woman in her efforts to be more of who she really is. I started to feel strongly that the increasing acceptance of women in the work world, including middle management isn't enough. It's time for the feminine—how we think and feel as women, not as man clones—to have a voice. And that's a whole different story.

A major reason many of my clients experience so much pain in their work lives is that, on the job, they're expected to behave like men and/or be seen as inferior and treated accordingly. For too long, they—like me— bought into that model and didn't question it.

It became clear to me that the archetypal feminine invites women to be powerful in ways different from the ones to which we've grown accustomed. Not only can individual women benefit by being true to themselves rather than role playing all day long, but they have significant, as yet unacknowledged, contributions to make to the organizations in which they work. The other side of power—the grounded, connected, passionate, and spiritual feminine—belongs in business, politics, and international relations.

I have written this book about feminine power at work for women. My goal isn't to exclude men, or the masculine. I've felt constant conflict about how to include the masculine balance that is an essential part of life, a key part of any decisionmaking or implementation. Men have suffered as deeply from patriarchal distortion of the masculine as women have. They need to learn about their masculinity as well as to honor their feminine side. In so doing, they can respect the depth and complexity of the feminine in women rather than accepting only those parts that satisfy, or at least don't threaten, the patriarchal power structure. Our view of the masculine is as limited as our view of the feminine. Another book that outlines the archetypal masculine as I have tried to do here with the feminine would be a real contribution. But that is truly another subject. As I wrestled to include both feminine and masculine perspectives at each point, an already elusive subject disappeared in the confusion.

Throughout my work on *Changing Woman Changing Work*, I've tried to honor what I've come to regard as archetypically feminine—non-linearity, receptivity, presence, process, emotion, connection, wholism, nature. I love Marion Woodman's four pillars of the feminine—receptivity, presence, process, and paradox—and have kept them in mind. I've listened to people and taken in what they've given me when it rang true. Sometimes that has drastically changed my views. I've tried to stay present—write the truth as I feel it, hear it, and see it rather than bending for convenience. The process of researching and writing this book emerged from my experience. In addition to my daily work as a therapist, increasing trips to the library and interviews, I attended workshops—both on writing and on gender issues. I gave workshops for working women (and one for men) on "Feminine Power at

Work"—heard and saw their responses to the model that was forming. And I lived with paradox—logical contradictions in the feminine, such as those between solitude and connection, power and openness, passion and containment—and included them, knowing that linear logic says you can't have it both ways.

Living that paradox meant staying connected with the important people in my life while trying to find enough alone time for the book. Throughout my five years' research and writing, my friends' support has been legendary. Phyllis Watts read every word of the early manuscripts and offered supportive, insightful feedback. Mary Bolton gave me gold earrings to wear at my book-signing party when I had only just begun and has been an inspiring friend and consultant throughout. Ruth Ghio said, "Even if this book never gets published, your work has affected me deeply." Phyllis, Mary, Ruth, and Peggy Northup met with me to brainstorm when confusion and overwhelm took over. Karen Davis and Melissa Lawler, in addition to their encouragement and faith in me, generously arranged contacts and interviews in New York and Indianapolis.

Countless other friends and colleagues encouraged me, gave me material and suggestions, and attended or referred women to the workshops that helped me clarify the model. My daughters, Erica Schafer and Karen Fleming, assumed that "Mom's book" was a *fait accompli* from the beginning and offered candid, helpful comments from time to time that kept me in touch with younger women's issues at work. Judy Wavers, my sister and loving friend, also helped me tune in to work groups that I might not typically have access to. These women and too many others to name, create the web, that deep, feminine connection that supports my efforts and keeps me centered when uncertainty and self doubt threaten. They have my deepest love and gratitude.

Clients, individual and organizational, created both the inspiration and the grist for this book. Their pain and joy have shaped me as well as my writing. Over time, I've integrated bits and pieces of their stories that form the patterns of feminine power—both the strengths and the shadows. I feel privileged to have shared the lives of so many people, and I thank them for their trust in me.

The fifty or so people I interviewed in different parts of the country thoughtfully answered my open-ended questions about the feminine presence and expressed their opinions and feelings. Some influenced the structure of the book, while others added color and music. When I started the interviews I was just looking for information. When I finished I knew my soul had been touched. I'm deeply grateful to them all.

I had professional help too. Paul Aikin, my therapist and teacher of many years, taught me to value my own femininity and honor myself as an ordinary woman. Eleanor Vincent validated the conceptual strength of my earliest drafts and launched my interest in learning to write as more than an academic exercise. She told me in all sincerity that anyone could write a book if she were willing to work at it long and hard enough. Those words buoyed me when I nearly sank in the mire in the middle. Marj Stuart's editorial assistance helped me create a creditable proposal and manuscript. Consultant Jennifer McCord, in her succinct way, informed me, "You have three books here; make one chapter for each dimension and take all this other stuff out." That's when I thought I was finished, but I followed her advice, and took another year to integrate her recommendations. Katie Gartner pulled my proposal from the stack at MacMurray & Beck Communications and called me on my birthday to ask if I had sold the book yet. Her grasp of my message and capacity to transport it to the marketplace thrill and amaze me. Fred Ramey's understanding of the feminine dilemma in the workplace, his substantive suggestions, and his editorial artistry transformed the book that was almost there to a finished product.

And through it all, Dave Krebs has been my partner, friend, and confidant, reading and listening to unending versions of the feminine presence at work. Occasionally, he's offered suggestions and feedback, but mostly he's been there—unwavering in his emotional, homemaking, and financial support, understanding that it takes time away from other aspects of a relationship to write a book. His sustaining love has taught me the possibility—reminds me each day of the warmth and joy in true partnership.

It's one thing to live and study feminine process. It's another to name it. Starting with *Melting the Monolith* (too esoteric), living for a long time with *Feminine Power at Work* (too scary), I searched for a title that embraced what I wanted to say. I had pages of brainstorms—ideas from friends and family as well as my own. I felt like Coleridge's ancient mariner with the albatross around his neck. I asked anyone I thought might be remotely interested if they had suggestions for a title. I was thinking of sponsoring a contest. Throughout, I trusted that the right title would appear, but the time had come and it wasn't there.

When I admitted my woes to publisher Fred Ramey, he said, "Why don't you consider something that reflects the Native American theme you've woven through the book?" I shared Fred's suggestion with Dave who, in his own quiet way, started some serious reflection on the title project. At five o'clock one morning, he startled me by sitting up in bed. "I've got it!" he said. "Your title."

That certainly woke me up. "*White Buffalo Woman Roams the World Making Things All Better for the American Working Woman*," he said. Only years of self discipline as a therapist and consultant kept me from saying, "Oh, honey, that's interesting, but it would never fit on a book cover and besides most working women probably won't relate to White Buffalo Woman." Instead we spent the next hour or so musing about Native American spiritual images, including Changing Woman, and how those relate to the feminine and what I was writing about. I happened to have Hausman's book, *Meditations with the Navajo*, by the bedside. When I read "Changing Woman Said It So" (you'll see it in the first chapter), I wondered how finding a title could ever have been so hard.

I could write a book about writing this book. It has taught me, entertained me, challenged me, threatened me, hurt me, and given me great joy. I've had to examine myself in both sides of all thirteen dimensions that you'll find between the covers. I've tried to be honest, both with myself and in the writing, and that hasn't always been easy or pleasant. I've been surprised repeatedly to see the right quote, example, or research material appear when I needed it. That includes this little piece I found at the end of a travel book review in the *Women's Review of Books*:

> We need many more intrepid women who set out to expand both their and our concepts of the world. We need them in writing just as we need them in politics. We need that sense of adventure, of reaching wider, delving deeper, pushing further afield, whether that field be geographical intellectual, political, personal, or all of these and more. Enough with decorousness. Let us risk preconceptions and treasured philosophies, bodies and souls. Let us be big and bawdy and full of courage. Let's go.

Lesley Hazleton's paragraph proclaims what we need to do to give voice to the diverse, archetypal power of the feminine in places that count. *Changing Woman Changing Work* is a map for that brave journey.

—Sacramento, January 1993

Changing Woman Changing Work

The women's movement made it possible for women to charge into the world of business and public service and, to a limited extent, into positions of power. That we've done, with enthusiasm and competence—and with great pain. Strategically, we learned to think and act like men in order to fit in—to compete and win on a level playing field. But now, recognizing that the field will never be level, many women are sick of the charade.

A woman who has her own business and makes much less than she did as deputy director for a major state department told me, "The workplace demanded that I sever my relationship with myself to play man. I had aready been ripped off in all the right places to be a good student. I did it well. It took a long time to know that I was losing myself at the same time I was so successful. I made the decision to do without the money. Now I find that I've internalized those patriarchal values so deeply I have myself on a production quota. My loss is greater than I ever would have imagined."

Less bitter, but reflective, a government official who's still in state service said, "I used to spend hours arguing with men friends and colleagues about women's place at work. I asserted, adamantly, that there were no differences between women and men. Women just needed equal opportunity to show what we could do. I made sure that I

> *In beauty it is done*
>
> *in harmony it is written*
>
> *in beauty and harmony*
>
> *it shall so be finished*
>
> *Changing Woman said it so.*
>
> Gerald Hausman,
> *Meditations with the Navajo*

acted tough and logical to assure my credibility. Only recently have I discovered—much to my surprise—that when I look at things in my own way—which doesn't always fit the tough and logical path I learned in graduate school—and pay attention to all those feelings I work so hard to control, I'm much less stressed. Speaking from this more personal place opens new avenues or adds a different twist to what we're doing. I could have taken better care of my uniqueness all along—and made a contribution—if I had valued my differences as a woman rather than trying to erase them."

Another woman—a psychotherapist who made the transition from a hospital setting to private practice fifteen years ago—told me, "I can't believe I still do things to make men in authority like me, even when I can't stand them. I walk away wondering why I did that. When I left my job and started my own practice, I had hardly anything to do with men. My clients were nearly all women. Most of my colleagues were women. It took a long time not to lose myself—to hold my own around men. I do much better now, but I couldn't stand working in a system where my ways are automatically put down because I'm a woman. Or where I have to cater to men in authority just to do my job."

Not only does the glass ceiling still hang over the heads of women in most companies, but the feminine way—the deep, connective, reflective side of human experience—remains undervalued in our culture. Decision-making is still linear—tough and logical—throughout the business world. Authority in the workplace is almost always hierarchical. And most major government and business decisions are made as though the world were populated only by men like the decisionmakers.

Women are still not routinely heard in ways that count. Even when we get into positions of influence, we lose contact with what we know and value and can't—or

rarely do—express what we know *as women*. Instead, as Rosabeth Moss-Kanter, author of *Men And Women of the Corporation*, has pointed out, our voices and actions echo those of the men around us, though our feelings and perceptions may be in serious disagreement.

What is missing?

If women are truly to have a place other than in the lower ranks of private industry and public service, we have to do more than fit in. We have to know and value the legitimacy of our feminine viewpoint so that we can bring its wisdom to work with us and express it so that others comprehend its depth and importance. Only then will there be a real place for us as women—at the top as well as at the bottom of the pyramid. Only then will it be possible for real change to occur that brings balance to the patriarchal emphasis on power and acquisition.

We need to rethink what we mean by authority—to redefine that concept from a more reflective, feminine position that takes into account the real experience of the female half of the world's population. The bottom line can be very positively affected by feminine approaches that enhance productivity. But that isn't the only determinant of what makes good business. The quality of our lives at work and at home, the condition of our planet, the future well-being of our children and their grandchildren are important factors too.

Women have always been strong and have assumed incredible responsibility for the personal side of life. But women's ways—our focus on relationship, our emotions, our intuition, and our cyclical biology—are deemed unacceptable in the masculine work world. The feminine—mistakenly understood by many to be a prissy, fluffy, sanitized kind of thing—has been second class for so long that we assume the dominant culture is right about how we ought to be. In our attempts to fit in or to get ahead, we squeeze into masculine modes that pinch and hurt us and abandon our good judgment and best interests. In the process, we deprive the world of feminine wisdom. The result is a workplace that continues, out of balance, to follow partriarchal values that benefit the minority and ignore the long-range effects of doing business as usual.

"I can't imagine working again in a setting where men run the show and I have to be careful how I dress and what I do. Tiptoeing around fragile egos takes a tremendous amount of energy that I don't want to put out." This woman's ten-year career as a department store buyer ended abruptly over a disagreement. Recovering from that jolt, she established her own successful business as a consultant and loves the difference. "We should be able to take for granted that we can go to work and be comfortable, able to work in ways that suit us, free of harassment and other gender-related hassles," she continued, "so that we can focus on what we're trying to accomplish."

Hard-won freedom to express ourselves in our work and to be powerful in accord with our talents and interests is an important part of being a woman. But big barriers— **territoriality, sexism, prejudice, intolerance** of "women's issues"—still stand tall at work. Nothing in this book should be interpreted to deny or minimize the existence of those barriers. Collective legal and social confrontation of those long-standing problems must continue. The need for change has yet to be thoroughly digested by those in charge. But necessity is ever so slowly nudging changes into place.

The part of the process that's in the dominion of each individual is self-development. We must energetically uncover, value, and work with our feminine strengths. This happens when we pay attention to ourselves and take our own perceptions and experiences seriously. We have to understand that feminine power and wisdom are as

important and necessary as the masculine view of the world. We have much to offer a culture that currently suffers gravely from corporate inefficiencies, decreased national competitiveness, bureaucratic sluggishness, an inordinate concentration of wealth and power, and a crushing national debt.

To be taken seriously, we first have to take ourselves seriously. We must define our personal characteristics in terms of what we know and believe rather than how we've been defined by men who are threatened by our difference. Then we'll be positioned to give up our second-class roles at work, to trust ourselves, to say what we have to say, and to offer much-needed feminine balance to the daily decisions that affect all our lives.

We need to know how to be powerful *as women*—to support ourselves emotionally as well as financially—and to stay well. And we need to know how to deal with the failures that inevitably come when we take risks or push. In our own way, not as Madam Macho or a behind-the-scenes-helpmate, we can offer the strength, connectedness, passion, and spirit of the feminine to the organizations that employ us and the communities where we live.

Women who know, trust, and express their deep feminine presence offer balance to the workplace. We can shift. We can bring harmony. But first, we have to reclaim our feminine birthright.

Deep personal loss occurs when we abandon our femininity or define it narrowly in ways that conveniently support existing stereotypes. The erosion is such a subtle thing, and so culturally common, that it isn't noticeable in the early stages. It's not as if we're giving up anything we've learned to value. But to awaken at mid-life and discover we've traded our feminine souls for someone else's dream aches bitterly.

One of the great stereotypes that haunts the workplace is that to be feminine is to be weak. Little wonder. I checked my 1983 *Webster's* and found "feminine" defined this way: "having qualities regarded as characteristic of women and girls, as gentleness, weakness, delicacy, modesty, etc." The word *feminine,* isn't even listed in a leading computer thesaurus, although *masculine* is strongly and clearly defined. Learning about and expressing feminine strengths empowers us to make a dent, at least, in such limiting, outdated definitions of what it means to support and express a very important life force.

Beyond "gentleness, weakness, delicacy, modesty, etc.," the heartier stereotypes of sex goddess, maternal hearth warmer, office helpmate, teacher, or assistant to the healer only begin to express the depth and variability of the feminine. They're important aspects. But we're also equal partners, leaders, decisionmakers, lawgivers, judges, jokers, artists, and healers. We have our own ways of working that, when we're true to ourselves, differ from our masculine colleagues'. When we honor those ways, we break the roles, stereotypes, and limits we've bought into and redefine ourselves to include the full power of our femininity.

Women inherit a long line of feminine strengths. It is said that before duly recorded history, life centered on the feminine. All creatures were connected with the Earth, Gaia, the Great Goddess. Women were the lawgivers, decisionmakers, judges. It's probably too good to be true, but it is said, at least, that when the feminine principle guided all life, harmony reigned.[1]

In America, as in other parts of the world, pockets of indigenous people whose life patterns follow the cycles of nature, still honor the feminine as a major life force. Balance is central in the mythology of our country's largest group of first citizens, the Navajo. They too, have their struggles with contemporary life, but the old ways haven't been completely lost. Changing Woman, the "most highly revered and dependable" of their deities, holds amazing

We need to know how to be powerful as women— to support ourselves emotionally as well as financially.

power in the Navajo creation story. Not only can she be different elements at different times, but she loves and cares for all living things.

> . . . Holy People are powerful and mysterious, capricious and capable of every human emotion. They travel on sunbeams, rainbows, lightning . . . . Changing Woman . . . never harms Earth Surface People and can always be depended upon for aid. From her symbolic image comes the strength of Navajo woman . . . . Changing Woman confers female qualities upon the world . . . . She is the source of life, the giver of sustenance and destiny to all beings.[2]

The typical American working woman has no such symbolic image to support her strength—in part because "female qualities" aren't part of the balance. They just don't have a place at the top echelons of American business. As a result, the everyday lives of women who work away from home are out of harmony. We work in masculine ways in masculine settings. Even "feminine" occupations like teaching and nursing exist only within patriarchal structures. Since, in our culture, men define the feminine, we abandon our female qualities at work and do our best to comply with masculine expectations, as though there really is no difference between women and men.

The American way has been to attempt a blend, to create a "melting pot," rather than to accept and benefit from the rich contributions of differences. The mistaken idea that equal rights means everyone is the same—that there is a "right way," the dominant white male way, to behave and that we just have to know how to do it—leads us to cancel ourselves out. Either we become white male clones or we work hard to please the men in power. As women and people of color we've shrunk our differences to allow this blending. The scary part is that most of us have blended so matter-of-factly that we don't even know what we've lost. But the cost of abandoning our "female qualities" is too high to continue.

This book offers you an opportunity to explore your feminine presence on the job. You can become much more self-supportive and expressive at work as well as in your personal life when you understand the power of the feminine. We have to learn to take our feminine energy to work in such a way that it makes a difference. As changing women in a changing world, we have the opportunity to change work, by being who we truly are.

When she was chair of her university department artist/professor Cornelia Schulz observed that:

> For women in the workplace, the dance is very delicate. We *must* really know what we feel and think. We're not just one of the guys out there . . . .
>
> We as women are operating within a dominant masculine system with feminine bodies and souls. If we continue operating by the same value standard, we mess up in the same way they do. The only way it will be different will be if we have done very significant work on ourselves.[3]

STRENGTHS FOR TODAY'S WORK

Women are not better or worse than men, but we bring some very different qualities to work with us.

The traditional patriarchal approach to work is to maintain a clear chain of command—to know who's at the top. The resultant scramble up the pyramid requires competition and autonomy. Feminine connectedness and creativity flow more freely when women can work in collabo-

rative ways—in "web"—with less importance attached to status or position.

These approaches, of course, are diametrically opposed. Each creates different standards for what needs to happen—and how. The conflicting fears—women's of floating free and unsupported, dropped from the web, and men's of being caught in it—give rise to different feelings and ideas about what is worthwhile. As Carol Gilligan puts it: "Each image marks as dangerous the place which the other defines as safe."[4]

So our perceptions are probably accurate when we feel that we're not being heard or taken seriously. When we suggest something that smacks of collaboration rather than individual competition—a team approach where an individual has done it before, attention to childcare or job-sharing—we're flying directly in the face of an important "difference." When we try to do something in a perfectly reasonable way, the way we might do it at home, it may be unacceptable because it doesn't follow protocol or match the "correct" masculine approach. This could be true even if our way is more efficient, less costly or otherwise "better."

As she recounted a little herstory for the 20th anniversary issue of *Ms.*, founding editor Letty Cottin Pogrebin wrote:

> Trying to choose a single representative anecdote is as impossible as conjuring a soufflé by cracking open one egg . . . The *Ms.* Kids? (My twin daughters and son, along with other employees' kids, spent many a school vacation at the office—surrounded by an extended family of women—crayoning, photocopying their faces, playing in the Tot Lot . . . .) But especially I remember the cramped (donated) space at our first office, where my 'desk' was a large cardboard carton with holes

Think about what we're missing because we censor our energy and creativity until they slide un-ruffled into environments designed and defined by men.

cut into it for my knees—a far cry from the office I
had had as a book publishing executive. More than
20 years later, I have a clear image of that funky
carton, and a sense memory of the exhilaration I
felt helping to translate a movement into a magazine—surely the most fun a woman could have sitting up.[5]

So, you say, "That's the rarified feminist atmosphere of
Ms. They could do what they wanted. Most jobs aren't like
that." Right. That's the problem. Think about what we're
missing because we censor our energy and creativity until
they slide unruffled into environments designed and
defined by men.

Women who've squelched their feminine styles to succeed in business have as much trouble with webby, cooperative work patterns as men do, sometimes more,
because their sacrifice has been greater. One such woman
said as she walked out in the middle of a seminar I presented, "This is all very pretty, but I want something that
will work!"

It will.

A male attorney who is comfortable with his feminine
side, observed, "Women attorneys deal with secretaries
and legal assistants differently—they don't yell and scream.
They get their work done in a softer way, cultivate loyalty.
When I was administrator at the Court, I worked this way
and felt very effective."

An archaeologist working in an environment that most
would agree is dominated by masculine values, described
to me her experience supervising the rebuilding of an his-
toric cabin: "I greased the wheels—talked on the radio,
made sure we had what we needed—made sure people
had something to do and didn't have to just sit around and
wait for the jobs that took lots of hands. It was an exciting
thing! I don't tell people what to do. I encourage participa-

tion in planning, as well as execution—say thankyou, thankyou, thankyou. My boss said he was amazed at how I get people to work for me."

Teaching space law and policy to Air Force missile and bomber crews in North Dakota, Attorney/Professor Joanne Irene Gabrynowicz (see Wholistic Thinking) stayed very connected with her feminine presence even while she worked with defense personnel. Working tirelessly in Congress and on the campaign trail, Congresswoman Patricia Schroeder exemplifies our rich feminine heritage, the strength and energy that has been channelled through women from past ages. Facing the nation at Senate hearings in 1991, Anita Hill dared to speak about the shadow in public, relying on her core strength to sustain her.

The power of the feminine is not always so obvious, but the strength and stamina required for pregnancy and child bearing provide a physical prototype. Patience and endurance that underlie childcare aren't usually dubbed power, but they are. Finding a way to move into our power as women in a culture where we've been defined as helpmates, or "the hand that rocks the cradle," takes some doing. Poet Ruth Gendler provides imagery on the subtleties of this subject.

> Power made me a coat. For a long time I kept it in the back of my closet. I didn't like to wear it much but I always took good care of it. When I first started wearing it again, it smelled like mothballs. As I wore it more, it started fitting better, and stopped smelling like mothballs.
>
> I was afraid if I wore the coat too much someone would want to take it or else I would accidentally leave it in the dojo dressing room. But it has my name on the label now, and it doesn't really fit anyone else. When people ask me where I found

such a becoming garment, I tell them about the tailor who knows how to make coats that you grow
into. First, you have to find the courage to
approach her and ask her to make your coat. Then,
you must find the patience inside yourself to wear
the coat until it fits.[6]

Think of your feminine presence as a "power coat."
Not a man-tailored number designed to straighten your
lines and toughen your armor, but a "coat that you grow
into," that "you must find the patience inside yourself to
wear . . . until it fits." As with any garment, there will be
times when it's too heavy, pulls in the wrong places, or
just isn't right. But usually it will be warm, comforting,
attractive, and dependable wherever you go. If not water-
proof, it has the capacity to recover from an occasional
drenching.

Since you create your coat yourself, you can experiment with design—vary it with color, texture, weight, and
style. When you finish, you can say with certainty, "It has
my name on the label now, and it doesn't really fit anyone else."

DIMENSIONS OF THE FEMININE PRESENCE

The first step in bringing feminine presence to the
workplace is to name the lost dimensions of our womanly
selves. Then we can reclaim them and rely on them as
resources at work. We have to know clearly who we are,
both our strong sides and our shadows, and embrace the
dimensions of our inner selves so firmly that we don't lose
them, become fabulous fakes, or quietly fade into the
woodwork on the job.

So just what is this "feminine," this way that women
are different? Here are two big factors that make this a dif-

ficult question to answer:

1) "Feminine" characteristics shared by women and girls cover a lot of shifting ground—they change throughout a woman's life. The girl, young woman, mother, and crone (older woman) all present different feminine images. Different aspects of the feminine emerge at different stages of development and in different life situations.

2) Each of us (just as is true with men) is unique. Individually, we create our feminine presence in very different ways, and none of those ways is right or wrong, better or worse. Astronaut Sally Ride, poet Maya Angelou, glamorous star Michelle Pfeiffer, and social activist Delores Huerta are all feminine. Each of these women has emphasized different dimensions of her personality. There is no specific way to be feminine, or to be a woman.

In addition to "gentle, weak, delicate, modest, etc.," "feminine" has been stereotyped as mentally unstable, passive, and self-sacrificing. As Susan Faludi has written, the "feminine" woman has been defined as "forever static and childlike. She is like the ballerina in an old-fashioned music box, her unchanging features tiny and girlish, her voice tinkly, her body stuck on a pin, rotating in a spiral that will never grow."[7]

Does this fit you? It doesn't fit the working women I know. And it doesn't fit me either. People unconsciously confuse "femininity" with "sexuality" and with passivity.

The great archetypal energy of the feminine has had a bad rap. By continuing to define femininity so narrowly, rather than understanding it as half of life's energy in a balanced world, we forfeit our own power. This understanding must be embraced by each individual in her own way.

The measure you'll need to create your new (or refurbished) feminine power coat can be divided into thirteen dimensions. They're intangible, inexact—even contradictory at times. But they offer a framework for self-exploration and new consciousness about your strengths as a working woman.

As you work through the next chapters, you'll get better acquainted with your strengths and weaknesses in each of these dimensions: 1) Body Energy, 2) Persistence, 3) Core Strength, 4) Receptivity, 5) Flexibility, 6) Nurturance, 7) Affinity, 8) Sexuality, 9) Creativity, 10) Aggression, 11) Intuition, 12) Wholistic Thinking, and 13) Wisdom and Spirituality.

You don't have to have all of them to claim and enjoy your femininity. Some may fit better than others. Some may not fit you at all. That doesn't mean that you're not feminine.

Nor are these thirteen dimensions necessarily exclusive to women. Men are certainly intuitive, creative, and persistent, for instance. But they tend to experience and express these qualities differently from women. The thirteen dimensions emerged through my research—reading, interviewing, and working with people as a therapist and consultant for many years. If someone used the same process to identify the components of the masculine, different and similar aspects would make themselves known.

In combination, the thirteen dimensions stretch and flex to hold the complexities of the feminine. I've organized them into four groups—I) Strength and Stamina (Earth), II) Connectedness (Water), III) Passion (Fire), and IV) Spirit (Air)—to make them easier to learn and remember. If you learn to call up and rely on the strong side of each of these qualities, you'll have a firm base of self-support that will help you to move out and express yourself at work.

REAL WOMEN CAST SHADOWS

We take another step when we acknowledge the shadow side of our femininity. Of course women are intelligent, creative, and strong. But we're not all good. Like men, we have our darker aspects, which we need to deal with at work as well as in our private lives. A woman's shadow side darkens and grows when she ignores or denies it. Without the light of exposure, it distorts her vision and stains her whole personality.

All bodies cast a shadow and if we deny this body, we cease to be three dimensional and become flat—without a shadow.

C. G. Jung

Unpleasant as it may be at times, our dark side serves a purpose. As C. G. Jung so aptly put it, "Life is born only of the spark of opposites."[8] When we embrace our shadow, it fills us out. Our shadow energy propels us into contact with who we are. And if we don't take the journey consciously our shadow will sneak up behind us.

While you work to understand each of the thirteen dimensions, look at the shadow side as well as at your strengths. This is a major step in avoiding the "sweetness and light" feminine stereotype that none of us can—or would want to—live up to. We can ground ourselves with our own inner experience and pay attention to what our fear, anger, frustration, or vindictiveness tries to tell us. We don't usually need to act on these feelings, but we do need to listen to them. Here's how my shadow spoke to me one spring day.

Two weeks had passed since I had sent six chapters of a manuscript off to New York for review by a woman I hoped would work with me as a literary agent. It seemed like a major accomplishment when I paid my money at the Parcel Plus counter and, feeling as though I were giving up a body part, handed the stack of neatly printed white pages over to the clerk. Along with a whisper of vulnerability, I felt excited and optimistic—anxious to get a fresh opinion from inside the publishing profession.

I took a little vacation, tended to several long-standing obligations, read Tom Robbins' new novel, and prepared to write about the shadow.

I had collected material to write this book for months (or years, depending on how you look at it). I'd thought of several possible approaches and was ready to get my hands into the goo.

At 2:30 Easter morning I found myself wide awake. Sleep had slipped out the sliding glass door. Plunked on my stomach, right beside Ajax the family feline, was another almost equally tangible weight. It was the presence of the shadow man himself, C. G. Jung, the great psychoanalyst who gave us the shadow concept in its most developed form. For some reason I had chosen this moment to grasp the significance of a passage from his writing that implied that all of Freudian psychology was about the shadow. I got up and reread the reference:

> The result of the Freudian method of elucidation is a minute elaboration of man's shadow-side unexampled in any previous age. It is the most effective antidote imaginable to all the idealistic illusions about the nature of man . . . . [Although Jung did more than any of the early theorists to support the feminine principle, his writing resounds with "man" as the whole human race.]

That didn't help much. I slid back under the covers, tossed, and turned some more. What did I think I was going to do? Write about "the shadow" in a few paragraphs? And deal with the feminine aspects to boot?

As my husband Dave and I walked along the river, a little after the Easter sunrise, I couldn't ignore the pain that was beginning to surface. Out on the river bank with the

sun streamers lighting the purple lupine and warming the licorice-fragrant fennel, I felt small and weak.

I admitted my doubts.

"Maybe I can't do this book. It's too hard. I'm not sure that any of what I'm trying to do has any meaning to anybody but me. And how can I write about the shadow? Jung said it's all of Freudian psychology. That's overwhelming. I want to be clear and helpful to women who struggle with these issues at work. They may find this whole idea off the wall, or even repulsive. And now I'm going to try to summarize the equivalent of Freud's life work in one chapter?"

By this time, I felt like a lump of lead. To my embarrassment, tears dribbled down each cheek. Dave put his arm around me but didn't say anything. We just kept walking.

And then somewhere in my awareness a tiny bell tinkled. I was in it—deep in my own murky depths of self-doubt and criticism. I was belittling myself in a mean and sneaky way. Once again I was face to face with my shadow, staring at personal phantoms that I try to keep pushed out of sight. But they creep out and surround me when I'm insecure. I was overwhelmed by a feeling that I had no substance, no power, and that I was very, very small. A familiar refrain dinned in my ears: "I don't count at all."

I realized where I was. I could start.

My anxiety—which had stayed hidden before—about whether the agent was going to like the manuscript had nudged me without my conscious awareness into the abyss of my inner darkness. Feelings that I hadn't let myself feel had taken over. When I realized what had happened, I looked for the message I knew I'd find. It was like reaching behind a mirror.

By opening up to my pain and talking about it with Dave, I found a moment of clarity. Even though this was my unique experience of the moment, I realized it was a very familiar one. This is how my shadow feels to me. I was experiencing what I wanted to write about. That was the message that was waiting for me and what I needed to take home from the river bank. The gift in discovering my shadow—openly admitting and experiencing this hidden part of me—was that I could write about it for you. The shadow is more than theory. It's real.

As modern working women, we're encouraged to reject our shadows. To succeed, we have to be *good*— good to look at, good at our work, and good at getting along. We develop those parts of our personalities that please the people who can reward us—first our parents, later our employers. When feelings from the dark side pour into the open, they terrify or overwhelm us and those around us. We try to push the fear away. We run to the bathroom, hide our tears, or take a sick day and stay home. We can't be small and weak in public—or weepy, angry, out of control. We're simply not supposed to have, or at least display, these feelings. And the more rigid and monolithic the expectations are, the thicker our defenses become. The "woman with the flying hair," that perfect creature who lives on the cover of working women's magazines,[9] casts no shadow.

We don't need to act on our shadow urges at work. In fact that's rarely a good thing to do. But we do need to hear what she has to say. It's time to invite this shady lady into the open and view her scary features more clearly—to admit our discomfort, give her a hug, welcome her wisdom and energy. When you're so mad you see red, or feel like collapsing and throwing it all in, or get rigid and stubborn and won't move an inch no matter what, your shadow is talking to you.

Whether we acknowledge them or not, our shadow aspects are visible to others. Our defensiveness and denial, the subtle and intricate ways we try to fool ourselves,

As modern working women, we're encouraged to reject our shadows.

don't fool others. And beyond being visible, the shadow aspects act as magnets—attract the shadow energy of others—just when we need it least. We need to own these parts of ourselves without embarrassment and choose how we want to work with them. The Self-Assessment in the next chapter is a tool that can help.

We can recover from treasures that have almost been lost to modern women and bring the complexity of the feminine tangibly into our everyday lives. We can wear it to work. Before you move on to the Self-Assessment and all that follows, sit with the ancient wisdom of Changing Woman's imagery. Let her beauty and power inspire your journey:

CHANGING WOMAN SAID IT SO

CHANGING WOMAN is not changing her hair
      to suit the times. She wears it long
      when it rains. Her black hair rains down.

CHANGING WOMAN wears her heart where
      her People can see it. She has bled
      for centuries of love, none of it wasted,
      none of it lost. Out of her heart's blood,
      the corn grows green.

CHANGING WOMAN is White Shell Woman.
      She lives in the Pacific
      where Sun Father shines.
      She gives us her blessing,
      these little shells
      we wear on our neck.

CHANGING WOMAN wears white when it is cold.
      In winter we walk softly
      upon her snowy skirt. Those who leave
      hard tracks upon her do not
      receive her blessing. Those who take
      from her, rape her—spoil her
      goodness. Those who steal
      her treasure out of the soil
      cannot know the beauty of

CHANGING WOMAN; nor can they harm her.
      For her loyalty
      is beyond our measure . . .

IN BEAUTY it is done,
      in harmony it is written.
      in beauty and harmony it shall so be finished.
      Changing Woman said it so.

                Gerald Hausman,
                Meditations with the Navajo

Self-Assessment

To do it in beauty and write it in harmony, we need to embrace those qualities in ourselves. A step in that direction unfolds as we broaden our understanding of our feminine presence.

The Self-Assessment scale on pages 26-28 helps you begin your personal exploration in each of the thirteen feminine dimensions. Take a quick look at it. Then return to this page to learn more about how to use it.

The more clear and specific you make your understanding, the more available it will be for you in the future when you want to rely on it.

Changing Woman Changing Work is designed for your active participation. Since our culture rarely provides us with models of the strong feminine, we have to create our own. Like building a house or designing and making your "power coat," this task has many steps. You may first find the materials, then choose the design. Or you may know exactly how to shape your coat and then search for materials to do the design justice. Similarly, after you complete the overall Self-Assessment, you may choose to start with Body Energy and work through all thirteen dimensions in the order that suits you. Or, you may want to dash straight to Creativity or Sexuality or some other dimension that grabs your attention. It doesn't matter, so long as you work through the dimensions in a way that feels right for you.

Whatever your approach, it's important to keep track. The more clear and specific you make your understanding, the more available it will be for you in the future when you want to rely on it. Your imagination is a powerful tool. As you work through the exercises that follow, you'll think of examples—words, pictures, sounds, people—that, pieced together, form your power coat and portray who you really are. This collection of your feminine strengths, rounded by shadows here and there, will grow brighter as you learn more about all thirteen dimensions.

You may prefer working through the exercises individually if you're a person who enjoys solitary soul-searching and reflection. Or it may be easier and richer to do this self-exploration with a friend or a group so that you can discuss and compare notes. Either way (one is not better or worse than the other), the more you participate, the more you gain. Open to your experience and solidify your self-understanding.

A journal is the best tool for keeping track. When you put your thoughts, feelings, or impressions on paper—in either words or pictures—you give them form. You then can look at them and take them back in. The part of your brain that reads them is different from the part that writes or draws. You get to see who you are from a different perspective. You learn something new about yourself.

You will become better aware of your insights or emotions if you will work through the exercises, write or draw them in your journal, and then reread them. In this way, you "handle" the issue at least three times, and that will help you clarify and remember what you've revealed about yourself. As your collection of images grows, you will get to know yourself from different angles. Putting the collection on paper creates a history that will become much more meaningful as its complexity and depth become apparent.

First, though, take as much time as you need to look inward through the lens of the Self-Assessment and map out your own unique patterns. Respond to each item with

your most honest intuitive guess. Try to avoid agonizing. You're only trying to put together a rough estimate at this point and will have ample opportunity to rework your views as you proceed through the book.

The left side of the Self-Assessment represents your connection with each dimension as a source of strength. When you get acquainted with each of these parts of you, you'll see that they fit together piece by piece until your coat takes form. You'll begin to see how you share these characteristics with other women. You can learn how each of them fits you and what to expect and trust from each.

The right side, the shadow, will help you pay attention to parts of yourself you attempt to ignore or underplay. When you get them out in the open you can make some decisions about how you want to work with them. The exercises in each chapter will help you with this task.

Remember, these dimensions are clustered into four elements so you can work with them a few at a time: I) Strength and Stamina (Earth), II) Connectedness (Water), III) Passion (Fire) and IV) Spirit (Air). These categories symbolize the dynamic tension and positive contributions of the feminine. Different though they are, together they create a complex whole. They weave the thirteen dimensions of the feminine presence in a sensual way we can comprehend with our bodies as well as our minds. The "elements" provide a matrix, a web within which to explore the dimensions.

The Self-Assessment gives you an introduction to the thirteen dimensions and an opportunity to estimate the intensity of your personal response to each. You may simply want to note your place on the line. Or you may want to use the numbers as suggested. If so, 5 is a strong response and 1 is weak. It's possible to have strong responses on both sides of the continuum, weak responses on both sides, or unbalanced responses.

There is no right or wrong. This simply gives you another way to know yourself.

The most straightforward approach is to base your assessment on how you see yourself at work. But feel free to base it on the way you are at home or to register your impressions as they have been at different times of your life. Just keep your framework of time and place in mind for each completion. You might want to use different colors to record different perspectives.

Here's an example. If you think you are very nurturing in a good way, give yourself a 5 on the *Strength* side of "Nurturance." If, on the other hand, you think you provide those around you with way too much caretaking—or if you reject this quality in yourself and never do anything for anyone—that would warrant a 5 on the *Shadow* side. Work through the scale, one dimension at a time, and see what you add to your psychological self-portrait.

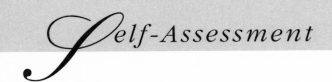
EARTH S T R E N G T H   A N D   S T A M I N A

	STRENGTH	THE SHADOW SIDE
	5 4 3 2 1	1 2 3 4 5

BODY ENERGY

Comfortable with my body and feminine cycles, good muscle tone and nutrition

Constricted, self-critical about body, out of shape, poor nutrition

	5 4 3 2 1	1 2 3 4 5

PERSISTENCE

Able to sustain; determined

Stubborn, rigid; distractable

	5 4 3 2 1	1 2 3 4 5

CORE STRENGTH

Substantial, solid self-trusting

Anxious, expect to collapse

WATER C O N N E C T E D N E S S

	STRENGTH	THE SHADOW SIDE
	5 4 3 2 1	1 2 3 4 5

RECEPTIVITY

Open, warm, compassionate

Guarded, jealous, rejecting

	5 4 3 2 1	1 2 3 4 5

FLEXIBILITY

Tolerant, open, resilient

Wishy-washy; rigid, scattered

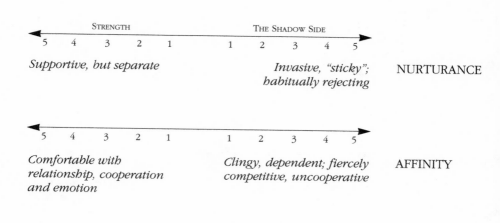

STRENGTH   THE SHADOW SIDE

5   4   3   2   1   1   2   3   4   5

Supportive, but separate   Invasive, "sticky";   NURTURANCE
                                  habitually rejecting

5   4   3   2   1   1   2   3   4   5

Comfortable with   Clingy, dependent; fiercely   AFFINITY
relationship, cooperation   competitive, uncooperative
and emotion

P A S S I O N *FIRE*

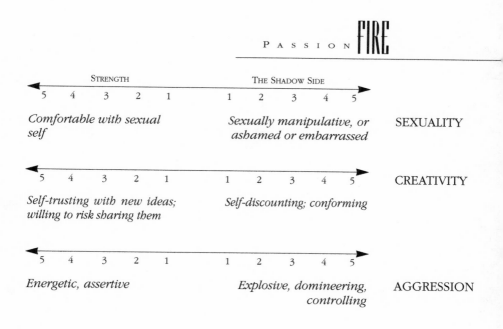

STRENGTH   THE SHADOW SIDE

5   4   3   2   1   1   2   3   4   5

Comfortable with sexual   Sexually manipulative, or   SEXUALITY
self   ashamed or embarrassed

5   4   3   2   1   1   2   3   4   5

Self-trusting with new ideas;   Self-discounting; conforming CREATIVITY
willing to risk sharing them

5   4   3   2   1   1   2   3   4   5

Energetic, assertive   Explosive, domineering,   AGGRESSION
                                  controlling

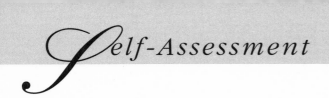

Self-Assessment

 SPIRIT

	STRENGTH					THE SHADOW SIDE				
	5	4	3	2	1	1	2	3	4	5

INTUITION — *Insightful, "tuned in"* — *Self-doubting; exclusively linear*

	STRENGTH					THE SHADOW SIDE				
	5	4	3	2	1	1	2	3	4	5

WHOLISTIC THINKING — *Futuristic, inclusive, far-sighted* — *Limited to here and now, nit-picky, critical*

	STRENGTH					THE SHADOW SIDE				
	5	4	3	2	1	1	2	3	4	5

WISDOM AND SPIRITUALITY — *Compassionate, congruent, aware* — *Judgmental, self-aggrandizing*

GUIDELINES FOR UNDERSTANDING

The chapters that follow will help you understand each of the dimensions and your experiences with them. But it helps to have an overview. Here are some guidelines for working with your Self-Assessment results. Roll up your sleeves and get started with your journal. You could, but don't have to, have a gorgeous leather-bound "blank book" with goldleaf edges. A spiral notebook works great. So do bits and scraps of paper that you keep together in a box. The notes you take will give you a baseline for future comparison. They'll also help you track your goals. Treat yourself to the slowed-down reflective enjoyment of getting to know yourself in some new ways.

• Make a list of your pronounced strengths by writing down all the dimensions (Persistence, Receptivity, Intuition, etc.) where you have 4s or 5s. These are probably dimensions you rely on without even thinking about it. Does your list of strengths fit the way you see yourself? If not, what are the surprises?

• Now make a separate list of pronounced shadow areas. Any surprises here? These dimensions may be troublemakers for you.

• Did you have all 4s or 5s on the strength side in one or more of the four elements (Strength and Stamina, Connectedness, Passion, or Spirit)? If so, you may feel more secure with these elements—less threatened by events that challenge you. This provides you a base from which to expand.

• On the other hand, if in some elements the shadow side pulled mostly 4s and 5s, you have spotted discomfort or uncertainty. Don't be self-critical. This is useful information as you work to understand some of the trouble you may have being yourself in these elements. Give yourself some time to explore and reflect upon what you have uncovered. It's useful to create a summary. Try something

like, "I am a woman who has experienced deep pain in these dimensions:_____. My fears seem to be concentrated in the (EARTH, WATER, FIRE, AIR) dimensions. I don't want to think about the way I manage my life in (EARTH, WATER, FIRE, AIR) dimensions. The shadow sides of _____ push me into situations I wouldn't consciously choose for myself."

• On dimensions where you have 4 or 5 on both the strength side and the shadow side, you are in conflict. If you have several of those in one element (Connectedness, for instance), you might want to take a look at whether you have to "play a role" in order to get by at work. If so, this probably causes you a lot of stress.

• If you're very high on the strength side in an element (Passion, for instance) when you feel safe, and exactly the opposite when you're vulnerable, you have discovered a problem area. You won't always be able to predict whether you'll feel safe or vulnerable in any particular situation. It will be important for you to avoid making commitments from a strong place that may overwhelm you at another time when you feel less sure of yourself.

• If 1s and 2s are the most frequent numbers on your Self-Assessment, it's hard for you to name and respond to your various inner communications. You will be able to learn more about yourself as you pay more attention to these inner messages.

• Note your overall impressions in your journal. Here's an outline: "I am a woman who feels more substantial with the (Strength and Stamina, Connectedness, Passion, Spirit)_____ element(s) than with the others. I feel strongest in the dimensions of _____. It appears that my least developed element is (Strength and Stamina, Connectedness, Passion, Spirit)_____. My areas of exploration and work (my 4s and 5s on the shadow side) are_____. I seem to have conflicts in these dimensions (4s and 5s on both ends of the same continuum)_____. I have trouble being clear in (1s and 2s)_____ and look forward to exploring these dimensions more. Overall, it appears that my greatest strengths are_____.

A Shift Into the Feminine

In order to know and express yourself, you have to live in all of you, including your femininity. It won't do to hang out in a few safe parts. You can be who you are at work as well as in your private life. That's what this book is about.

This will be something new and different for the American workplace. If you've been working overtime to beat men at their own games, or to please them so that you'll be appreciated, it will be a major shift for you. But when you shift securely into the feminine at work, you'll find that your confidence grows. Your approach might differ from the standard way of doing things, but it will feel right for you. If others criticize you, you'll be able to listen for the constructive parts. Differences won't feel so threatening or demeaning. Compared to your masculine colleagues, you may invest more time and energy in the personal part of work or in solving values conflicts that emerge there—and you'll feel good about doing so. Moving around at work will become easier and help to generate a sense of well-being about your body. You will be able to contribute your ideas, trusting that they are worthwhile and that you deserve to be taken seriously. Your power coat will fit.

For now, you've sketched your feminine strengths and completed a preliminary assessment. The next chapters will take you more deeply into each of the thirteen dimensions and their shadows. Before you continue your exploration, take time to reflect on what you've learned about

yourself so far and to write down new ideas that came to you as you worked through your Self-Assessment. There will be more to come, but your early impressions are important ones.

As you read through the rest of the book, return to your Self-Assessment and update it based on the new understanding you acquire with each chapter.

EARTH

STRENGTH AND STAMINA

Earth: The Element

In 78 percent of subsistence cultures surveyed, it is usually women who gather and carry home fuel—usually firewood. In 15 percent, men usually do this work . . .Women are the usual water-carriers in 89 percent, and they usually carry the other burdens in 59 percent.[1]

From the beginning of time, women have done heavy work as the water carriers and burden bearers in most places in the world. We do tasks that require physical strength, persistence, and stamina. "But," you say, "that was then, this is now. That isn't me. That may be true in third world subsistence cultures. But ours is different!"

Take another look. Here's what Arlie Hochschild found in her research for *Second Shift: Working Parents and the Revolution At Home*:

. . . I began with the measurable issue of time. Adding together the time it takes to do a paid job and to do housework and childcare, I averaged estimates from the major studies on time use done in the 1960s and 1970s, and discovered that women worked roughly fifteen hours longer each week than men. Over a year, they worked an extra month of twenty-four-hour days a year. Over a dozen years, it was an extra year of twenty-four-hour days. Most women without children spend much more time than men on housework; with children, they devote more time to both housework and children. Just as there is a wage gap between men and women in the work place, there is a "leisure gap" between them at home. Most women work one shift at the office or factory and a "second shift" at home.[2]

As much as the nature of the work may have changed, the need for endurance seems to stay the same. Where did we get this business about being the "weaker" sex? It doesn't reflect now, and never has in any major way, the experience of any but a few women's lives.

Most women are different from most men in terms of muscle mass and short bursts of energy. But that is not to say we are weak. Feminine strength and stamina are formidable forces, and we can take better care of ourselves when we know how those forces operate in each of us. We can contact and appreciate our own energy shifts, ebbs, and flows, if we understand our *Body Energy. Persistence* and *Core Strength* are reliable dimensions we can develop and trust to keep us together in hard times.

Here's one example of a petite, "older" woman, trusting her strength and stamina to accomplish the almost impossible, which made a difference in a lot of people's lives.

Sacramento's Mayor Anne Rudin, in her mid 60s, had been on the City Council for twenty years—in the top spot for eight. Her leadership style evolved over that time and she weathered the pressures of life at City Hall with her integrity intact. When I asked her about some of her accomplishments as a leader,[3] she shared this example of strength and stamina that supported her skill and feminine strategy in solving a very tough problem:

"When the symphony almost went under in 1985, I stepped in between the musicians and the board. Persistence was one of the qualities that helped me. It had been a long, bitter dispute and everyone had nearly given up. We were on the verge of losing one of our city's major assets.

Feminine strength and stamina are formidable forces, and we can take better care of ourselves when we know how those forces operate in each of us.

"My way of doing things is to bring people together. I always see that as mobilizing resources that you need. I knew the right people to call. It happened that our labor negotiator was not busy with other city issues at that time. I called on the Chair of the County Board of Supervisors, Illa Collin, and she agreed to help. We told the players and the symphony management that we were willing to sit down with them.

"We began on a Saturday morning and we met, literally, day and night. There were some nights we got away, but sometimes we met through the day and through the night.

"One morning around 4:00, I was beginning to read the signs, when it was time for pushing, when it was time to hold back—when they had put enough of their demands on the table—the give and take. Anyhow, everybody got angry and the musicians just stormed out. They said we weren't getting anywhere.

"But I could see that we were. I could also see, though, that they did not know how to present what they needed. So at 6:00 A.M. I called a representative of the local musicians union—told him that I needed help. He called the musicians and offered his assistance if they would accept.

"By the middle of the afternoon, we had an agreement. He knew how to present their demands for them and how to give and take a little. . . ."

Mayor Rudin didn't give up. She used common sense and good judgment, creativity, and contacts to make the process work. Her sensitivity to non-verbal communication helped her read participants' emotional reactions and work effectively with the embattled groups.

But the part that all of us can learn from is that she provided leadership by hanging in there. Through the long days and nights of tension and disagreement, she refused to fold. "Women do things differently. It was different to have Anne and Illa involved," she heard later from the secretary of one of the men who had participated. The power inherent in the Mayor's position and her skill were certainly factors. But her feminine presence and that of her colleague—the special qualities they brought to the process—also made a difference in the way things went.

The Mayor felt that one of the differences was that she and Illa could see people's reactions—body language and movement. And another was that she asked for help.

When I questioned her about how she sustains herself in the midst of the conflict and controversy that are part of her job, her response reflected what I call core strength. "When I feel like I'm doing the right thing," is how she said it. "And from knowledge. I make it a point to understand the issues." She also dips into that deep well of feminine power, connectedness: "I do get upset sometimes. But I get strength from other people—from constituents. My public gives me emotional support—moral support—and the feeling that I did the right thing."

Although this example portrays the experience of a feminine political leader, the same strengths that helped her through that long week and through other times of stress can support you in your work life. Manager, line operator, secretary, nurse, executive vice president—whatever your job—you face intense demands on your physical and emotional energy. The earthy, everyday qualities Mayor Rudin relied on to sustain her—endurance, persistence, core strength—along with learning more about how to appreciate and nurture your body energy—are the focus of the next three chapters.

Regardless of the work you do, the power in these dimensions, *Body Energy, Persistence,* and *Core Strength,* is available to you. They provide a solid foundation that differs from stereotypes of the "weaker sex" and from much of what we've learned by imitating the masculine way. They have to do with being grounded and staying in your center, rather than indulging in "learned helplessness" or toughening your shell.

The qualities of vulnerable strength (the capacity to withstand, flex, and not collapse) and endurance are legitimate in the business world, as well as at home, for both women and men. The energy and stamina of the strong feminine in a woman who knows and trusts herself grow from a different center than the facade of macho toughness she has learned to use as armor to survive at work.

Susan Griffin's portrayal of earth and sisterhood symbolizes the strength and stamina of the feminine—the deep connection with nature that sustains the species.

> . . . This earth is my sister; I love her daily grace, her silent daring, and how loved I am, how we admire this strength in each other, all that we have lost, all that we have suffered, all that we know; we are stunned by this beauty, and I do not forget: what she is to me, what I am to her.[4]

The power of this poem calls for images that differ from stereotypes of femininity as weak or passive. It speaks to that part of womanhood that "the woman with the flying hair" flies right past. It does, though, give us a glimpse of the strength and stamina of our feminine presence.

Body Energy

Generations of

working women

have learned to

dress like men,

move like men,

think like men.

But we can't feel

like men.

The feminine presence is physical, and so the atmosphere shifts when women move into settings that have been dominated by the masculine way. Whether it's vibrant, sensuous and earthy, or quiet, calm and airy, feminine energy changes work. The female body brings a basic connection with nature—with birth and death, with moon cycles, and with the continuity of human life. When we know about and value this precious dimension, it energizes our work. It's exciting. And it complicates matters for men who are accustomed to working mainly with other men, or with women as support staff, not as equals.

The mysteries of feminine biology—bleeding and not dying, pregnancy, the end of monthly bleeding in midlife—are profound. The feminine life cycle doesn't fit neatly on the competitive, upward angles of a career ladder. We deal with frustration, shame, blame, and, in our struggles, can come to regard our biology as negative—an inconvenience, a hindrance to our careers. Feminine energy, this connection with life cycles in the workplace, offers a form of rebirth if we can learn to recognize its value and listen to it rather than trying to hide it.

Increasing numbers of women hold positions of responsibility at work as well as at home. The patriarchal establishment can't ignore family needs the way it always has. Now organizations have to take seriously things like childcare, flex-time, family leave, and other so-called "women's issues." Maybe someday in the distant future it will become apparent that the solution is to provide space for these needs in all the places women work, so that birthing and caring for the next generation escape the label "women's issues." But for now, the difficulty and threat of making these changes erects blinding barriers that interfere. It's much easier to expect inconvenience and disruption than it is to grasp the contributions our feminine ways of working can offer. When we regard our biology as negative, we buy into the notion that we are the problem.

One way we've tried to secure our position, and to make ourselves less trouble, is to masculinize—to ignore or reject our feminine bodies. This has been a slow and subtle process and it's causing a lot of damage. (See the Sexuality chapter.) Generations of women have learned to minimize feminine differences on the job—to dress like men, move like men, think like men. But we can't feel like men. And so we develop two personalities, one for work and one for whomever we are without the armor. Men do the same thing, but since the workplace is, by design, usually more compatible with masculine style, the differences aren't as dramatic for them.

There is another way. That is to appreciate our very real, feminine difference and use it to enlighten and inform our work, whatever it is. We have a wonderful opportunity to bring the feminine presence to the workplace. One of the simplest, most direct ways we can do this is to pay attention to what our bodies tell us.

Nancy K. Jungerman, a psychotherapist respected not only for her work with individuals and families, but also as a resource to other therapists, shared this story:

> A therapist in one of my consultation groups became pregnant with her first child in her late thirties. Although she had many years of psychotherapeutic experience in a variety of work situations, she admitted to becoming uncomfortable with her clients and so unsure of how to deal with the reality of her

pregnancy that she found herself pretending that nothing would change. Her denial and self-criticism temporarily blinded her to the creative possibilities that her pregnancy offered in terms of enriching and deepening the therapy.

In the workplace, if you're trying to do something that is not in accordance with your feminine nature, you feel like you're not doing it right—feel inauthentic. We get into self-evaluation that comes from a model that isn't felt as inherent.

The young therapist I mentioned was able to shift—to use what was forming in her to work with her clients. When she didn't get defensive about clients' responses to her pregnancy and planned absence, those feelings became part of the therapy, as they should be.[1]

Whatever job we do, we can use our feminine presence to enrich the workplace. Obviously, since they can't be masculinized, pregnancy, lactation, even premenstrual syndrome (PMS) and menopause, add qualities that change the usual way of doing things. These very feminine conditions may be inconvenient on the job. They may reduce certain kinds of efficiency. But when we pay attention to them, they can also contribute an awareness of the life process that makes a difference in workstyle, policy decisions, the very products that are created. Subtle and not-so-subtle forms of abuse that men have tolerated or perpetuated stand out prominently when pregnant workers are involved.

It's not just the drama of menstruation and childbearing, though, that deserves attention. Whether motherhood is part of our lives or not, women aren't just men with curves. Our bodies, our rhythms, and our energy flows differ from masculine ways of being. Learning to honor our feminine body energy on the job is a function of how we dress, move, and feel about ourselves, as well as of how we go through our cycles. We work best when we know and respect our body energy.

Strength and stamina, the capacity to endure, are very much a part of feminine body energy. Achieving hard-body toughness is a questionable goal for most women, but learning about and appreciating our physical strength and stamina, as well as accepting our vulnerability, is invariably reassuring to us. Childbirth, childcare and other "women's work" have always required physical strength and endurance. As we've shifted to a culture where most women work away from home, while taking most of the responsibility for home and childcare, we ignore our needs for physical exercise. Who has time? But physical well-being and activity help both women and men to develop self-confidence and ease with our bodies.

Care for and trust your physical competence—based on how you feel, not necessarily how you look—and you will establish a strong base for self-reliance. One summer—in the face of a long history of dedicated non-exercise—I trained for and successfully completed a ten-mile run. For a non-athlete, middle-aged at that, the feeling of physical accomplishment provided real support for the long, hard days my work requires at times. My increased physical stamina helped me feel much stronger emotionally—more able to stand my ground, less likely to cave in to manipulation.

You don't have to run ten miles to tune in to your physical strength. But it will help if you create your own physical conditioning program. When you learn to listen to them, your muscles can provide you with potent information about how you are affected by what's going on around you. Through exercise and conditioning, you can know and love your female body, a key to understanding your feminine presence.

Another step requires coming to terms with the ebb

and flow of hormonal cycles. Other than attempting to deny they exist, we haven't dealt with the realities of female biology on the job. To reduce our threatening presence, we've pretended that the mysteries of the feminine don't exist. We make believe that we're just men in skirts.

Painful menstruation or agitating PMS become inconvenient, for some women even difficult, enough to interfere with daily activities. Psychiatrist Lesley Schroeder, a specialist in this area, estimates that 15% of women suffer from PMS that is so disruptive they seek treatment.[2] In a world organized around men's ways, women buy into negative, self-critical views (the popularity of PMS jokes might be a clue) and we reject ourselves at this deepest, cellular level. An alternative is to acknowledge the realities of emotional ups and downs and take special care of ourselves when we need to.

We need to find ways to be practical, productive, and efficient, and to honor our feminine biology as well. If we know ourselves and respect our physical and emotional fluctuations, we can learn to work around the difficulties we have rather than denying them or feeling inadequate. This means taking time off or arranging for a lighter work load if we need to, reducing our work schedule during some times in our lives, knowing the times when we may be particularly vulnerable and when it requires more energy to focus. At times, we may really need to work alone, or really need to work with others. Our strengths fluctuate, too. At times, we may have the energy to "move mountains" or more than usual access to sharp intuition.

Historians tell us that menstruation was seen as magical, valuable in some ancient civilizations. Women took part in rituals where they returned their menstrual blood to the fields to fertilize the soil.[3] This approach probably doesn't have much appeal for today's woman, but we can learn, with new respect for our femininity, to love our bodies and cease to regard our periods as "the curse."

Those menstrual huts we've heard about where anthropologists tell us women went during their periods weren't necessarily about being ostracized from the rest of the group. They were also about women being together to tend to women's interests—education, humor, tradition, and taking a break.[4] What a concept!

Your feelings about your body—your level of self-acceptance or self-rejection—determine whether you relate to others openly or defensively. If you hate your body, you're likely to assume that others hate it, too. Bogged down by your own negative views, you may maintain a defensive stance—expecting to be criticized or ridiculed. If you talk about hating your body, or what you don't like about it, you invite others to think less of you. Each of us is in charge of how we live in our bodies and present them to the world.

To reduce our threatening presence, we've pretended that the mysteries of the feminine don't exist.

Routinely, feelings about our bodies are complicated by the "dress code." The uniform for professional or office jobs has been dresses or suits, high heels, and pantyhose. Some women find this way of dressing comfortable and enjoyable. Many, especially large women, suffer daily in attempts to fit round bodies into the straight (masculine) lines of "business" clothes.

The project was a success if the goal was to design clothing to keep us off balance. Just try to ride your bike to work, pick up your three-year-old, or move boxes in your professional straitjackets. Traditional women's business dress style cramps the healthy nobility of our body energy. It also communicates the feminine in a safe, male-defined way, rather than in a way that feels comfortable or expressive for women. "It's a good idea to wear shoulder pads; they de-emphasize your breasts," her female boss advised one of my clients. Maybe this is necessary protection around some men, but consider what it says about being a woman.

Here's what Catherine Steiner-Adair found in her

research with fourteen- to eighteen-year-old girls.[5] When asked how they think the culture views the ideal woman, they said: She's thin, rich, fit (hard-bodied), youthful, tall, pretty, dressed-for-success, energetic, carries a brief-case. Doesn't this fit the images you see on the newsstand? Except for "pretty," this describes a young, privileged, adult male.

When asked what would make them happy in their own lives—in other words, what do they value?—the young women in the study said: girl friends, a relationship (husband), children, money, career, and home. Their personal goals have more to do with their femininity—with connection and relationships—than with being at the top.

The young women who were grounded in their own values, who didn't buy into the "ideal image," were the ones who felt more sure of themselves. The researchers found that the woman who doesn't realize that her personal values are central and important—regardless of her body shape and size—is much more likely to suffer from one of the most prominent emotional disabilities of our time—eating disorders (anorexia, bulimia, obesity). This sometimes life-endangering form of self-hate is disturbingly frequent among women today. While, on the planet, large populations are starving and others have food stored and spoiling, we have become a culture that is fanatic about what and how much we eat.

The rounded feminine form, the basic female body shape, has become an object for self-hate and for rejection by others. Catherine Steiner-Adair estimates that in the female population 10-15% may be naturally tall and thin. Most of us aren't. Just like men, we're energetic sometimes but not all the time. Unlike men, we're likely to spend the money we make on our appearance—having something done to our hair, skin, bodies or buying clothes.[6]

If, in fact, our culture sees the successful woman as a tall, thin, hard body, then round women—that is most of us—have a harder time with credibility. We need to know how to take care of ourselves in this situation, how to talk about feminine strength and the reality that women's ways make an important contribution. And if we do happen to fit in that tall, thin picture, we may need to be especially supportive and compassionate with our own femininity. In that spot, not only are we more likely to be accepted as one of the boys and supported for our masculine side, we're more vulnerable to the jealousy and suspicion of our rounded sisters.

In some areas, slight changes are afoot. Broader ranges of dress, workstyle, and scheduling are increasingly acceptable. But these shifts need encouragement from all of us. When you're willing to push the limits and create traditions of comfort rather than conformity, you free up your energy and support the powerful feminine—not the stereotype or the male-defined idea of attractiveness.

For some women workers, physical fitness is not an option. Many do strenuous work because that's all they can get. Others choose heavy work to get equal access to high-paying jobs in non-traditional areas or to satisfy a personal preference. Those of us who perform non-traditional work have to be strong emotionally as well as physically. We can learn to deal with taunts and tests in ways that fit our femininity—to connect with others and with our own strength. Then we won't have to prove that we're one of the boys. By teaming with another woman or a supportive man, we can check out our viewpoints and don't have to endure the stress alone.

Women who do non-traditional work are a serious financial threat to the male blue-collar establishment and usually have to deal with harassment. But we are more successful on the job if we avoid attempts to compete in a masculine way. We can learn to rely on our own inner resources—what feels right for us—rather than copying the way the tough guys do it. Feminine strength and stamina are about holding our ground, staying with the task, and weathering it through to completion. There is tremendous power in this approach.

Janet Nielson, an urban police detective with more than twenty years' service, the first officer in her city to get pregnant and the first of her department's women officers to win the Medal of Valor, provides a classic example. Out of uniform, Janet's round, open face and easy manner wouldn't tag her as an officer of the law. She melted the stereotypes I had about women who do this work.

She told me that she learned to develop "a presence" when she was on patrol rather than rely on physical force. Knowing that a tough, intimidating style wasn't right for her, she learned from other, male, officers who maintained authority through body language and de-escalated conflict whenever they could. She found she was taken seriously when she carried herself with authority, maintained eye contact, and spoke in a firm but gentle way. Effective use of humor helped, too. She didn't have to use he-man tactics to be taken seriously.

Janet's realistic, understated approach fits her femininity even though she learned it from her male colleagues. Her strong feminine style has been successful for her in a stressful and sometimes violent occupation. Not that it's been easy. She put up with hazing and rejection from some of the other officers, including some potentially dangerous harassment.

When she was pregnant, she said the only rule was "you were out of uniform, off the street. Pregnant police officers weren't assigned to public duties. They put me in the radio room, treated me as if I were sick, not pregnant. I got swing shift projects and was labeled 'long term disabled.' After a while I changed shifts and went back to running investigations."

"Some women," she continued with a frustrated tone, "have been absolutely confined to office work, not allowed to have any contact with suspects or go out on investigations while pregnant." Pregnant women, like women in all other phases of our lives, are capable of deciding how much and what kind of work to do throughout our terms. Treating pregnancy as illness is discriminatory and undermines women at work.

Janet observed that years ago, when pioneering women first joined the department, they tended to masculinize themselves so they could fit in. She pointed out that when women go into patrol, many try to become one of the boys. In her view it takes them two to five years to find out that they'll never gain acceptance in that way. The first weeks on patrol, she had to learn to walk differently, with her arms out so she didn't bump them on her gun all the time. All of a sudden she became aware that she wasn't 'feminine' either. Lots of women try to get into manly sports, get really good at shooting, go out hunting ducks or deer, or go drinking after work. It can't work. "Each of us," Janet concluded the interview, "has to earn respect. If you're a woman, you have two strikes to start."

Through it all, Janet created her own effective style in an occupation where masculine toughness and aggression are the standards of comparison. She listened to others, tried different ways of working, and persisted until she found a way to maintain her deep connections with her feminine presence.

THE SHADOW

Body Energy casts its shadow with subtlety for many, cruel obsession for others. We may experience it through the perpetual search for the perfect body—addiction to exercise—the tyranny of the bathroom scale. Some of us attempt to deaden personal pain or fear with alcohol or other drugs. Others experience life from the neck up only—denying the existence of a physical self. We mirror the cultural negativity toward the feminine when we hate our bodies for the inconveniences that are part of PMS, menstrual cramps, pregnancy, or menopause. When we hate our bodies we are living in our shadow.

At work, we may express discomfort with our body energy in different ways. We may be compulsive about how we look, obsessed with having to be perfect. Or we might pay no attention to our appearance. We're likely to be catty about how others look, and feel vulnerable and insecure when something or somebody reminds us of our own discomfort.

All bodies are beautiful, contrary to what many of us have learned.

The shadow can restrict movement so that we walk rigidly, stiffly concealing anything that resembles femininity. Insulation becomes thick. No expression leaks through. One woman said to me, "I'm totally asexual at work—don't feel anything. I never get harassed. And it has cost me a lot. I've been doing it for so long, I don't have a clue about how to meet and relate to a man outside work. Either I'm totally discombobulated and fall head over heels for him, or I keep him at such a distance there's not a chance to get anything going." Although she's struggling to contact her feminine presence again, this woman has spent a major part of her career experiencing her body energy as a liability rather than an asset.

We can become so busy—or so sedentary—that we ignore the body's basic need for exercise. "I don't have time, I don't like exercise, I'm not the athletic type," the shadow says to justify neglect. Sleep problems, general sluggishness, and poor muscle tone clue you in to this one.

One of the shadow's meanest forms is illness. One symptom after another grabs the foreground. The body speaks about pain or self-hate you can't deal with directly. You may become preoccupied with physical symptoms; or accidents may happen to you, and happen again. If this feels like your history, consider the possibility that your shadow's trying to say something to you. One of my clients said to me, "My husband must get tired of hearing about all my illnesses. First I have a cold, then I sprain my ankle, then I get a bladder infection. I'm always sick." This basically healthy woman hates her job but doesn't want to risk looking for another. Her shadow is screaming at her.

If you find yourself driving down the street thinking, "If I had just a little accident I could be off work and someone (?) would take care of me. . . ," listen! Get more assertive about asking for what you need. Or, "maybe I'll get the flu and not have to finish the budget by the end of next week. . ."—take a look at your relationship with your body, at how you may be working against yourself. All of us face work crunches from time to time and dive into overwork. But if getting sick is the way you take the time off, create more active strategies for getting the rest you need. The time off will be the same whether it's spent in misery or on scheduled "mental health days."

The shadow side of body energy is a basic rejection of self, so it makes just about everything else problematic. All bodies are beautiful, contrary to what many of us have learned. If this is an area that's difficult for you, as it is for many women, give yourself permission to explore it now, and linger with this dimension as long as you like.

SELF-REFLECTION

Use the following ideas as guides to estimate how comfortable you are with your body energy. Look at your strong points first. Learn all you can about your strengths. Then begin an exploration of the part of yourself that is more difficult to accept—the shadow side. Often, what we learn by delving into the murky, confusing chaos of the shadow helps us understand and become more open to what our darker feelings are trying to tell us.

STRENGTH: I love my body. I exercise regularly and stay fit. I wear comforting clothes to work. I'm comfortable with my feminine cycles. My body is a source of pleasure. I feel grounded most of the time. I trust my body.

SHADOW: I hate my body. I exercise to attain perfection. / I never exercise. I hate my periods. I hate being a woman. / I ignore my body, wish I didn't have it. / I abuse my body with alcohol or other drugs. / I know I have a beautiful body and use it to control men. / My body betrays me.

Take time now to design and commit to a fitness plan that supports your body energy. Work on one that you know you can complete. Avoid fantasies of a total "remake." You may want to select one or two of the exercises that follow as a primary focus. Start today by shaping your routine to pay attention to your body energy. Write this commitment to yourself in your journal, and keep track of how you're doing as time goes on.

TIME FOR YOURSELF

Women aren't just men with curves. Give yourself permission and time to regard your body energy at work as important, even if your job requires little physical exertion. For many of us, just getting to work takes stamina. When you're securely grounded and your energy flows freely, you're in a stronger position to expect others to take you seriously.

Here are exercises—some mental, some physical—that have to do with your body energy. It helps to make clear in your mind what you're trying to accomplish. Select the steps that appeal to you and take notes in your journal. Then stretch, bend, breathe, and enjoy the glory of your body energy!

As you read through the exercises after each dimension, select a few that are most appealing to you. The idea is to experiment and become more conscious of each dimension. If you try to do them all, you may get overwhelmed and stuck—which will do you no good and just may keep you from addressing the other dimensions covered here. Go easy on yourself; sample and enjoy.

• LOVE YOUR FEMALE BODY—whatever its shape or size. If you find yourself being judgmental, see if you can figure out whose judgment you're using. Is it truly your own? Would you trust the source of this judgment in other important areas of your life? In your journal, write a loving statement (a list, a poem, or a description) that honors your body.

• FIND A WAY to take exercise seriously. A regular exercise program that conditions your cardiovascular system and muscles is by far the best for stress reduction and maintaining your strength and stamina. If you're basically healthy, check your bookstore or library for books on basic conditioning. Consultation at the gym or workout center can help you design a program that fits you. If you have physical limitations or health problems, your chiropractor, physical therapist, or physician can help you design a program to meet your needs.

• COMPROMISE if daily exercise is impossible. An option is a 30-40 minute jog or walk, three or four times a week. Coupled with some stretching and deep breathing, exercise also serves as a chance to think your thoughts and feel your feelings.

• IF YOU ABSOLUTELY CAN'T FIND TIME to exercise on a regular basis, use household activities as a way to breathe deeply and stretch your muscles. Exaggerate your stretching movements if you make the bed. Bend from the waist and breathe deeply if you pick up the daily mess. Use deep breathing while loading or unloading the dishwasher. Stretch as you reach into the cupboard. Romp with the kids—yours or a friend's. Use the stairs at work rather than the elevator. Remember, perfection isn't an issue here. Every little bit helps.

• TAKE A CLASS. Yoga, aerobics, and dance classes provide opportunities for exercise, reflection, and social contact. Even learning a few simple yoga positions can make a real difference. "Mountain" pose is great for standing in grocery store lines and the "Salute to the Sun," in just a few seconds, wakes up all your muscle groups to start the day.

• PAY ATTENTION TO YOUR BODY ENERGY AT WORK. If your job requires that you sit most of the time, get up and walk around every hour. Stretch and breathe deeply. If you spend most of your time at work on your feet, find ways to stretch, relax, and breathe.

• WEAR CLOTHES THAT ARE COMFORTABLE—even comforting—things that feel good and allow for easy movement. If you wear a uniform, find some way to be yourself. Treat yourself to underwear that you really like, a special pin that has meaning for you or a scent that you can enjoy all day long.

• STASH A PAIR of walking or running shoes for lunchtime walks. They can be just the ticket to letting go of some tension on an impossible day—even if you use them rarely. Better yet, use them often.

• TUNE IN TO YOUR MUSCLE STATE at work. Are you holding tension in your shoulders? Your jaw? Your back? Exaggerate the tension and then relax. Breathe into the tense places. Pay attention to what the tightness is telling you. Is the location meaningful? The source? What are you holding in—or out? This focused attention requires no extra time and can be done at your desk or work station without drawing attention to what you're doing. If you take notes in your journal, you may begin to identify a pattern that you can work with.

• PAY ATTENTION TO HOW YOU SIT. Think about being grounded—centered. When you let yourself curl over, you squeeze the energy out of your center and become more tired. When you find yourself collapsing of your own weight, get up, walk around, stretch, and breathe deeply.

• FIND OUT whether your nutritional practices help or hurt your body. Eating disorders have become a common way for us to express self-rejection. If you're a junk food junkie or fad dieter, you might want to ask yourself why. Write the answer in your journal in some detail.

• KEEP TRACK of your menstrual cycle if PMS or other symptoms cause you stress at work. Learn when your emotional and physical ups and downs are most likely to happen. Develop a strategy for self-care that reduces your work load at times you can guess are going to be most difficult for you.

• IF YOU HAVEN'T DONE SO already, look into some of the ancient feminine lore that is positive about the feminine body—including the cycles of fertility, reproduction, and old age. *Women Who Run with the Wolves*, by Clarissa Pinkola Estes; *The Crone: Woman of Age, Wisdom and Power*, by Barbara Walker; *The Chalice and the Blade*, by Rianne Eisler; and *To Be a Woman*, by Connie Zweig, all provide different glimpses of this material.

• HERE'S AN EXERCISE for home. Try a body awareness exercise when you have some time to yourself at home. Margaret Fjelstad, Ph.D., suggested this one that takes about twenty minutes and is amazingly grounding and self-loving.

Sit in a comfortable place. Close your eyes. *Slowly* feel your hair, touch your scalp and massage it. Feel your face; stroke it. Give yourself a neck massage. Explore and massage one shoulder and arm and hand. Repeat on the other side. Feel your chest and breasts. Breathe and expand. Explore and massage under your ribs and across your belly. Move your shoulder blades, reach around and massage down the spine with your thumbs. With your hands, squeeze and massage both hips. Lie on your back, explore and massage each thigh, calf, and foot.

We usually don't massage ourselves long enough to get any effect. This helps you see that you can lovingly care for your own body.

Return to the Self-Assessment Scale on page 26. How powerful are the pulls for you on each side of body energy? Are you happy with this? If so, great! Would you mark it now the same way you did when you read through the Self-Assessment the first time? Take a minute to make any adjustments that will make it reflect your self-understanding now. It helps if you make changes in a pen that's a different color from your original markings.

STAYING GROUNDED

In the first two chapters, as you initially worked through the Self-Assessment Scale and explored the thirteen dimensions of your feminine presence, you tuned in to your strengths and weaknesses. You have new possibilities to explore in self-development and new awareness of your shadow side and how you express it. As you gain comfort with both sides of each of your thirteen dimensions and how you experience and express them, new confidence should emerge. How can you live them on a daily basis and bring them into the workplace in a way that supports your feminine power there?

It's one thing to travel inward—to gain appreciation for your feminine presence—in the protection of home with a friend, in a workshop, or in your therapist's office. It's another to take your vulnerable new way of understanding yourself to work.

Ground yourself first by taking stock of where you are. Find a quiet minute or two each day to bring your current state into your conscious awareness. Here's a quick checkup you can do at your desk or while you repair your frazzled hair.

- Are you centered or off balance?
- Are you breathing?
- What old images about how you're "supposed to be" do you hang onto? (For example: thin, rich, hard

bodied, youthful, tall, pretty, dressed-for-success.)
- What is your energy level?
- Are you feeling heavy and loaded down?
- Are you focusing on your inadequacies or short-comings?
- What are your choices?
- Are you feeling mean and hateful—picking at others out of your past or present hurt?

If you're humming along in a centered way, enjoy the flow of your feminine power. If you're off-balance, tune in to your body energy. Let your muscles inform you about where you're tense and need to relax. First tighten and then relax the places your tension has gathered. Give yourself time to take some deep breaths and let the air out slowly. As you grow more confident about your body, no one may notice specific changes, but you will *feel* different. You will be more substantial and better able to feel your strengths and accept your limitations. You'll be able to take on work or stand your ground emotionally in ways that might have been too much for you before.

BODY ENERGY GOES TO WORK

One of the barriers that pops up here is an old familiar one. **Feminine Biology is Inconvenient**. We've been taught that women aren't dependable—can't be trusted with important decisionmaking or responsibilities—at "that time of the month" or when pregnant, lactating, or menopausal. Women, we're told, aren't tough enough.

When you feel strong enough, try fitting your work schedule more to your needs:

"I don't feel well now, but I'll be back and ready to work tomorrow/Wednesday afternoon/Monday morning."

"I'd like to arrange time off to nurse my baby—from

2:00 to 3:00 in the afternoon for the next six months. My co-worker is willing to cover for me during that time while I take a late lunch."

Yes, women's emotions are cyclical—more up and down. Let your supervisor know that you still have the capacity to take responsibility and make excellent decisions. If you're familiar with your own biology and are willing to deal with it, you can guarantee the quality of your work.

It is a reality that feminine biology creates inconvenience at work. But *that* is not the barrier. The barrier is the exaggerated idea that your biology renders you incompetent as a worker or leader.

As you read through the "do's" and "don'ts" below, check the possibility that the "don'ts" describe some of the ways your shadow sneaks out at times. If you act on the "do's," the "dont's" aren't as likely to be the way you choose to express your feelings.

Do	*Don't*
Learn to confront put downs about female biology.	Collude with comments or jokes about female biology.
Keep track of PMS or other symptoms you experience.	Whine or complain about your aches and pains.
Assume you have a right to care for yourself. Arrange time off when you need it.	Assume that male supervisors are knowledgeable about feminine biology.
Admit to limited energy when that's the case. Learn to say, "I'm not in a place where I can do that. I'll do it tomorrow."	Be intimidated about explaining your needs to a male supervisor.

Do	*Don't*
Stay aware of your strengths and limitations if you work while pregnant or lactating.	Expect women who have denied their own needs to be sympathetic to yours.
Teach the long-range view of getting work done. Most crises aren't really crises.	

Protective Males Watch over Little Women is another barrier that relates to body energy. This way of keeping women from being powerful emerges from a loving aspect of masculine energy—the urge to protect the pregnant female or new mother—and from the physical fact that the male body is designed to lift more weight and carry heavier loads. But in the contemporary workplace, what appears to be "helpful" or "protective" can be anything but.

It's hard to sort out truly supportive good intentions from the kind of "protection" designed to keep you in your place. One way to tell the difference is in the response you get if you tactfully refuse help when you don't really need it. If your refusal is greeted with a pout or a jab about "liberated women," you just encountered the protection barrier.

Do	*Don't*
Be realistic about what you take on.	Play "poor damsel in distress" when you need help.
Learn to say, "I appreciate your concern, but. . . ."	Accept help you don't need. If you don't need it, say so.

Do	*Don't*
Express yourself clearly about your strengths and competencies.	Accept physical assignments that are beyond your capacity.
Accept help gracefully when you need it.	Try to be one of the boys.
Be ready and able to express your needs clearly.	Diminish yourself by playing the "daughter" role.
Equate what you do at work with what you do in other parts of your life, i.e. lifting a wiggly young child.	

Through tactful, supportive limit setting, you have the opportunity to demonstrate your competence and help change some stereotypes. "Thanks for your offer to help me, but I've learned to handle this equipment comfortably and safely," is a clear message that respects a good intention if that was the offer.

SUMMARY

Your body energy, including the inconvenience your feminine cycles cause at times, is a rich resource for you at work. Value your feminine body. Let your clothing and the way you present yourself increase your comfort with your body energy. If you need time off to care for yourself, find ways to coordinate with your colleagues to provide this self-care. Listen to the messages your body sends to you about what is right, what is humane about the work you're doing, and how you're doing it.

To whatever extent each of us asserts her body energy as a legitimate, important part of the workplace, she increases the comfort zone for herself and for other women. We can then work in a place that feels good. It's much easier to concentrate on our work and not have to put energy into excusing, protecting, or defending something as basic as our biology.

Being there is a first step in bringing feminine balance to the decisionmaking that affects all of us. The changes that the feminine presence brings to the board room, the engineering department, the inner circle at the White House are positive ones. We make it harder to forget that all humans are connected with families, with the earth, and with future generations. As we learn to care for ourselves, in addition to our personal benefit, we teach others that concern for the feminine is legitimate and important.

Persistence

rains of sand. The daily effort to hold a relationship together. Type, type, and retype—and retype. An assembly line. A toddler's unrelenting demands for attention. A twelve-hour work day. The repeated practice of an intricate musical passage. Quilting, knitting, crocheting—hobbies that create their wonders stitch by stitch.

We don't think or talk much about persistence in our fast-paced times. It's an old-fashioned virtue. But it's a central part of the feminine, and it's still around. "Women are more persistent," was a comment I heard repeatedly as I asked people about femininity at work. One man put it this way. "What is feminine energy? Persistence. Women will stay with something, just keep plugging away at it, way beyond the point where I would have said forget it." Not a particularly glamourous portrait, but it implies the power to move mountains—like water cracking stone, drop by drop, year after year, century after century, winning the right to vote and changing the course of history. Women have had to knock on closed doors long enough to get a response. And the needs for persistence persist. It's important for you to know how yours works—or doesn't work—for you.

Men may lift the big boulder. But women can move rocks over the course of the day. And they do. Day after day all over the world.

Chuck Baroo,
New York City

Masculine-style persistence paints with a broad brush; it tends to be aggressive and goal-oriented. It's designed to accomplish something that is clear and obtainable: to win a heart or a game, to solve an engineering problem, to make a point. When a man is persistent, you know it.

Feminine persistence, by contrast, can be almost invisible, low-key, assertive repetition. Other words that come to mind are patience, tenacity, self-discipline, perseverence. At first, energized by a feeling, not a clear goal, the outcome may be unpredictable, because only the small steps are visible. But the goal may become more obvious as the small steps make their mark.

"I think about my mother, who would do things nonstop, never still, driven," Delores Jimenez, a community organizer, shared with me. "She could have chosen not to live that way, but she had incredible energy related to the family. It's hard to believe the number of things she took care of." Delores continued to describe some of her work with community groups: "And women who don't have children may have this same energy in a different way. I've seen them take on community projects and drive themselves when they feel that it's best for their people. They do insurmountable amounts of work with very little regard for their health and sleep. From men may come a different motivation—more likely to be head commitment not heart commitment. The man says, 'I'm committed to my family, but. . . .' The women sacrifice themselves. The 'buts' aren't as prevalent."

Most women's lives aren't built on great deeds. Watching a young substitute kicker score a field goal from fifty plus yards to win a football game, my husband remarked, "He'll have something to tell his kids!" What we have to tell our kids is something very different. It's, "I'm here for you. You can count on me." Every day, we spin the thread, weave the fabric that holds our lives together. We get good at being consistent, and dependable, because we know it's important and nobody else is going to do it for us. We assume that we'll do what needs to be done. And we take this capacity to work with us.

Persistence is the energy that pushes you to do something over and over and over and over and over and over and over. Or to return to a task after repeated interruptions. You work either until you get it right or you get it done. The drive may not be clearly conscious or thought out, but it's powerful, often in an understated way. Persistence is a quiet dimension that gives us the capacity to endure pain and tedium—to stay with the process, ill-defined as it may be, to make sure the job is done. It's the kind of thing that wins out over time.

Or it can be a well-organized effort toward a clearly defined but distant goal. Although it feels much better when there's some validation, feminine persistence can live a long time with neither recognition nor reward.

Nobel Prize-winning geneticist Barabara McClintock, brilliant and highly trained but unable to secure academic appointments reserved for men, persistently conducted experiments in her own garden for years. She could see that, under certain conditions, genetic strains in her corn samples changed in particular ways. Further complicating her attempts to gain support from the scientific community, her observations didn't fit the theories of the time. But she continued working in her own way, painstakingly crossing and re-crossing strains of corn and studying the results. The will to keep at it came out of her own interest and personal conviction. She was not trying to meet another's needs or get approval; she just believed what she saw and refused to give up.[1]

Basic survival in so-called primitive societies—food preparation, infant care, educating children (the original "woman's work")—all require patience and persistence. "Upingarrlainarkta—Always Getting Ready," was the title of a photographic exhibit I saw at the Anchorage Museum of History and Art, James H. Barker's Solo Exhibition portraying village life in the Yukon-Kuskokwim River delta. Tribesman Walky Charles' comments next to a photograph of his people's time-honored fish-curing process captured both the central importance of this dimension and its invisibility:

> Me and a cousin, we've just finished doing herring. Our aunt's too old to work so we had to do all the fish. I never realized how much work it was. You know, going out fishing and hunting is easy and fun. But we had to sit hour after hour, six hours one day, five another, gutting them and then stringing them up. It is so tiring. There I was, sitting and working all those hours, thinking the same thoughts my mother would think when she was doing fish. Well, it's incredible the amount of work these women do. I'll never eat fish again without thinking about all the work these women do.[2]

And the same is true of feminine survival techniques for our culture and time. We may not be stringing fish, but many of the tasks associated with educating ourselves, getting a job or promotion, finding good childcare and keeping it, demand the same tenacious capacity. Whether it's biological or learned, this ability to persist in small, repeated tasks supports women doing what's necessary in everyday life. It's a force of unmeasured power in the workplace. And it becomes even more potent for each of us when we recognize it for what it's worth. Small, routine tasks then become part of life's foundation. They take on meaning that makes them less tedious.

THE SHADOW SIDE

The shadow of persistence builds a living tomb. We know this when our repeated, stuck, action goes nowhere—too much persistence with too little direction. No matter how carefully done, re-arranging the deck chairs on the *Titanic* doesn't save either the ship or any-body's life. Persistence provides a distraction, a hiding place, when fear stops us from plunging into the unknown and risking change. "As soon as I get my files caught up, I'm going to apply for a fellowship to teach overseas," a colleague tells me—and has been telling me for the past five years. The filing is safer than risking either the rejection of the application or the changes that teaching overseas would really mean.

Persistence is a quiet dimension that gives us the capacity to stay with the process, ill-defined as it may be, to make sure the job is done.

Persistence that becomes rigid or compulsive shuts out new information and ignores the feelings of others. Single-mindedness that doesn't have room for the facts but just keeps on going is the voice of the dark side. It keeps out needed feedback so that confusion or conflict won't stir up all those insecure feelings that flare when we don't know what will happen next.

Perfectionism—doing something over and over to reach some ever-elusive state—is another way to spend a long time in the shadow of persistence. If you can't take the risk of exposing some flaws, persistence is a good place to hide.

The shadow side of persistence has been emotional home base for working women who are trapped in non-opportunity. Compulsive attention to detail, nit-picking, and a sense of martyrdom provide some release for feelings of worthlessness and frustration. This has been a survival mode for women who haven't been able to move beyond detail-oriented, routine jobs that go nowhere. It contributes to negative feminine stereotypes that women are drones who don't have initiative and can only handle minor responsibilities.

Learned helplessness, "Somebody else will do it; I can't," enlarges the shadow side of persistence. This is a vicious cycle. By not trying, by giving up, we miss out on the practice or learning experiences that make us better at any task or skill. The unrealistic expectation that we

should be able to do a tough assignment on the first try or
without practice darkens the shadow here: "I submitted a
proposal and the boss didn't like it. That's it! I'm not
putting myself out again."

Persistence is very powerful in pushing for a goal or
learning how to do something really well. On the shadow
side, it can mean drudgery, loss of self-direction, and ultimately, defeat. If you're captured by the shadow here, ask
yourself what you're hiding from.

SELF-REFLECTION

Look at the way persistence weaves in and out of your
work life. Pay attention to how this dimension pulls at you
from both sides.

STRENGTH: Persistence is part of me. I trust my
capacity to stick with something until it's done. I might not
like it, but I can do something over until I get it right. My
persistence helped me get my present job. I learned to
(sew, play the violin, climb a mountain, etc.) by practicing
small steps over and over.

SHADOW: My persistence turns into compulsivity. I
get started on something and can't quit until it's finished. I
get tunnel vision and persist in self-defeating ways long
after it's clear that whatever I'm doing isn't working. / I try
once and give up. / I can't stand to redo something I've
completed. / It drives me nuts to see someone else do
something over and over.

TIME FOR YOURSELF

How do you feel about persistence—in you and in others? Do you like it? Does it bore you or irritate you?

Experiment with this quality in your own work life. Select a few of these exercises and work through them.

• THINK OF SOMEONE you know who has sustained herself at work or in her outside life through patient little steps done over and over. Why was persistence needed? How did it pay off? Would a more action-oriented approach have been effective or was persistence necessary? Answer these questions in your journal.

• HOW MUCH PERSISTENCE do you have? Think of a time when persistence and stamina paid off for you. Were you conscious of being persistent or did you just do it? What kept you going? In your journal, write about ten tasks at which persistence has been or will be productive. (Examples: learning a new computer program, creating a network, building a mailing list, writing in your journal.)

• PERSISTENCE AND STAYING POWER are central to developing any skill, craft, or art form. Think about actions you have done or plan to do over and over to develop skills. Select an example from your experience and list the tiny steps you did to accomplish some part of it.

• LITTLE TASKS MATTER. Contrary to media images of the rich and famous, much of life *is* repetitive or boring, not particularly glamorous or exciting. When you can let go of inflated ideas of how your life ought to be and appreciate your everyday competence, a wonderful thing happens. You can do the small, necessary parts of life—pay bills, run the Saturday errands or fill out insurance forms—with a sense of harmony and centeredness, and with little impatience. Write about one example in which you have found this to be true.

• WHO IS THE MOST PERSISTENT person you know? How do you feel about that quality in her/him? Do you have a tendency to discredit or discount persistence as picky? Brainstorm a list that describes the positive aspects of this person's persistence.

• IS PERSISTENCE ONE OF YOUR STRONG DIMENSIONS? Is it just part of the way you are, or did you learn it? If you learned it, who taught you? What do you admire about that person? In your journal, compare the way your persistence flows with the way this "teacher" persists. What do you need to learn? Write it.

• IF PERSISTENCE ISN'T A STRONG PART of your personality, is it something that would help you feel grounded and secure? The opposites of persistence are impatience and impulsiveness. Do these qualities get in your way at work? Describe ways you undermine your persistence.

• IF PERSISTENCE IS AN AREA of your work style that you want to develop more fully, create a plan to follow through persistently and learn more about this dimension in your life. Identify a particular skill or process that you would like to improve—nothing grandiose; just a little step that needs some work. Make a plan, a time line, for doing this work. Write it down. Do it.

• IF YOU TEND TO SLIP FROM PERSISTENCE into shadowy compulsivity, create some techniques to help you let go. Set a time limit for yourself and stick with it. Stop whatever you're doing, relax, and ground yourself when that time is up. Give your self an imaging break. Imagine a special, peaceful place to which you like to go. Take yourself there in your mind and enjoy it. Stretch and breathe. Give yourself permission to clear your head for a while. Everything worth doing is *not* necessarily worth doing well.

• IF YOU ARE A PERSON WHO HAS TROUBLE with persistence, are you likely to try a task two or three times and then forget it? Think about what gets in your way—what contributes to your self-defeating style. Make a list of these barriers in your journal. Is this what you want? Try again with some different approaches.

• MAKE A LIST OF BLOCKS you face that undermine your persistent efforts. (Example: get caught in perfectionism; easier to repeat than to move on to something new; haven't experienced succeeding as a result of persisting; prefer detail work because you can hide in it.) Underline one or two that you think you can reduce. Explain in writing or pictures how you will do this.

Success in self-development lies in choosing a project that is within your grasp—something that you care about that is really workable. If you have trouble persisting in something that's important to you, look at the messages you give yourself. You need to confront whatever blocks you creatively—and you need to confront it with persistence.

Return to your Self-Assessment on page 26 and see if your rating still fits. Make the adjustments that reflect your persistence as you understand it now.

PERSISTENCE GOES TO WORK

Every parent who first sees a baby walk thrills at the tiny faltering steps. No matter that they are unsure, awkward, and lack direction. No one expects them to be perfect. The image of those little steps as you take your own first steps in learning a new skill or tackling a big project can be a great support. The toddler doesn't give up when she falls down. Mom and others will spend years helping her learn to walk and become competent in thousands of other ways. When you take the long view, when you understand the importance of shaky, repetitive first steps, you can appreciate persistence when things are tough at work.

Tiny steps make a real difference in your learning process. Over time, you see your accomplishments accumulate. Try to find another person with whom to share your small accomplishments. He or she will benefit from hearing about them as much as you will from sharing.

When you can accept and value your own small accomplishments, you can appreciate the work of others in the same way.

Boring, non-glamorous tasks that contribute to getting the work done over time are a major part of life. And women do more than their share of this work. Charles Baroo, a community worker whose travels have taken him into the homes and lives of ordinary people all over the world and whose quote opens this chapter, talked with me about immigrants in New York.

> They're able to transition into this culture mainly because the women persevere at menial tasks much longer than men can—stoop, labor, do domestic work. In one of the Latino communities, the women easily find jobs—do mundane tasks repetitively. The men can't do this. Maybe their expectations are higher. Some of the new-wave Asian groups are having tremendous difficulty adjusting to NYC. I sense this is more true for the men. Black West Indian men in England have an incredible incidence of breakdown, but the women keep on going.[3]

It's important to know how to take good care of yourself emotionally and to take the time out to do so. When you can nurture and encourage your persistence at work, rather than fight it or feel ashamed of it, you open up another way to support your feminine power.

Persistence is feminine strength at work, subtly, and often behind the scenes. Water dripping carves stone, but it takes uncountable drops and a long time. Persistence doesn't require tremendous physical strength or high rank in an organization. The persistent person who's committed to her goal takes small steps—a comment here, a reminder there—but she comes back again and again. She doesn't go away. And because she doesn't make it easy to forget something that is uncomfortable or difficult, she may get put down or characterized as a pain in the butt.

She is just being stubborn may sound familiar if you persist at trying to change things where you work. This popular barrier falls into place if you push a little too repeatedly against the way things have always been done. Or if you try to create conditions that are better for female workers. This barrier is designed to make you doubt yourself or think you're being bad.

"Stubborn"—refusing to yield, obey, or comply, resisting doggedly, determined, obstinate—has some of the feel of the shadow side of persistence. "Stubborn as a mule" catches the essence. It implies rigidity and closed-mindedness and gets applied in a negative way to women when we don't fit the sweet, compliant feminine stereotype. The "nag" is a concept that comes directly from persistence, and is used to devalue women who don't give up easily. When we've grown up thinking it's important to be nice, we don't like to hear that we are "stubborn" or that we "nag." Mayor Anne Rudin, who shared how she persistently worked through a week's round-the-clock negotiations to save the Sacramento Symphony, gets called "stubborn" from time to time, too.

She is just being stubborn is a tough barrier to deal with. It's not likely to be said to your face, but it is, nonetheless, an attitude that others may have toward you that hurts your credibility. It's belittling and it implies you're some sort of robot, that you don't think through what you do: "She is such a pain. She continues to bring up this childcare thing, when she knows it can't work! Why can't she just drop it?"

Here are some suggestions for those times when you realize you've bumped headlong into this hidden but dangerously undermining barrier:

Do	*Don't*
Trust your intuition and stick with your feeling even if your goal isn't clear.	Give in to manipulation like sighs or words like "stubborn."
Work persistently with small steps when bigger ones are blocked.	Get discouraged if others don't understand what you're trying to do.
Develop a sense of the long range. Time passes and new opportunities emerge.	Give up just because you feel uncertain of the outcome.
Give yourself breaks and come back when you feel refreshed.	Expect others to support efforts they can't understand.
Learn the rhythm and flow of your persistence.	Quit until you're quite sure you're headed in a non-productive direction.
Gain comfort with turning down offers that distract (and undermine) you.	Join with your critics in ravelling the fabric you're weaving.Give yourself breaks and come back when you feel refreshed.
Listen to yourself and try to hear what your persistence is telling you.	Learn the rhythm and flow of your persistence.

A Persistent Woman at Work

Persistence moves one grain of sand at a time and changes the landscape while it appears that nothing is happening. Similarly, Joyce Davis's efforts built an organization contact-by-contact, phone-call-by-phone-call. With compassion and determination over the years, she devoted

time and energy, made herself available, and stuck with
the small steps that needed attention in a subtle leadership
process.

Along with her consulting and therapy practice, Joyce
worked as Executive Director for a professional association. Members consult for diverse businesses and government agencies in the greater New York area as well as
nationally and internationally. Many travel constantly, keep
hectic schedules, and routinely work in high-stress, con-
flictual situations. They compete with each other for business and benefit from each others' support.

Quietly and persistently, Joyce served as a communication channel, a connector for this group, establishing the
groundwork for openness and participation. Through her
"connecting" energy, people with similar interests met and
found ways to benefit each other. She wove a safety net
that promoted interpersonal contact. Then, persistently,
she supported people who were willing to tackle the
countless details required to establish computer networking as a support tool when the group hosted their national
organization's annual conference. She facilitated this complex, time-consuming project and then managed the predictable opposition, disappointments and technical difficulties that came with interfacing with the national group.

Her matter-of-fact openness, compassion and optimism about people grounded her work. She avoided getting stuck in the gooey shadow side of feminine leadership that tends to bog down when receptivity and
flexibility aren't balanced by structure, closure, and decisionmaking. By empowering others, she smoothed the
rough places in the participative process which relied on
group wisdom for direction. Busy people, who can be
uneasy with a push for commitment and want a "strong
leader" to control and provide structure, increasingly
shared responsibility for the process. The successful development of the organization created a sense of identity and

connection among competing professionals where the jungle of alienation easily overtakes the cultivated fields of collaboration.

Now this organization provides a resource network, as well as a professional exchange forum, for individuals whose work has broad-reaching impact throughout the world. Joyce's low-key, behind-the-scenes efforts shaped the energy and contributions of willing members. They continue building a home base that serves them professionally and personally.

Creativity, persistence, and nurturance, over several years, supported Joyce's step-by-step efforts. Her style was to work individually but consistently to acquaint people with mutual interests, brokering business connections as well as supportive professional ones. As the group slowly came together, she supported others who emerged as leaders. She then handed over her responsibilities, after a period of transition, and left the group in the hands of a new board which continues an open, participative leadership process.

Subsequently, as a member of the national board for a similar association, using a comparable process, Joyce has heightened a global perspective and influenced the creation of an international focus in that organization. Her wholistic thinking, core strength, creativity, and persistence have been key in connecting consultants, particularly in Latin America, but also throughout the world. Her efforts, energized by her love, persist toward co-creating possibilities for diverse people to work together.

Joyce's example affirms that one persistent person can make a difference and create fundamental change through small steps over time. Working against the constraints of busy schedules and competing motivations, Joyce served as a glue in a loose, unwieldy organization. Now she directs her efforts at doing the same in a fragmented world. When she started her work, she didn't know how it would come together, but she stayed true to her own process. She didn't have, or need, a clear picture of the outcome to be persistent.

SUMMARY

Persistence allows for a gradual unfolding and deep connection with self and others. Let your energy speak to you and inform your actions. When your feelings push you to hang in with an idea, goal or relationship, pay attention to them, whether or not you know where you're headed. If you get stuck, if you feel like you persist only because you're afraid, listen to what your shadow is telling you. Get some help confronting your fear, if you need to.

In our "have it all now" lifestyles, we don't take seriously that it's possible to build something worthwhile over a long period of time. But, in fact, that's what women have been doing for many centuries. Our capacity for taking small steps consistently and endlessly can be very sustaining and reassuring when more immediate goals seem out of reach. The ability to stick with the process when the going gets tough makes a real difference. Those drops, grains, stitches, and small assertions are important parts of your daily life, and they mold your imprint on the world.

Core Strength

Sarah Olds was a Nevada homesteader who, when her son became ill, found it her job to check the trap lines. "On my first trip around the trap line I caught a bobcat," she remembered painfully. "I hadn't expected to catch anything, and now I was faced with the task of killing what I had caught. . . . For a while I stood there and bawled good and loud. . . ." She finally stunned the animal with a tap behind the ear, followed by a death blow to the heart. She also devised her own method of rooting out fleas and lice from hair and clothing. "We all took baths with plenty of sheep dip in the water. . . . I had no disinfectant . . . so I boiled all our clothing in sheep dip and kerosene."[1]

Stamina, hope, conviction, a dash of creativity, determination. Core, underpinnings, not-to-be-messed-with primal center of the feminine. Every woman has it. Glaciers brush off half her soul and she emerges with invented energy for a sick child, one more hour with a dying friend, a finished piece of work that dawn's light welcomes, or the job she really wanted but thought was out of reach. She stands firm when crumbling would be so much simpler.

Core strength is constitution, mettle enlivened by determination and hope. It's the bedrock of feminine authority, the quality that communicates, "I'm in charge of myself. My presence makes a difference. You may disagree, give me a hard time, or love what I have to offer,

but you must take me seriously. I'm not to be ignored."
More importantly, it's the quality that each of us can trust
and reach into when we need to get through hard times.
Core strength is the foundation of the inner self.

It's not the kind of thing you think about or choose.
It's just there. Core strength, endurance brightened by
hope, carried Sarah Olds, the pioneer woman in the quo-
tation that opens this chapter, through the incredible hardships she faced. And it is there for today's women as we
pioneer new paths for our complex lives—giving birth and
caring for our children while we endure the hardships and
challenges of work. Of course, core strength isn't just
about children. Married and "childfree," lesbian, or living
the life of a single person who has total responsibility for
all the details of keeping her life together, including her
work—it keeps us going and nourishes the spirit long after
exhaustion sinks in. This strength is personal and inner-
directed, and it has nothing to do with having power over
someone else.

Core strength

is constitution,

mettle

enlivened by

determination

and hope.

Do you know your core strength? Do you recognize
and trust it? Is it easy to reach? Or is it subtle and hard to
find? Depending on how you learned about your feminine
self, your core strength may be easy or difficult to contact.
It may or may not be well-developed, but it's there. Use
this chapter to identify this dimension in your personality.
Learn to use your core strength both for self-nurturance
and for confidence. It's yours to rely on.

Nor is inner strength limited to the feminine. But
being strong is one of the stereotypes men live with. Their
struggle more often involves accepting their own gentility
and vulnerability. In our culture, men expect themselves to
be strong, though they're more likely to think about their
strength in external terms like winning and losing, being
the best, being on top. They see a "strong man," as someone who's physically powerful, in charge, perhaps concerned about the welfare of others, but not to be pushed

too far. "The strong, silent type," another masculine stereotype, raises a different image—someone who isn't expressive but will be there for you. Neither concept fits core
strength in the feminine presence.

Each of us builds her core strength in a different way
by collecting a broad base of information about life, the
world, who she is. Hard experiences test us and we grow
from them. People who care tell us how we're strong.
Information that we trust and believe comes to us from
many sources—education, growing up, relationships. We
preserve this information in conscious memory as well as
in that cluttered and mostly inaccessible emotional storage
shed, the unconscious. This lifelong, growing collection
reminds us we survive in spite of difficulties and underlies
our core strength. Unless we pay attention, we won't catch
its full significance as a resource. It's there for us, but we
have to learn to believe in it and trust in it.

A sense of being in and of ourselves, a feeling of personal authority, arises when we trust the floor of our inner
resolve. It's based on willingness to risk doing what seems
right—succeeding some of the time.

Knowing our limits is as important as knowing our
strengths. Then our expectations for ourselves are realistic
and we can stand firm without collapsing.

Melissa Lawler, an Indianapolis professional, shares
her reliance on core strength:

> I know when I'm truly responding to my inner
> knowing about an issue. I feel calm and open to
> hearing all the data from others. When I'm defensive
> and stubborn, I don't want to hear—I want to tell—
> and tell and tell! I feel an element of anger when
> others aren't convinced. But when I'm coming from
> my own centered strength, I usually don't feel angry
> when others see things differently. I just feel puz-
> zled. I say, "I need to stay open to the possibility

that I'm not right," but I proceed under the assumption that I'm correct, even when everybody else is saying something different.[2]

Powered by our own energy source, we're more productive than when our actions are attempts to please others. If we placate rather than living in ways that are true to our core strength, we lose touch with our inner emotional reality and feel off balance.

The quality of our work reflects who we really are. It saps our energy when we diminish our judgment or creativity and compromise what we believe is right. Not only do we have to generate more energy to do it somebody else's way, but when we undermine our integrity, we do a real disservice to ourselves and depression may begin to set in. Then we have to plow through its heaviness to get anything done. When we spend the day pleasing others at our own expense, we end up feeling very tired—and very empty—especially when the person we're trying to please doesn't notice.

Reaching into core strength is a private and unobservable process. Both male and female leaders appearing in the media typically present themselves in ways that match images of power and male-defined success. If they don't easily communicate this quality, they create such a persona for themselves—or worse yet, have one created with the help of media consultants. Political candidates of either gender speaking in sound bytes rarely give us an idea of their soul searching or inner struggles. CEOs rarely disclose their self doubts, or the process used in decision-making.

It's hard to identify public examples of prominent people sharing an honest, centered process that portrays their vulnerabilities as well as their strengths. We have adopted the myth that, if a leader does not always look strong, authoritative, and "together" then he/she is not to be trusted. And so we are typically presented with the polished exterior, a "finished product," not the unlovely gymnastics all men and women must go through to get there. We miss out on the human tussle with insecurity, vulnerability, and uncertainty. And we get skewed ideas of what it means to be strong.

These public figures are the models that women who aren't celebrities think they have to live up to and struggle to imitate in highly visible or difficult situations. Reading a draft of this book, a sensitive professional woman said to me, "Revelation of lack of certainty, such as in the first part where you're talking about your own shadow, may be a marketing minus. People want to know that 'This woman knows what she's doing, and believes in it'—that it will work for them." The contradictory nature of the feminine allows us to know what we're doing and have doubts. Core strength is about going on *in spite of* the doubts.

Core strength is something very different from a manufactured image. It grows within; it's not painted on. It acknowledges imperfection, uncertainty, and vulnerability and goes on anyway. Here's an everyday example.

Diana, a woman who had worked several years in health care, described an experience in which a much older, powerful male physician attempted to intimidate her. In her job as Director of Nursing, she confronted him when he ignored an important charting step. He had omitted this step many times before and hadn't ever been challenged because no one was willing to deal with his overbearing style. When she called the omission to his attention, he raged and threatened her.

This capable woman found herself shaking—feeling deeply frightened. Suddenly, from the depths of her being, calmness flowed through her as she realized that she didn't have to tolerate bad treatment from this man or capitulate to his demands. She didn't have to take the

Core strength—

power from an

inner source

that sets a limit,

draws a line,

or asks for

reflection—

is a balancing

response to

oppression.

attack personally and respond like a scared and powerless child. She reached inward, gained control, and confronted her colleague in a professional, matter-of-fact style.

She looked him squarely in the eye and said, "I know, Dr. Blank, that you're mad about this. And I know that you haven't ever had to chart this step. It's your job, though, not mine. It's hospital policy and your liability. I won't accept the chart without the notation." He slammed the chart on the counter and left. But he came back and completed his work.

Diana wasn't able to deal with this man effectively until she tuned in to her personal authority, her basic right to stand up for herself and for what she knows is right. The "structural" power she had through her administrative role was not enough. Her *personal* power, rising from her core strength, energized her self-confidence. This confrontation of a senior male physician by a woman in her twenties breached the accepted power structure in an industry known for its rigidity and patriarchal traditions.

The masculine way, or more correctly, the patriarchal caricature of the masculine that is prominent in our culture, relies on the hierarchy. The group with the most power controls what happens. The "in-group" uses rules and regulations for support when convenient, but underplays them when they get in the way. Diana enforced the rules by confronting the physician. But she had to have personal courage to do so. Enforcing, or calling attention to, rules that have been long overloooked is one of the ways women break barriers in organizations run by informal trade-offs among the "old boys."

Core strength—power from an inner source that sets a limit, draws a line, or asks for reflection—is a balancing response to oppression. Diana's encounter with the physician gives us an example of core strength in action. Her capacity to hold her ground kicked into gear before she was even aware of what was happening. Core strength helped her make her stand. But, "This very inner strength is most threatening to the rule-bound patriarchal structure," consultant Ed Tamson pointed out to me, "It is often attacked, as in many sad cases of 'whistle blowers.'" The patriarchal structure may be rule-bound, but the old boys' club is even more powerful. Women who challenge the informal power structure, even by following the rules, need all the core strength they can find.

Core strength contains elements of softness and resilience as well as hardness. So it often isn't as obvious as more immediate masculine responses. As with other dimensions of the feminine, the submerged quality of core strength may make feminine ways appear, on first glance, weak or disorganized by masculine standards. We get treated as if we are weak, since weakness is part of the feminine stereotype, making it even harder to break through and stand up for our convictions.

"Feminine" is strong and receptive when we learn to trust ourselves in this dimension. We can be true to ourselves and stay connected at the same time. We have room for negotiation, for hearing the voice of the other without losing ourselves. We don't have to be perfect or to win every time. This complex capacity is strength, not weakness. And it helps even more if we can talk about it.

Those who've learned to trust core strength know that even when it's not apparent to others, they can trust themselves and take the risk of trying to get what they need. Until more men understand and respect this process, it remains necessary to talk about thoughts and feelings that come from this centered place so they can become part of the language of the workplace: "I understand that you disagree, but I feel strongly about this and will stand by it." "I know this is a different way. I believe it will make our company better. It's worth the effort."

We can rely on our inner process, our core strength, for information and support. The next step is to speak about the results in a way that's clear to people who habitually see women as weak: "I've invested five years in this program. We've met our goals each of those five years. It was a struggle all the way, and I'm proud of our work." The emotional intuitive shorthand of women's ways of talking, and our habits of being humble, confuse those who haven't learned to appreciate our strength. We need to explain how we are strong and how we find the strength to do what we need to do.

The Shadow Side

It's no wonder if the idea of core strength, a feminine quality, is hard to take for granted as the basic design structure for your feminine power coat. In our culture, strength is too often associated with "masculine": "She's as strong as a man" or "She'll have to work like a man to keep that job." "Strong woman," for many, sounds destructive, devouring—someone who walks over people to get what she wants. It isn't a compliment when used in this way. A young minister I interviewed candidly described a "strong woman" this way:

> We have these typical strong domineering mother types—physically big, full of power. She's like a viper for the minister. How do you avoid being devoured by her? Walk a very straight and narrow line. She has the power of a mother. You don't want to be punished by her. She's more moral than we, the ministers, are. We're there, trying to please our mothers. The Church is seen as a "she." We're there worshipping that typical male God, but we don't relate to the devouring mother. We build fences around her so she doesn't hurt us. I don't think we know how to enter into a relationship with

her. We "be-friend" at great personal cost. They
show up at all the church functions, and they either
tell us that we did a great job, or that we really
messed it up. On staff, we do a tremendous number
of mother jokes.

Not a pretty picture. A powerful shadow image of the
strong feminine. This man clearly and courageously talked
about what remains unspoken more often than not. The
devouring mother image, in its countless varied forms,
raises fear in women as well as men.

We fear our own strength, fear that we'll be perceived
as domineering, "too powerful," frightening to the men we
would relate to. Generations of women learned to defer,
learned even that helplessness was attractive. We are good
at diminishing ourselves. Of course, when we do so we
miss out on getting to know and trust our own core
strength. We need to know as much about our core
strength as possible. This major dimension of our central,
sustaining femininity gives us both the endurance and the
resilience to deal with our lives on our own terms.

Core strength becomes pathetic either as weakness or
as stubborn dominance on the shadow side. Both are
exaggerated aspects of this dimension that take over when
we lose our capacity to be vulnerable and strong at the
same time. Remember the example at the beginning of the
chapter? First Sarah Olds "stood there and bawled good
and loud," and then she killed the bobcat. Her vulnerability surfaced first and then core strength kicked in.

Pathetic weakness gives us permission to hide within
our low aspirations. We don't expect much of ourselves
and neither does anyone else. Helplessness becomes our
style, and so we act and get treated like a victim.

It's time to take a look when we find ourselves feeling
victimized.

• How am I making myself look inept?
• What do I fear?
• What am I avoiding?
• How am I denying my core strength?

The answers to the questions give us direction about where we need to make choices and be assertive.

Attempts to control the behavior of others substitute for a feeling of inner confidence on the stubborn dominance side. We may appear "strong," but in fact we've developed ironclad defenses that block personal contact with our inner selves and with others.

At work, this stubborness or hardness makes for the unapproachable "iron maiden" style. What many people think of as "strong women" are stuck in this impenetrable frozen shadow. The old-style "organizational" man or woman fits here. When we're in a place like this, it's very hard to recognize our vulnerabilities, but that's just what needs to happen.

Feelings of tightness, frantic desperation, and cynicism are clues that can lead us to examine our hardness. If we're truly operating from core strength, we're not "brittle"—we're not easily defeated when our armor is pierced. We also have the capacity for vulnerability and softness.

We can be overwhelmed by our shadows when we mistake being strong for taking responsibility to do it all. We criticize others who don't do enough, according to our standards, rather than monitoring our own tendency to over-extend. When we find ourselves in this place, our shadow may be suggesting that we take a look at why. How are we abusing ourselves? How can we be more self-nourishing? How can we get better at setting priorities and limits?

Because our culture tends to see strength as masculine, the shadow side of feminine core strength is seen as typical feminine behavior. Woman as victim and even as iron maiden are stereotypes that may not be loved, but they're tolerated. When we slip into these robes, we're not likely to get feedback about it. Our own shadow, in that case, is our best informant.

Perhaps the main shadow quality of core strength is that age-old feminine process of holding back. We defer, don't live in our power, because we're afraid of being too visible, too far "out there" or more powerful than our companions. We hold back from taking risks or enjoying our strength. We opt for what's easy or available rather than facing up to challenges that are important to us. Then we project our dissatisfaction onto our partner and blame him or her for not being enough.

Our shadow is trying to get our attention when we blame our partners, children, or colleagues for being less than we think they should be. It's time to take a look at how we're holding back—being less *ourselves* than we want to be.

We can get into this same process with people on the job. Holding back gets to be a way of life and we defer rather than going after what we really want. Our shadow speaks to us through blaming or bitterness. When we're wise enough to listen, we can move into our core strength and out of the darkness.

SELF-REFLECTION

Grapple with your personal concept of core strength. Let the following items suggest ways to estimate your position on both ends of this continuum.

STRENGTH: I know and trust my center. Under stress, I can tune into my inner strength. Sometimes I'm surprised at my calm in difficult situations. I can rely on myself to stand firm. I have the capacity to sustain myself in difficult or painful situations when I need to.

SHADOW: I feel frightened most of the time, even when things are going OK. I hardly ever say what I really think if I believe others will disapprove. / I keep order in my world by attempting to control those around me. I'm seen by others as a "strong woman." / I hold back because I don't want to seem more powerful than my (partner, boss, friend).

TIME FOR YOURSELF

The capacity to contact and rely on your core strength allows you to be self-supportive in tough or frightening times. And core strength supports your confidence in complex situations. Here are some ways to dig into this dimension and expand your capacity for self-support on the job. Read through them and select several for deeper exploration.

• MAKE A PICTURE of your own core strength. When you think about "core strength," what comes to mind? Sexuality? Physical strength? Endurance? Intelligence? Emotion? Draw it in your notebook. Your symbol might be a mountain, a deep canyon, a rock, a generator, a favorite building, a tree, or anything that comes to mind. Let your thoughts drift until you find an image you like.

• MOVE WITH YOUR CORE STRENGTH. Imagine yourself as an energy source that moves with nature. You are in tune with all of nature and all of time. As you let yourself fill up with this image, move around. Buzz, hiss, sizzle, hum. Let your body be a container for this energy that you can use as needed. In your journal, write the key words that describe your experience.

• CLOSE YOUR EYES and visualize your core strength symbol now. Make it become very clear for you. Practice pulling it into your awareness easily. Learn to reach it. When you're in a difficult situation, you can rely on this symbol to remind you of your core strength.

- LIST FIVE TIMES in your life when your core strength emerged for you in a tough situation (a job interview, a confrontation, a board exam, personal loss, conflict with someone you love). These may be small or large events in your life. The key is that you relied on your inner resources in some stressful situation and were true to yourself in a centered, nondefensive way. The outcome may not have been what you wanted; it might even have been painful. But you know your process was right for you. How did your core strength make itself known or grow stronger in each case? Write about it in your journal. The greater your understanding of how your core strength works for you, the more consciously you can nurture it. Self-support grows over time as you learn to trust your track record.

- LEARN WHAT METHOD YOU USE to contact your core strength. (Your symbol, a certain feeling, or self-talk like, "This is hard, but I know I can do it.") If you really understand how you do this, you can readily start the process when you're under stress. If not, work to create a consistent method as you become better attuned to this dimension of your feminine presence.

- LIST IN YOUR JOURNAL five times in your life when you have purposefully or without any conscious awareness gone against your core strength. As you look back on those events, do you understand how and why you betrayed yourself? Are you in a better position now to stand your ground? If not, what needs to change for you? Name and note this needed change. List the steps you will take to make it happen.

- LEARN TO BELIEVE in your inalienable *right* to your feelings, perceptions, and experiences. They are resources that reflect your own truth. And that truth is worth expressing. Your way has value. List three important feelings or beliefs you want to trust more.

• CREATE OPPORTUNITIES for personal reflection, meditation, or guided fantasy. Make room in your life for quiet time that allows you to make contact with your grit and bedrock at a deep level. As you get to know more about who you are, write about what is really important to you.

• WHAT VALUES ARE MOST PRECIOUS to you? Are they violated at work? What prevents you from expressing your concerns about what is happening at work? (WARNING: If you decide to speak up, your style and timing are important. Good judgment and communication skills are essential if you are to be heard and taken seriously. In some places, there can be no hope for change and your only choice is to walk—speaking up as you go—or deal with the ever-deadening consequences of work in an emotionally toxic environment where you get little or no support and validation.)

• LEARN TO DEAL WITH hearing "no." Others also have rights to their truth, which may differ from yours. When you can accept disagreement or rejection without collapse, you communicate your strength to others and invite trust.

• WHEN MANAGEMENT TRAINING or personal growth opportunities are offered at work, take advantage of them to learn more about yourself. If they teach compliance or conformity rather than leadership and creativity, pay attention to the strong part of yourself as it resists. Ask yourself, "Can I help create change here? Can I accept what's going on? Or do I need to get out?"

Rely on your deepest personal strength to know and interpret your world. Your inner awareness provides a significant balance to what others have to say as a new rhythm emerges between the inner and outer flow of information. Learn to look inside first, to trust your intuitive process; you will gain a sense of centeredness and self-confidence that can't be obtained by imitating someone else. Of course, it's important to be responsive to what others have to offer, but know and trust your own position as part of your response.

Now return to your original Self-Assessment on page 26 and update your rating. You should have better understanding of both sides of your core strength. Add this new data to your Self-Assessment, using a different colored marker than the first time you completed it.

CORE STRENGTH GOES TO WORK

Core strength in the feminine presence is different from more masculine styles that emphasize territoriality or competition. It's the strength to know who you are and to act on your integrity. It provides you the courage to say no when something doesn't feel right or to set a limit when you need time to think. Talking about core strength combats the prejudice that women are weak either emotionally or physically. Say things out loud like:

"I know this is a big assignment, but I have the stamina to carry it through."

"It's true a woman hasn't done this job before in this company. I can understand it might feel a little strange to you to think that I'm taking over this responsibility. Let me tell you about my qualifications. . . ."

"You seem worried about whether I can finish this work. Tell me your *specific* concerns, and I'll tell you how I plan to address them."

Old stereotypes are hard to change. As you rely on your core strength over time, you begin to trust yourself more and more. It may still be necessary, with those who expect women to collapse under stress, to point out your track record, your ability to come through in the crunch.

Two barriers have a lot to do with recognizing core strength on the job. One, **She Can't Do It; She's Too____**, tunes in with the negative messages you've always heard about your femininity. The other, **She Can Do Anything; Assign It To Her**, jumps up as your competence becomes evident.

Since it vibrates so well with your inner experience at

those times when you doubt yourself, **She Can't Do It; She's Too _____** is most likely to fall off the cliff and land on you when you already feel overwhelmed. When that's the case, you feel like the weakest, dumbest, most inept person who ever did a job like yours—or maybe any other job. The whole idea that women are too something (sensitive, weak, volatile) to do challenging or desirable work is a very old one. What it really implies is that we're too feminine, which of course is not an acceptable way to be at work. It's designed to scare us into not being very daring, and it has worked too well. Here are some things to think about when you find yourself confronted with **She Can't Do It; She's Too_____:**

Do	*Don't*
Ask for what you want.	Be manipulated by thinking you have to do it perfectly.
Confront sexist ideas that women shouldn't travel.	Collude by calling other women too _____.
Talk about your strengths and interests.	Feel inferior because you have emotional ups and downs.
Agree that you're sensitive and have limits	Cave in when others "power trip" you.
Learn to mend fences.	Agree with others if they call you too _____.
Learn to negotiate for time when others "power trip" you.	Think you have to win every time.
Get good at being assertive.	

The twin brother of **She Can't Do It** is **She Can Do Anything; Assign It To Her**. In an attempt to gain acceptance and survive sexist attitudes at work, competent women learn to be super-competent. It doesn't take long for this process to reach monstrous proportions. This barrier has risen too high when you've become so buried in responsibility you can't finish what you start or make choices about where you want to devote your energy. Deep in this ever-growing pile is the need to please and to get approval. Although it may look like you're being honored and rewarded with responsibility, you're being exploited. Your core strength can support you in saying no as you get selective about your pace and direction. Here are some guidelines for dealing with **She Can Do Anything; Assign It To Her**:

Do	*Don't*
Understand that your purpose is to get to be who you are.	Be manipulated by attempts to inflate your ego.
Respect your personal limits and vulnerabilities.	Feel obligated to accept assignments just because you can do them.
Learn to set and maintain your priorities.	Buy into the idea that you're indispensable.
Learn to share your expertise with others who are less skilled than you.	Take responsibility for implementing an idea just because you have it.
Protect your personal time and nurture your personal life.	Expect your colleagues to be sympathetic when you get over-extended.

It takes courage to honor your feminine presence at work, especially if you are in an environment where women and human issues are put down. Learn to stay connected with yourself—with your experience and perceptions. Don't give in to those who imply, or say outright, that you're wrong, you don't count, or you're not enough. Contain your energy until you're ready to release it. Create your own way of being at work.

Recognize core strength in your female colleagues. Talk with them about it—about how they sustain themselves over the long haul. Acknowledge their efforts and let them know that, even though they don't flaunt it, you know they are strong.

Your energy system is yours. As you rely on your own worth, it becomes easier to create your own personal boundaries and take yourself seriously so that you will not be invaded and exploited.

ANOTHER KIND OF PIONEER

I met Mary Bolton in the mid 1970s. Her amazing wit and brilliant capacity to understand the complexities of the feminine struggle were the first things that grabbed my attention. She is present, up-front, and warm. A nonconformist, she says outlandish things and gets away with them. Passionate about life, she notices beauty and comments on it.

Mary's energetic approach to life was instantly appealing to me. But it took a while for me to understand the core strength that powered that approach.

We started working together soon after we met and continued for the next fifteen years. Both of us were committed to doing something about the flagrant abuse experienced by many working women. We worked as independent organizational consultants, tackled some hard projects, and learned hard lessons. I started to catch on.

Rather than being defeated, Mary would say, "That didn't go over too well, let's try this. . . ." And she'd be ready for another attempt. We gave up our first effort to break into working with women in non-traditional jobs after bruising our knuckles on closed doors for a year. Our second effort, in the same general area, was a success, technically. But we were deeply disappointed that the agency which had hired us didn't implement our recommendations. The operation was a success, but the patient died.

We learned from the second project that you need real support—not just consent—from decisionmakers at the top of an organization for any change effort to succeed. That painful lesson gave us the stamina to hold out for what we needed in the negotiations and contract setting we did from then on. We knew where we stood and that we couldn't be successful unless our conditions were met.

Mary knows about doing things the hard way. As a child she had asthma. "After I got over being very frightened, I began to understand I wouldn't die—it would go away. Then I began to *hope* it would go away. When the attacks came late at night, I was too scared to get up and ask for help. If I could stay awake and be brave, it would soon be daylight.

"I learned about endurance, hope—and later—creativity. I think core strength combines those three. I had two strong grandmothers who were good models for me. One of them endured a lot of death. She had eleven children. Lots of them, I don't know how many for sure, died. And the other grandmother was physically strong. She'd get out and work hard—sweat would pour off her and her hair would curl—and get a lot done. She gloried in it. She'd say, 'Look at all those peaches we canned,' or 'Look at all the wash we did,' and be obviously pleased about it. They were both helpful and supportive to me—models for my real self."

She also learned to be responsible for more than her share and to protect her younger brother and sister. As the oldest child, she learned self-reliance. And, "In order to avoid blame, I saw that things got taken care of."

Responsibility for others continued as a central theme for Mary. Sorting out what to hold and what to release in order to make room for her many talents and interests has been an ongoing dilemma. Mary walks this tightrope better than most.

About the same time that she divorced, Mary finished a Master's degree in Medieval English. She moved her four teenage daughters and multi-handicapped son from the suburbs of Detroit to California. It took nearly a year to find a job—clerical work that didn't begin to use the skills her new degree provided, but a job as an administrative assistant at a university counseling center. When I met her, Mary had wound her way out of the clerical ranks. She'd written a grant and was Assistant Director of the university's Learning Assistance Center. Shortly after we began working together, she left the university—once again facing the void of absolutely no job security. Her telling comment was, "I haven't starved yet!"

Our consulting work increased. We grappled with the intricate human relations problems our major client presented to us. We dealt with rejection, conflict, distrust, and skepticism. Mary never wavered. We drove thousands of miles together, providing training and consultation to our major client's widely scattered business sites.

Mary's first angina attack seized her in the middle of a training session in Modesto. Neither of us knew what it was. We were both terrified. As we left the hospital later that day, she said, "You don't need to worry. There's no way I'm going to die in this client's bathroom!" And then, six months later while caring for her daughter and infant

I learned about endurance, hope—and later—creativity. I think core strength combines those three.

twins who had hepatitis, she contracted that disease.

Time passed and Mary slowly recovered. She learned what she could about her heart condition. It was scary for her, but she dealt with the frustration of limited energy and having to be selective about her activities. She kept on keeping on. Our client continued to grow and we became more and more deeply involved in the organization's processes.

That wasn't enough. Mary's difficult, aging, and ailing mother moved in with her. Various daughters and now, grandchildren required assorted levels of support. Her disabled son continued to live at home. She patched together a support system of part-time caregivers who could lend a hand when she was out of town. And she continued to live her life.

Mary worked with our mutual client after I left. Her last project there was to help them institute a childcare program for employees.

Over the years, Mary has personified core strength, the inherent authority of the feminine, for me. She matter-of-factly deals with her responsibilities, disappointments, and personal pain. And she finds life very much worth living. Late one afternoon as we were driving along, I was particularly aware of how burdened she must be. We were talking away, but the other track in my brain was focused on the many stresses that fill her life, wondering, once more, how she does it. Suddenly, she lifted both hands upward toward the glowing, backlit leaves of the giant sycamores that arch the downtown Sacramento street we were on. "Look at that light," she said. "Isn't that glorious? I feel like the luckiest person alive!"

Core strength is more than being tough or hard or strong. It also has to do with appreciating the light.

Summary

The dimensions you've worked through in this section provide a solid base for moving on to the next chapters. As you allow yourself to understand and appreciate your strength and stamina, your grounded self-trust becomes realistic and solid.

Spend some time with your journal now to create a personal summary for this section. Describe yourself in terms of *1) Body Energy, 2) Persistence,* and *3) Core strength*. Make three columns on a page, one for each of these dimensions. List the ways that you rely on each of them at work. You can add to the lists as you learn more about each dimension on the job. Write the specific ways you intend to concentrate your attention on one or more of them. Tell a friend what you plan to do.

Before going on to the next section, which swirls and bubbles through water's connective dimensions, get up and move around. Feel the floor beneath your feet and appreciate your connection with the Earth. Walk hard and feel securely grounded in your *body energy, persistence,* and *core strength*. Better yet, take the opportunity if you can to go for a walk outdoors. Concentrate on the way you place your foot for each step. Think about connecting with the very center of our planet—about yourself as a part of the earth. A sense of being well centered in the Earth dimensions is a strong base for moving on. You can swim from that base without losing yourself. Go for your walk. Relax. And then dive in.

WATER

THE FLOWING CONNECTION

Water: The Element

A s one male vice president said to me, "Whether she makes it or not is determined by a woman's ability to kick ass." It has become O.K. to be a woman in more and more places, but getting along in womanly ways remains taboo for the most part. "Feminine" isn't a positive label in the business world. In order to survive the standard work environment, the feminine takes a deep dive out of sight.

It's time to find ways to get the work done that honor rather than violate relationships.

Energy for closeness—contact and caring—flows from the heart of the feminine presence. Can we create pathways that permit and foster connectedness in corporate life and politics? How can we use this energy to ease stress and work together productively? The previous section focused on individual strength and stamina. This one explores the dimensions that thrive in relationships.

Understanding your own personal experience is first. What is your way of being receptive or flexible? How does each dimension in this section help you or get in your way? How can you find these strengths in yourself when you need them? How does your shadow side express itself? When your inner experience seems clear, you can speak out and be self-supportive on the job.

For many centuries, masculinity has had center stage to solidify the patriarchal values of law, order, form, and science. The flow of connection brings feminine balance to these important contributions.

Concern and caring wash through this element. It's the

aspect of the feminine that is most different from the masculine, and it's the part that suffers most at work as women move into positions of authority. It's where women sacrifice themselves beyond reason in jobs that provide support or care—secretarial work, teaching, nursing, social work.

To elevate the qualities of caring into the decisionmaking aspects of work life—into management and executive board rooms—is to change the way business is done. That can happen only if women value staying connected and climb the ladder at the same time, a very tricky maneuver that requires highly developed balance and skill.

In an office where "winning at any cost" is emphasized, feminine needs for connection lose out. Who wants to compete with someone she cares about for a promotion or stab her work partner in the back to get preferred hours? Research tells us that girls learn to hang back rather than hurt a friend's feelings by beating her,[1] and this style goes to work with us. Flowing connection is the power of the feminine that is most undervalued on the job.

When the company's priority is to move in a straight line—to observe order—then feeling-based logic falls behind. Women's ways of knowing, personal and experience-based as they are, don't fit. We need to be secure enough to recognize the ways we think and feel as legitimate tools for getting work done.

But it's also important to look at the other side. The organization bogs down of its own weight when structure and power needs are ignored and connection is overvalued. Talented, productive artists can't support themselves with their art when they don't develop the structures necessary to finish or market their work. Groups that can't progress for fear of hurt feelings over disagreements *don't function.* There has to be a way to "cut the losses" and move on to a decision. A balance between masculine structure and feminine unboundedness is most effective.

Part of feminine sensitivity is knowing when to make the shift and having the flexibility to do it.

Work relationships, and then work practices, can change only when we're each secure in our womanhood. We have to be willing and able to lower our Superwoman shields and risk a different kind of honesty and vulnerability in our work relationships. This is asking a lot. So, understandably, we hide our feminine needs and feelings and move over to the dominant masculine mode in systems that run with strict attention to rules and protocol. For short-term, high-pressure situations, this approach may be the most direct and efficient. But as a lifestyle it has a very high price. Alice's story provides a case in point.

The Very Familiar Story
of Lost Feminine Connection

Alice checked the last item on the agenda and closed her briefcase as the meeting ended. She had run the planning session by the book. Assignments were clear and complete. Everybody had eventually agreed to do her or his part. Sparks had flown over whether simply to inform the supervisors who would be responsible for carrying the project forward, or to ask for their input and consent. Alice had put a lid on the discussion when she said, "In the interest of efficiency, I prefer that we just let the supervisors know what we expect of them." The energy in the room slackened as tired staff members complied. After all, the supervisors would *have* to cooperate. It was their job.

Alice knew the ropes. She'd been with the company for fifteen years. After college, she had captured a stellar job in aerospace with one of her present company's competitors. She had known it would be a challenge, that she was a "token woman," but she was very skilled at being one of the boys. She felt good about her style: "In college

I was a top seeded tennis player," she told me, "I spent days on end travelling and kibitzing with men. I speak their language." She could talk sports with the best and clearly understood the importance of "chain of command." And, more importantly for her new job in middle management, she could glide through "administrivia" without ruffling feathers.

Alice's education in human relations had started early. She was her father's daughter. She learned how to get his attention by doing a "good job." She could see clearly that he knew how to get things done and she learned to do the same to earn his praise. When he told her to do something, it didn't occur to her to hesitate.

In high school and college Alice didn't have much patience for her classmates who "questioned authority." She could be the life of a party and knew how to have a good time, but she most enjoyed her reputation for competence, leadership, and not rocking the boat.

At one point, she had thought seriously about marriage. But Stan couldn't ever get it together in a way that seemed secure for her. She knew he loved her, and at times she could imagine being very happy with him. They lived together for a while, but she found work more exciting—more stimulating than Stan's less than ambitious lifestyle. She couldn't take time for "doing nothing," as she put it. She could rely on her own efforts, her career, for fulfillment. She'd never been particularly interested in any other partner.

When I met Alice, she was 45 and her career, now that she was a VP, was no longer either stimulating or fulfilling. Her company loved her. She could run a meeting and get the company's work done with talent and skill. But still, as she said, "I'm the woman who has everything, and my life is a wasteland. I don't have time to turn around, but I'm bored to death. I wonder why I stick around."

A Look at the Spin-off

I'm not implying that marriage and children are the ways to fulfillment for women. On the contrary, I'm saying we need to bring the feminine along with us to work. We all also need the challenge and stimulation we find in the bigger world. But, like many of us who bought those grey pin-stripes with an air of excitement—"I'll show 'em"—Alice deadened some important dimensions of her feminine presence, and she had no conscious awareness of her loss. The fluid, complex, feminine needs, feelings, and vulnerabilities that are the focus of this chapter are the ones she worked hardest to cover up.

Oh sure. She could rely on them when she wanted to tune in to nonverbal communication and other "people" parts of work—or to move around men who followed more linear paths. But as for indulging them in herself, nurturing them, or expressing them in public, forget it.

At work, Alice had wrung herself dry in her flight from the ill-defined, boundless depths of the feminine. But could she have found a richer, more self-nourishing way to work? What other options did she have?

Water, the Feminine Metaphor

What better reminds us of both the constructive and destructive feminine urges toward connection than water? Water supports life, cuts canyons through hard stone, bubbles up in virgin springs, destroys everything in its course, or putrifies in brackish sloughs. Variable and boundless, it goes where it flows. Like connection, it's necessary for life but can be unwieldy to manage. On the job, it's tempting to build dams and reservoirs for control and forget about the wild beauty of white-water rivers.

Our capacity to live in our womanhood at work, to

find comfort in the ebb and flow of relationships, can grow as we discover ways of attending to rather than ignoring our connections—*Receptivity, Flexibility, Nurturance,* and *Affinity.* When we respect and promote these qualities, we can successfully nurture ourselves as well as others on the job.

To get into a watery frame of mind, let your imagination float freely for a moment. Imagine that you can splash yourself with sparkling bubbles. Bathe in water's mysteries. Allow other water images to pour in. A clear Rocky Mountain lake mirrors a summer day. A flood swallows half of Georgia and leaves thousands homeless. April showers, thunderclouds, icebergs, steam, rolling Pacific waves. Water isn't a simple element. It's surface calm hides riptides and dangerous currents. Water's soothing, reassuring qualities are legendary. Our bodies are full of it. We depend on it for life itself. It can cleanse us, buoy our spirits, sustain us, engulf us, or wash us away.

But it's hard to take to work.

Feminine eddies such as the secretarial pool support organizational work but don't direct its course. As a result, moving into the mainstream is still difficult for many of us. Women who have been "left behind" in the more "feminine" parts of the organization are often resentful and can be the toughest critics of women moving up. And women who have achieved power often did so at great personal cost. So they aren't inclined to welcome and nurture their sisters. And in a competitive system, they have no model for doing so. Their lives are further complicated by the fact that work at the management level isn't easily observable, which leaves ample room for projection, prejudice, and stereotyping. They easily become objects of suspicion or chronic attack. In the struggle to survive under such strenuous conditions, many set down the water jug and just climb the ladder.

To "live our feminine presence at work" we need to

To elevate the qualities of caring into management and executive board rooms is to change the way business is done.

communicate effectively that we feel comfortable and capable with who we are. We need to get the message through in ways that allow people to relax the unconscious barriers they maintain.

We also need to find language that portrays the subtleties and strengths of connectedness. We need to let men—and women who downplay their femininity—know that they can take us seriously even though we don't conform to masculine ways of working. Our communication can be indirect, through our actions rather than our words. For instance, when manager Shauna Granger enters a room, her presence is noticeable. And, even in her man-cut uniform jacket, her warm personal style, invites connection. She walks without self-consciousness, smiles directly, and hears your conversation. It doesn't take long to discover she says what she means and admits her mistakes. At the same time, it's clear that she is not someone to mess with.

To change things at work, we have to find ways to translate what we've learned about our feminine strengths into behavior. We can wear our own coat, unless the "corporate uniform" really fits.

Not everybody is going to appreciate a feminine, connected approach. Barriers that protect the status quo may become even more prominent in relation to this element. We need to know how to deal with those barriers when we encounter them—whether to go through, over, or around them, or simply sail our ship on friendlier seas.

You can truly appreciate your tendency to make connections as you wade in the water of the feminine presence at work. Net weaving is a legitimate, effective way to work that has increasing acceptance in the corporate world.

Companies such as Hewlett-Packard and Volvo have built their advanced organizational systems on the principle of cooperation in team-building, planning, and quality control. These concepts are difficult for men and women who've moved up in competitive organizations. They fly in the face of rugged American individualism. And to move from competition to cooperation requires a significant redirection of underlying assumptions—a paradigm shift. When this occurs, everything changes. The values, culture, and style of the organization may shift. Sometimes even the reason for being in business is different. The old assumptions are out the window.

But participative management, a collaborative, non-competitive approach to getting work done, is much more effective for running complex organizations than is the traditional "chain of command." The flexibility of the matrix (shifting centers of authority and control) increases confusion but ultimately handles modern work challenges better than the top-down pyramid can.

As Marilyn Loden points out in her book, *Feminine Leadership, or How to Succeed in Business without Being One of the Boys,* " . . . there is a growing recognition of the need for more people-oriented skills—a heightened sensitivity to nonverbal cues, creative problem-solving, intuitive management, participatory leadership—the same skills that women have been taught to cultivate since they were little girls."[2] All of these spring from flowing connection.

Inroads are starting to appear in noticeable ways. Joan Konner, Dean of the Graduate School of Journalism at Columbia University, made these observations:

> The female sensibility is growing everywhere in our culture today, in literature, in art, in history, politics, the media. There seems to be a great hunger for values that we associate with the private sphere of home, family and spiritual life. We see it in the concern for the environment, in the search for a collective spirit and relationships based on the awareness of the interconnectedness of all life.

Some believe that women, as they succeed in the marketplace, are retaining what is valuable in what used to be considered the domestic sphere and bringing that broader, more life-supporting perspective into view. On a threatened Mother Earth, some—women and men—are calling into question the efficacy of the instinct for the jugular. . . . [3]

As an individual working in an organizational system, you know about making connections. What you have to offer is valuable. But, because it rocks the status quo, problems accompany a personal, feminine style at work. The dimensions in this section offer some of the qualities that can help you stay afloat. Explore each of them, and keep your focus on how you can bring the gifts of each one to your job.

Receptivity

isten. Hear the music. Absorb the subtleties. Sense the emotion that flows behind the words. Open up.

The capacity to take in, to "allow" a connection, forms a significant dimension of the feminine presence. Receptivity is the quiet dimension of the feminine that receives—a lover, a child, a friend, an idea. It's the part we want from our partner or our boss when we say, "I just want her or him to *hear* what I'm saying!" It's quiet. But it's not passive.

The receptive feminine has been misinterpreted as "passive." So, we need to make conscious decisions about when to receive and when to shut the gate.

In making a connection, it's as important to receive as it is to reach out. Receptivity provides the fertile moment in which the seed is planted—the open gate that invites the visitor and welcomes the unknown. When the door is closed, there can be no invasion. But new thoughts and feelings are shut out, too.

Openness and gentleness reside here: a teacher who hears a student's pain and confusion about a late assignment, a nurse who truly understands the terror a pre-operative patient isn't talking about, a manager who remembers that her secretary's son collects baseball cards and brings one to him from a business trip.

Receptivity allows differences, even confusion. Because no immediate action is necessary, listening should come easily. The focus is on the other, not the self. The capacity to be there is enough.

Receptivity controls the sluice gate through which nurturance flows. If the gate's always closed, we dry up. We can't take in support, affection, love.

In the business world, time pressures and competitive relationships tend to squeeze receptivity dry. On the other hand, sitting around being receptive can get us exploited if we're seen as weak. The receptive feminine has been misinterpreted as "passive." So, we need to make conscious decisions about when to receive and when to shut the gate. And that's not an easy thing to do. Sacramento's former Mayor Anne Rudin (see pages 37 – 39) spoke of some of her struggles:

> In the development of North Natomas, I've been criticized as being unflexible, unwilling to support growth in this community. The opposite is true. We should have taken four years, not one, to plan that area and we would have been able to learn about the flooding before committing large tracts of land for development. The planning process has to unfold like the petals of a flower.

The capacity to say no or to set a boundary when we've had enough—and to make it stick—ensures our ability to be receptive. The receptive feminine is safe only when it can't be overrun. Many women who don't know how to set a boundary feel they have to submerge this part of themselves for fear of being seen as weak.

But receptivity is such a central part of us that its annihilation hurts after awhile. The absence of conscious receptivity is hard to detect. But when we work with our guard up all the time, we deaden our ability to accept a genuine connection. Relationships with others begin to be based on what works, an economy of trade-offs, rather than on honest human feeling.

Alice's story in the opening pages of the "Water" section (pages 106 – 107) demonstrates how a lack of receptivity and the fear of being overrun blocked her openness to the concern that her staff members expressed. They wanted to involve the supervisors—to be receptive and take in their advice rather than just inform them of a set decision. But Alice skipped over this information in the interest of "efficiency," and the people with whom she worked gave in to her authority. As a result, their energy collapsed, and Alice deadened herself a little more.

If Alice had been receptive to the concerns of her colleagues, things would probably have turned out differently. To invite and use input from the supervisors would certainly have taken more time and trouble up front. But the time spent listening to the supervisors and using their input would likely have been more than repaid in results. As it was, the policy was passed along and the supervisors had to make do. Order was maintained, but the messy richness of creativity was lost.

In today's complex organizations, the capacity to listen to others is a valuable asset. As organizations shift from clear chains of command to project-based management or other less clearly defined structures, our capacity to take in information, both content and emotional messages, helps us stay tuned to the constant processes of change. By paying attention, we can make decisions based on what's really happening or needs to happen.

THE SHADOW SIDE

A quagmire hides in receptivity's shadow. Generations of disempowered women live half-lives here. There are no boundaries, no solid places to take a stand. It's a terrible place to get lost.

The "doormat" is stuck here. She doesn't say no and she gets walked on. The shadow says to give in and conform, to pay more attention to the views of others than to your own. Years of habit make it hard to stand up for one's own view, or to know for sure what that is.

Closed-mindedness and rigidity are other ways the shadow forms this dimension. If it's too scary to be receptive, nothing new or different can enter. Only information that fits with preconceived ideas is allowed in. Alice lives in this place.

The ultimate "yes woman" also lurks on the shadow side of receptivity. She fits the feminine stereotype of "weak, passive, dependent." She lives in all of us and emerges when we are too frightened or overwhelmed to stand up for ourselves. She whispers, "Oh, I can't do anything about it anyway," and collapses when it's too hard or too much work to set a limit.

Receptivity's shadow opens the door for any and all ideas, suggestions, projects. *Just because something is worth doing, it's not up to you to do it.* If you find yourself distracted by more input than you can manage, look here. Give yourself permission to build a dam, to say no, to choose. Create a system for making priorities based on choices that are good for you.

Have you ever had the feeling that you have spent the whole day working as hard as you could and that you haven't done one single thing that has any meaning to you? Receptivity's shadow may be the culprit here. Glance over your shoulder and see if she is directing you in the service of others so much that you've lost yourself.

A finely tuned ability to receive, to hear, and take in, sensitizes the feminine presence to important information that waters all the other dimensions. If you feel you've taken in too much, that you're stuck in a quagmire of too many yesses, reach for the one word that shines light on receptivity's shadow: No.

SELF-REFLECTION

Where does receptivity fit in your personality make-up? Be as honest as you can when you estimate where you fit on both sides of this continuum.

STRENGTH: Listening is easy for me. I'm comfortable with differences. I like being emotionally close to others. I'm comfortable being quiet while others talk. I can hear feedback that I don't like and work with it. I can take compliments. I can hear my own inner voice.

SHADOW: I believe others' opinions of me more than my own. My feelings are easily hurt. I let other people walk all over me. / I shut out opinions that differ from mine. I keep to myself and avoid close relationships at work. / I will do anything to avoid hurting someone's feelings.

TIME FOR YOURSELF

Receptivity can be a frightening dimension because it has to do with letting go. The best way to understand how it works in your personality is to wade in and take a look.

If you want to spend more time on the Earth dimensions before receptivity becomes your focus, just list the ideas that come to you while you read through this section. Your first impressions will be useful to you later. Take your time and proceed through the following steps in a receptive mood. Choose a few of the exercises to explore in depth, either now or later.

- IN YOUR JOURNAL, describe your "receptivity" in a positive light. What does receptivity mean to you? Being passive? Exploited? Vulnerable? Having the capacity to hear another? Create your own *positive* definition that affirms this feminine dimension for you.

• THINK OF AN EXAMPLE of your "inner voice" trying to communicate with you in the past week. Receptivity includes the capacity to hear yourself as well as others. Self-confidence grows as you learn to allow your inner experience to inform you. Take that information seriously. It provides balance to what you receive from the outside.

• TAKE TIME TO LEARN more about your own receptivity. Is there someone at work with whom you feel comfortable in this dimension? How do you relax your guard with this person? Can you feel your muscles relax?

• WRITE DOWN THREE THINGS you've seen other women do that seem appropriately receptive. Do they differ from your own typical way of being receptive? Do you know another woman who can be open and receptive without getting pushed around? Ask her how she does it.

• TAKE A LOOK AT YOUR SHADOW. Think of the most passive "yes woman" you know. What about her behavior do you find most disgusting? Are these things you do yourself or are afraid you might do? We can usually see our shadow side more easily in others than in ourselves. Write about the ways you say yes when you really mean no. What is your shadow trying to tell you?

• LEARN TO LISTEN really well. It's safe to take in what other people say when you are secure in your self. You can be in sync with another person's feelings without abandoning your own point of view. You don't have to agree with what others say to be a good listener. Think of a time you've been able to do this, and describe it in your journal.

• LEARN TO BREATHE DEEPLY and relax when you're trying to receive. Your body energy sends information to your mind. Pay attention to your patterns of tension in various situations. Let your muscles tell you whether you feel safe enough to be open, vulnerable, and compassionate, or whether you need to be careful. Draw a stick figure in your journal. Highlight in red the places your tension increases when you block your receptivity.

• LEARN TO RECOGNIZE OVERLOAD so that you can speak clearly when you want to set a boundary. Develop skill at assertive limit setting. When you say something like, "I've taken in as much as I can for now. I need to think about what you've said," you set a clear limit that requires no immediate action or work overload on your part.

• BE CONSCIOUS OF WHETHER or not a particular person or situation deserves your receptive vulnerability. This dimension calls for an ability to say both yes and no—an ability to open and close by choice, not just by reaction. How you choose to share this dimension is up to you.

• TRY BREATHING INTO YOUR TENSION when you find yourself erecting blocks. Say to yourself, "I can relax and open up, because if I get overwhelmed, I know I can set a limit"—and *then* listen. Have you observed women like Alice at work who block their receptivity? Are you aware when you put up blocks unnecessarily? When you intentionally set a limit, you're making a choice. But when a block emerges without your knowledge, your shadow is in charge. Write about an example of each that you can remember.

• IMAGINE YOURSELF AS A POWERFUL, open listener who can deal with another and set limits when needed. What images come to mind when you think of powerful, feminine receptivity? Making love? Holding an infant? Listening to a friend? These feelings are so personal they're difficult to transport to the workplace, but you can do it. Write a brief scenario that describes both your receptivity and your limit setting at work.

• TRUST YOURSELF TO STAND your ground. Core strength and receptivity work together. The woman whose resolve is clear doesn't get thrown off course by criticism or differing opinions. If you trust your core strength, you can afford to open up, take in what's useful, and discard the rest.

Now, turn back to page 26 and make any necessary adjustments to your Self-Assessment Scale. Mark it with a different color than your first note so you can easily compare your original beliefs with your more educated response.

FLOW WITH YOUR CONNECTION

You've had the opportunity to get to know both sides of your receptivity dimension in a personal way. Now let's move from personal experience to the work environment and explore what happens to this part of you on the job. Why do we work so hard to veil this dimension? Why is it so hard to benefit from this finely tuned instrument at work?

Research with young children as well as studies of adult group communication patterns,[1] provides help in understanding some of the negative aspects of receptivity in the workplace. If we follow the path of least resistance, get stuck in the shadow side of receptivity, we do more than our share of receiving. If we don't balance it with good limit setting and solid assertive communication, we run smack into a barrier: **Men Don't Listen To And Aren't Influenced By What Women Say**.

Women in business have dealt with this barrier by learning to behave and communicate like men. But in doing so, they dilute their ability to bring feminine influence to work. To get through this barrier rather than become a part of it, work constantly to improve your communication skills in ways that support your feminine presence. Say it in "feminine." Then translate to "masculine" if you need to. "Something about this just doesn't feel right. I can't say what" becomes, "I think we need to evaluate _____ and determine whether it's really feasible."

Do what you can—organize workshops or other educational experiences—to increase the numbers of people who support and accept feminine influence. People who are simply inexperienced are often willing to accept new views, and a lack of information just adds to gender bias.

Use feminine language that communicates feminine emotions—attitudes of caring and responsibility—rather than emphasizing more masculine passions toward domination and territoriality. Avoid language that is loaded with violent metaphors from war and male team sports, even though that may be the accepted mode of communication where you work. Use language that portrays your own interests and values. Be receptive to your inner voice and express it.

Patriarchal communication practices affect men as well as women because they address "position" rather than "person." It may not be an easy process, but it's worth it to try to find others with whom you can talk about their emotional experiences. If you can find a male co-worker who is open to this possibility, a conversation about what happened is a way of softening this barrier and building an alliance. For instance, check in with him when bad things happen: "When the vice president told us he didn't think we were doing a good job, how was that for you?" If he glosses over his pain, try a gentle confrontation: "That doesn't seem to fit with the amount of effort you've invested in this project. I'm surprised to hear you take it lightly."

If you know that this powerful barrier, **Men Don't Listen To Women**, is a reality where you work, you can learn to deal with it effectively. If you're tuned in to your own receptive capacities, you're in a good position to help others develop theirs.

Do	*Don't*
Make sure that your listener is giving you his or her full attention.	Participate in putting down your efforts or those of others.
Assert your wish to finish any sentence or thought you have started to say.	Consistently interrupt other women speakers.
Ask for the listener to say back to you what he or she has heard from you.	Expect that you will automatically get your "turn" in a mixed-sex group discussion.
Counter subtle or overt put-downs of your communication style.	Hesitate to point out that another woman's comments have been cut off or ignored.
Explicitly state that you expect to be taken seriously.	Let other people tell you how you should feel about issues at work.
Confront overt sexist comments or actions.	Assume that you will be heard and taken seriously.

The other side of this barrier is that women *do* tend to be influenced by men. This takes a tremendous amount of awareness and self-confidence to work through. It is so well-learned, unconscious, and deeply imbedded that it has the capacity to shut out feminine influence without your even knowing that's what happened. Your best efforts can be negated and you'll get no feedback to let you know why. Conscious, open communication with your male colleagues about this issue is very important.

When you can trust yourself, your own worth and power, you can stay open—receive—and you can relate to other women with openness and trust. You create the possibility of sharing information and knowledge, of contributing to a network of mutual trust and support. When you nurture this sharing, it can energize the best of your feminine presence at work—open and holding, contained and energetic.

Publicly acknowledge those who receive well, those who are good listeners. Call attention to the fact that you are listening, taking in information. Receiving is an active process that requires skill and concentration. It's a way of connecting.

Listen to other women. Your own self-hate and disrespect may run so deep that you not only discount yourself but also put down the contributions of other women. Try to listen between the lines for the music that sings beneath the surface. Hear what others are saying, what their feelings and concerns communicate. Support, share, learn to cooperate. Validate. Acknowledge. Corroborate.

The often unconscious patriarchal strategy of divide and conquer is a negative force for all women at work. When you compete for the attention of men you may win the "victory," but you defeat yourself and other women in vicious, destructive ways. The shadow side of the water dimensions invades the workplace and gives force to the patriarchal view that women are shallow and can't get along.

A FEMININE LEADER AT WORK

Ellen Steele, an executive officer in a New York manufacturing firm, told me a story that portrays the power of receptivity at work. At the time of the incident she described, her job as Vice President for Human Resources included responsibilities for organizational design, as well as other human resource functions. The more experienced of two women in the executive group, she was deeply involved in the company's massive efforts to reorganize.

The CEO wanted to improve the company's way of getting work done—to integrate historically different businesses within the organization, including a new acquisition. He looked to Ellen for help in making a major shift. As part of this effort, he proposed an off-site retreat that would involve the thirty top people.

Ellen dived in. She was excited about the opportunity and threw herself into designing a retreat experience. The company's business was to create experiences that involved learning. The retreat design would experiment with the ways people learn—physical, mental, emotional processes that address the whole person—as well as the hard-core business-oriented planning and development goals.

Ellen was well aware that many of the people involved felt threatened and would dig their heels in at the prospect of the unusual intimacy of a retreat experience. She put together a plan she felt would respect their needs and still provide opportunities for growth and change. The stakes were high. As an experienced, competent professional, she felt challenged, excited, and nervous about this major risky responsibility.

On a Friday two weeks before everyone was to leave for the retreat site, the CEO cancelled it. He said it wouldn't work. People—particularly the most senior members—didn't want to go. Ellen had expected resistance from the group but was dumbfounded by the CEO's announcement. She was hurt and furious. The CEO had *wanted* the retreat. She had supported the project and planned for it. More than anything, she felt betrayed. What had happened? Why?

Ellen confronted the CEO about his decision. He agreed to hold an emergency meeting of the top eight decisionmakers the following Monday.

Ellen's emotions swirled. What in the world could she

do? She was convinced that this event was necessary to get the diverse group together in one location to plan their joint future. It was a potential turning point for the organization. Not a person who is easily thwarted, Ellen became immobilized. She didn't know if she wanted to, or could, do anything to neutralize the resistance to this event.

Ellen's angry shadow loomed large, growled, and drooled. Conflict gripped her as she vacillated between giving in to company pressures and sticking to her own beliefs and feelings. Her struggle portrays one woman's efforts to stay in her feminine presence while contributing to her company.

She considered gearing up to create a presentation for the emergency meeting—logic, notes, pages of overheads designed to persuade them that this was the thing to do— good, solid, masculine logic to make the listeners change their minds. She also considered quitting.

Ellen worked. She agonized. She fumed and felt depressed. It wasn't right. Somehow, she was taking responsibility for convincing people to do what she believed was a necessary move. She knew this was against her principles. It pushed against everything she was trying to embody in her life and her organization to respond in this way. But she was at a total loss for an alternative.

Ellen began saying things to herself like, "Trust your wisdom." This was a little comforting but didn't have much form or provide security when she thought about the Monday meeting. She went to church and prayed . . . no answers. She returned to her apartment and plopped on the couch. She picked up a copy of Lao Tzu, searching for an eastern alternative, and even found herself looking through the Bible. No tangible help there either. She only continued to hear the faint refrain: "Trust your wisdom."

There were no peers or role models to hear her cry for help. She had to work her own way to an approach. After hours of confusion, reaching in and wondering what her wisdom and experience were going to offer, clarity emerged. Ellen began to feel calm as she understood what she would do. She would let go—give up investment in the outcome. If she didn't hold a position, it wasn't her retreat. She would not have an agenda. She would walk into the meeting empty.

Feeling centered and in herself, an open if somewhat uncertain vice president, did just that. As people arrived and settled themselves, she waited. When time came for her presentation, she said, "I understand nobody wants to go. What do you want to do?" Her executive colleagues began talking to each other. For three hours they talked to each other.

Ellen held the space—listened, stayed receptive. She maintained a truly open hand, neither pushing nor pulling. She served as a resource and support while the decision-makers, through their own heated discussion and in their own wisdom, became clear about *their* needs for the retreat and the importance of supporting it. It became their event, a company retreat, not Ellen's or the CEO's.

Ellen would most likely have been able to convince the group to hold the retreat through direction and persuasion. But two things would have been different. The group would not have owned responsibility for the decision, and she would have been less true to her feminine self. Ellen's personal experience was important. But the real difference for the group had to do with whose retreat it was going to be. No longer was a retreat being imposed on resistant participants, or cancelled by a frightened and frustrated CEO. The executives had responsibly taken ownership of the decisionmaking process. They would work *with* Ellen rather than giving in to the company's power to require their attendance. Now the participants would be present in a real way, not just making an appearance.

First, Ellen was receptive to her own inner experience—hurt, anger, confusion. She listened to her unhappi-

As organizations shift to project-based management, our capacity to take in information helps us stay tuned to the constant processes of change.

ness about doing a high-powered persuasive presentation. She used that information to guide her decisionmaking. Then she had the courage to be receptive to the needs and opinions of others who disagreed with her. She walked into the executive committee meeting "empty." She was a vessel ready to receive.

But her receptive process was far from passive. She was open, vulnerable, capable. Although it may have appeared that she was doing nothing, that was not the case. Holding and supporting is active, not passive, and at times can require tremendous psychological effort. To sit by, stay out of the fray, may require more energy than to get involved, especially in our culture where non-directiveness is often interpreted as inept or weak.

SUMMARY

Receptivity is the underlying dimension for all connectedness. It fits so much devalued and stereotyped feminine behavior in the business world that it may be difficult to see it as a powerful resource. But it's 50% of every relationship. The fact that women have done 95% of the receiving and are trying to turn this habit around sometimes gets in the way of developing and appreciating receptivity's gifts. For the record, they include the ability to hear, to have empathy, and to predict intuitively what's going to happen next.

Being receptive takes courage. It isn't being passive. It's agreeing to hear new information, differing viewpoints, someone else's pain.

Develop your receptivity as an equal partner with your core strength. By doing so, you take in what's available from the outside world, combine it with your own feminine wisdom and experience, and create a new mix that adds feminine sensitivity to what happens at work.

Flexibility

S–t–r–e–t–c–h, b–e–n–d, t–w–i–s–t. Feel your muscles relax and tingle. Now do it all over again. And keep doing it. No, it's not aerobic exercise. It's just life. This magnificent quality of flexibility runs throughout the feminine presence. It lets your attention flow to wherever it's needed and changes directions with little notice or awareness in order to keep you connected with your surroundings. If receptivity is working well, flexibility follows.

Both genetics and learning influence feminine flexibility. Your body may be in one state or another, depending on the time of the month or the time in your life. You learn to ride the hormonal roller coaster and go about your business. When you're a mom or a person who works with babies and small children—not to mention adolescents—flexibility is the key to maintaining a sense of personal balance. A basic feminine strength is your ability to take care of children while you cook dinner, plan a schedule, watch TV, and think through tomorrow's meeting. At the office, this translates into the ability to take a phone call, work on the computer, talk to someone who walks into your office, and respond to a crisis, all within a few minutes. "Women are more flexible," I heard over and over as I asked people around the country questions about the feminine. "Women can do a lot of things at once, and it doesn't seem to bother them too much." This is one of the advantages confirmed by Sally Helgesen in *The Female Advantage: Women's Ways of Leadership*.[1] She found that women executives expect and flow with interruptions—see them as part of their job, not something outside the job—rather than getting upset by them.

The capacity to attend to conflicting needs of several different people and relate to each of them is a part of this, too. This quality is often under-appreciated, even ridiculed as fickle or two-faced. Men, and women who have adopted masculine standards, sometimes find flexibility threatening and diminish it by calling it "flaky." Other women who identify with this evaluation often reject their own gifts in this dimension.

When transferred to the work environment, flexibility delivers small miracles. Secretaries who type letters while they answer the phone, manage an appointment schedule, and keep track of who is who and who is where, develop their flexibility to a fine art. Supervisors who have a sixth sense about what's going on, or account executives who move from one client's problem to another's at a rapid rate, rely on this dimension without giving it a thought.

And it is revolutionizing such major industries as healthcare. A physician with whom I spoke pointed to ways that the flexibility of female physicians allows them to find ways of practicing medicine and managing their complex lives:

> Women physicians see their work differently than Western-trained male doctors. We're willing to work fewer hours. Involvement in our private lives is important to us. We take different jobs. Many women work in situations where they can count on regular hours—in agencies, HMOs [health maintenance organizations], part time, in government positions. Benefits and flexible hours are priorities.
>
> Usually, women-centered health care networks are all women—a team. They provide alternative referrals to nurse practitioners and chiropractors, and for acupuncture and therapeutic massage.
>
> Women physicians take time out for maternity

leave and child care. But they practice longer, live longer, survive the profession longer.

New ways don't come easily. This same physician described a professional meeting focused on "Women in Medicine." About half the male physicians walked out after the first twenty minutes. "You are ruining medicine!" one of them said to the speaker as he exited.

Misunderstandings between women and men happen when we take our male colleagues' ability to be flexible for granted. In working with groups of men, I learned after a few uncomfortable confrontations that it was important to *announce* a change in direction if I shifted a meeting agenda. Admittedly, that's good practice with any group. But I've noticed that women "go with the flow" much more easily. Minor adjustments or shifts are less likely to throw us off track.

A good, clear, straight line to the goal has become the accepted way to get work done. Men seem to have a more difficult time shifting their attention from task to task and prefer a focused approach. They experience darting from item to item as disconnected and upsetting. Seen through their eyes, this "flightiness" isn't flexibility but lack of focus. If we look to these men for their stamps of approval, we are likely to agree that our way is inferior and reinforce this misconception. We need to know about our flexibility and speak up on its behalf.

Even if your job requires concentration and focus rather than flexibility, getting along with your co-workers is easier with the help of this dimension. Flexibility, like persistence, is one of those qualities that you probably take for granted unless, for some reason, its absence is called to your attention.

THE SHADOW SIDE

Of course, a darker side shadows flexibility. That wonderful radar that tunes in to nearby activity can distract you too easily. You can be so flexible that you automatically pick up on work items that fall through the cracks as if they're discarded and forgotten toys. Soon you're doing everybody's work but yours.

One of the hardest things women who have been at home have to learn to do in the work environment is to build personal boundaries and stay within them. At home, especially doing the work of mothering, *everything* is your responsibility. Mom is usually the person who keeps track of the toddler while folding the laundry and helping the eight-year-old with her homework. It doesn't work to say to the toddler, "Stay in one place, now, I'm focused on helping Jenny with her story." For those who are accustomed to taking responsibility for whatever presents itself it takes self-discipline to walk by and leave the toys on the floor.

Old-time practices in the office assume that men do the "important" work and women "pick up after them." And without giving it a thought, many women fall into the trap. This can change only when we look our flexibility in the eye and say, "No. I see that needs to be done, but I'm not the one."

Flexibility gets shadowy when we slip into another's emotional space and get stuck there. It's great to have the capacity for empathy, but we need to stay on our own side in emotional relationships. We can get so flexible that we lose our ability to take care of ourselves and try to be all things to all people in situations where others need a lot. In the helping professions, many women struggle with this shadow until experience or burnout helps them learn about setting limits clearly, if not comfortably.

Rigidity is another aspect of flexibility's shadow. Fear

of being overrun stiffens the response before any bending can be allowed. A colleague said to me once, "I always say no. Then I can change my mind if I want to." This practice protected her, but it also made her a tough person to work with.

SELF-REFLECTION

Take a few moments to estimate how your flexibility works for and against you. Focus on how this dimension serves you at work (strength)—or gets in your way (the shadow side). The following ideas can help you with your self-assessment of this dimension.

STRENGTH: I can shift from one activity to another with ease. When my attention is disrupted, it's not difficult to return to what I was doing previously. I can deal with opinions that are different from mine. I can change direction when I get information that lets me know it's important to do so.

SHADOW: It's hard for me to stay focused on anything. My attention is easily diverted, and I constantly skip from one thing to another. / I'm fairly rigid and can't take in ideas that differ from my own. Changing direction is very difficult for me once I get going on something.

If flexibility is a dimension you want to develop further, the first step is to heighten your awareness of ways you find yourself being either rigid or wishy-washy. After you get better acquainted with this dimension, identify one or two areas at work and experiment with flexibility in a conscious way. For now, make a note or two in your journal about what these areas are, and how you can go about working with them. Then sample a few of the exercises for greater self-understanding and a chance to work in this dimension.

TIME FOR YOURSELF

As you think about yourself in this dimension, see if you're as psychologically supple as you might hope. Here are some ways you can experiment. Try to determine the degree of flexibility that's comfortable for you. Think about whether you need to s–t–r–e–t–c–h your capacity or work to define your boundaries more clearly.

• LIST IN YOUR JOURNAL the things that are happening around you right now. Music, machinery noises, other people? Were you aware of them as you were reading? Is it difficult to shift your attention from the book to your journal to your surroundings and back to the book again?

• NOW SHIFT YOUR ATTENTION back to your immediate environment. Do you find it difficult or easy to shift your thoughts and focus on your surroundings? You can choose either concentration or scanning. Pay attention to whether or not you resist change—whether previous thoughts trail into the present activity. Then shift your concentration back to your reading.

• GIVE YOURSELF PERMISSION to focus on your own flexibility for a moment. List the ways you are flexible at work. Can you shift easily from task to task? Do you deal with differences well? Are you able to relate to people who disagree with each other? And you?

• THINK OF A RECENT EXAMPLE in which you dealt with conflicting information and kept or modified your own position. Write about it in your journal. If you trust your own capacity to sustain your beliefs, you can afford to hear conflicting information and selectively change your views without losing your sense of self. Do you accept information or ideas that differ from your own view? Can you put your preconceived views aside and evaluate the relevance of someone else's opinions?

• LOOK AT YOUR SHADOW SIDE. Think of the most wishy-washy person you know—first she's on one side and then the other. Write down what you like least about her exaggerated flexibility. Which of these character-istics are part of you? Or are there some you work overtime to keep under control? Listen for the message under your urge to comply too readily. What are you frightened about? Write it in your journal. What's a more direct way to deal with your fear than giving in?

• LEARN TO RECOGNIZE whether you're following your own inner direc-tion or doing another's bidding in order to avoid rejection or anger. Co-dependency, getting your needs met by taking care of others, contributes to hyper-flexibility for women who haven't been powerful in their own right. The capacity to bend to another's needs as a way of maintaining control is a dark side of this dimension that has trapped many a woman. If you hear yourself saying, "If I don't do this for so and so, she or he will be mad at me," you're in your shadow. List examples of co-dependency in your relationships at work.

• LIST SOME EXAMPLES OF PATHS you haven't followed. How do you capi-talize on flexibility without being either wishy-washy or co-dependent? The down side of flexibility means that you never follow a job through to the end. In order to trust your flexibility, you must also trust your capacity to concentrate when that is your task.

• PAY ATTENTION to how you express yourself when you're with an all-female peer group at work. Experiment with using "feminine" expression at work. Be ready to translate into "business language" when you need to. In their book, *The Feminization of America*, authors Elinor Lenz and Barbara Meyerhoff point out that women are much more able to adopt masculine language style than men are to communicate in feminine lan-guage.[2] Do you find yourself shifting from feminine to masculine lan-guage in order to be understood or taken seriously at work? List some examples.

• IF YOU WOULD LIKE TO increase your flexibility at work, get in touch with your fears. If you tend to be somewhat rigid, you have probably been hurt in ways that make it difficult for you to tolerate enough openness to move easily in your environment. Identify an area in which you feel secure at work and stretch your flexibility there by relaxing your guard and risking less perfection. Then move on to another area that might be just a little scarier and do the same thing. Keep track of your progress in your journal.

• ASSERT THE BENEFITS of your flexible style if someone alludes to it as "flaky" or disconnected. "Yes, I have the ability to deal with a lot of things at once," or "this may look 'flaky' to you, but I'm tracking the issues we're talking about while I'm sorting through these files. I can pay attention to both things at once."

Return to your Self-Assessment on page 26 and update the information about your flexibility that you recorded there earlier.

LET FLEXIBILITY WORK FOR YOU

You've examined your own flexibility and have a sense of how it works for or against you. How can this dimension benefit you at work? What can it contribute to getting work done?

Whatever your skill or craft, your level of performance can only be what it is at any given time. When you can accept your skill level with its flaws and imperfections, you can be flexible and open to hearing about needed improvements. Flexibility helps you benefit from feedback, use suggestions, and change your approach when needed.

Even though you may work in a rigid system, flexibility is a part of your personality that you can nourish and support. If you stay conscious of it, you won't give in to the rigidity of the environment and lose your own form. You can bend when you need to while taking care to *choose* where you do the bending.

Use your flexibility where it counts. Doing several things at once can work to your advantage, but it's important to communicate clearly about what you're doing. That *you* know you're tracking several different projects doesn't make it obvious to others who may become anxious about their parts of those projects.

We no longer have to squeeze ourselves into rigid work patterns that were designed by men to fit what were once men's needs.

When you take in information that is new or contradictory and make adjustments accordingly, communicate about that, too. Otherwise people assume you're still headed in the same direction you started. Shifting gears may be relatively easy. The cumbersome work of explaining the process is tedious, but equally important. You make life easier for your colleagues if you give them a roadmap.

Avoid unconscious acts of rebellion like being late or demonstrating your flexibility in other self-defeating ways. If you work where rigid organizational limits frustrate and inconvenience you, find ways to be flexible within the limits of your control and responsibility. If organizational rigidity continues to thwart you, look for another place in your company, or maybe even another job that is more compatible with your style.

Learn to identify negative comments or attitudes toward feminine flexibility. Talk with other women about this. Learn to tell the difference between flexibility and irresponsibility. Point out the positive aspects of flexibility when they are part of the work process.

Avoid using "flexibility" to mask incompetence or lack of knowledge. If you're late or unprepared, just say so rather than implying that others might not be as flexible as you if they're upset.

Flexibility gives you new eyes for looking at the way things are done. Eight o'clock Thursday morning staff meetings might have been the best arrangement once upon a time. Now that it conflicts with childcare connections for two staff people, some other time might be better. Research the possibilities and propose a change.

Openness to working in different ways offers other options. Cross-training, making sure several people know how to do each job, is an important part of team-based management. Your flexibility as you participate in or support this process can help it flow more smoothly.

Staffing flexibility supports the needs of working women. Flex-time, job-sharing, and parental leave programs are all easier when people can fill in for each other. The ups and downs of menstrual discomfort that some women experience can be easily worked around if scheduling and work assignments are flexible.

We no longer have to squeeze ourselves into rigid work patterns that were designed by men to fit what were once men's needs. (These are changing, too, as more men take family life to heart.) With attention and consciousness, we can translate our inner flexibility to change the way work is done. By doing so, the place where we spend most of our waking hours becomes much healthier and more enjoyable. We can create balance so that feminine needs are taken seriously, too.

A WOMAN IN HER TIME

Sponsored by Women's Alliance, a group of serious-minded women and a few men gathered for a two-day seminar on the UC Berkeley campus in early spring 1991 to hear *Women's Voices in Troubling Times*.[3] Winona LaDuke had finished her formal presentation and moved from side to side on the stage so she could see the speakers behind the microphones in each of the auditorium aisles. Speaking from her background as a Chippewa Native American and a skilled change agent, she had outlined some of the economic and social issues that native people in our country and others contend with. Obviously under the weather, the much recognized leader had spoken just above a whisper, her voice ravaged by the flu. Conference participants asked Winona and the other nationally prominent presenters tough questions about motives, strategies, and future plans.

She had spoken in Los Angeles the day before, made the long trip to Berkeley by car with her two-month-old son, and now patiently listened and responded with clear, thoughtful answers.

One woman asked, "How do you find the energy to do all this? You have a new baby, another child, and you're actively working on political and economic issues on many different fronts?"

Winona must have been sorting her answer with each step as she walked to the mike at the center stage podium and said, "When you're clear about who you are and what you want to do, the energy comes." And then she spoke into the dark corner of the auditorium where her baby's voice had been heard a few minutes before. "You can bring the baby up here." It took a while. The woman who was taking care of the infant had slipped out an exit. But she returned with a very young man who appeared quite happy to see his mother.

Winona sat down in a chair, reached to take the microphone off the stand. A female sound technician appeared from nowhere to supply a chair-level mike on a boom. Winona smiled, lifted her blouse, offered the baby her breast and continued answering questions. She didn't apologize, she didn't make a joke and she didn't miss a beat. When spontaneous applause erupted from time to time, she gently covered the baby's ear with her hand.

The beauty of this woman, framed by a huge vase of blooming fruit sprays—her dark skin, purple blouse, turquoise necklace, and the baby nursing—communicated the essence of feminine strength and tenderness. Her capacity to sit in the bright lights and field technical and philosophically challenging questions and comments without losing connection with her feminine core spoke of an age-old flexibility that can serve us all very well. Winona seemed very grounded in what was right for her. She responded to the demands and needs of those around her from her comfort zone.

"Very nice," quipped one woman who read this vignette, "but she'd be *fired* if she were a vice-president at ____ and did this!"

The corporate world may not be ready to embrace the feminine at this level. But think about what might be possible when the feminine presence is seen as a legitimate half of that world. If women who choose to have children are flexible enough to manage microphones and breast feed at the same time and wish to do so, more power to them.

SUMMARY

Flexibility from a centered place is neither flaky nor co-dependent. It's a feminine strength that provides us the resilience to deal with life's hassles without losing ourselves in the process.

On the shadow side, women get so good at being flexible we forget to stand up for ourselves. This has been seen as "feminine" in the past and makes boundary-setting hard for many of us. The key is to know about and appreciate our flexibility but not feel required to bend at every pressure. Choice makes the difference. *You* choose when to be flexible, when to be firm. And *you* determine whether you're being flexible, or being flaky.

Nurturance

other's love, the milk of human kindness—nurturance. Women encourage, support, foster, warm, heal, teach, feed and comfort. We connect with others by giving and caring. And we feel good about ourselves in the process. What exciting gifts to bring to the workplace!

But in our lopsided culture where men are powerful and women serve, the joy of nurturing can expire from sheer exhaustion. In generations past, we carried more than our share of this dimension, but in trying to shift the weight of the burden today, we're in danger of losing the whole load—of sacrificing a precious part of ourselves. To give up the capacity to nurture on the job in order to maintain a tough, competitive stance is to block a major feminine connective path.

But how in the world can we nurture without losing ground at work or being stuck with all the caretaking responsibilities at home? Do we give away our hard-earned positions to support our competitors and co-workers? Do we refuse to nurture as a matter of principle? The struggle for balance has been going on for a while.

Nearly forty years ago, Anne Morrow Lindbergh wrote about her attempts to contain the rapture of a wonderful day alone at her beach hideaway. Her words betray the tension between her sense of personal richness and her tendency to give herself away as the hub of family activity:

> Is this then what happens to woman? She wants
> perpetually to spill herself away. All her instinct as a
> woman—the eternal nourisher of children, of men,

of society—demands that she give. Her time, her
energy, her creativeness drain out into these channels if there is any chance, any leak. Traditionally we
are taught, and instinctively we long, to give where it
is needed—and immediately. Eternally, woman spills
herself away in driblets to the thirsty, seldom being
allowed the time, the quiet, the peace, to let the
pitcher fill up to the brim.

—*Gift from the Sea*

We need to find a middle ground between withholding and giving too much. In our private lives, the nurturing
flow is dependent upon our resources and the levels of
need around us. A mother's milk appears at feeding time.
In the more structured work environment, where the need
is great—and constant—different rules apply. For many
people, work substitutes for personal life. If we unconsciously respond to their emotional needs then we can be
depleted without having done a bit of work. Many
women, especially in their early stages as managers, get
mired in this trap.

It helps to nurture and support others *in ways that
will get the work done.* Hours listening to the pain of someone else's difficult personal relationships probably will not
help very much. In such situations, a tactful referral to the
employee assistance program might be in order. But support and direction about setting limits, learning new techniques, or developing additional skills will help your co-
workers.

One of the hardest things for many women to learn is
to take care of themselves by ending a conversation while
the other's need is still intense. A pressured public relations director who spends an hour on an unscheduled
phone call educating a reporter about her client's product
has given too much. Twenty minutes and a referral to
other resources is enough. This is essential learning for

survival on the job.

Some women handle this dilemma by not giving anything. They buy into the "dog eat dog" philosophy and become simply unapproachable. But this leaves them to operate in a masculine style that serves neither them nor the people around them. It's worth it to learn about your own nurturing style so that you can negotiate the shades of grey between giving too much and not giving enough.

In recent years, the flowering of the Twelve Step programs, Alcoholics Anonymous and other Anonymouses, has made co-dependency a household word. The idea that we take care of people in order to be taken care of ourselves—a shadowy form of nurturance—has been explored from many directions, which has brightened possibilities for many otherwise hopeless lives. But it's hard to sort out what's co-dependency, what's nurturance, and what's generosity.

Jean Baker Miller is a pioneer psychologist whose groundbreaking 1976 book, *Toward a New Psychology of Women,* opened a new era of understanding. In a later publication, Miller talks about women's traditional roles as fostering the growth of others—that we empower others through our own power by increasing their resources, capabilities, effectiveness, and ability to act. She points out that a major component of nurturing "is acting and interacting to foster the growth of another on many levels—emotionally, psychologically, and intellectually." She asserts that what women have been doing all the time is a very powerful thing to do, but "no one is accustomed to including such effective action within the notions of power."[1]

And Janet Surrey carries the idea a step further as she describes "one of women's particular sources of strength—the power to empower others, that is, to participate in interaction in such a way that one simultaneously enhances the power of the other *and* one's own power."[2]

Now we're talking! All this giving we've been doing gives us something back. And that's neither sick, selfish, controlling, nor self-denying. Giving something to someone because you want her to have it, or taking care of someone, not out of guilt or obligation, but because you're concerned about him, is a very powerful act. As contemporary working women, we get to express ourselves, live our birthright as nurturers and empowerers, and empower ourselves in the process. So let's learn to make it work for us.

Traditional work environments don't foster generosity and sharing. Nurturance is contrary to the competitive expectation that we need to hold onto whatever we can grasp. Of course, women continue to do it anyway, even so.

Frustrated by the failure of female candidates to get elected, Ellen Malcolm found a way to turn her ability to nurture into a powerful political force. Recognizing that female political candidates have a chance only if they're well funded early, she created EMILY'S List (Early Money Is Like Yeast). She and her colleagues simply wove a network that collected donations from people (mostly women) interested in supporting female candidates for office. This campaign chest tipped the scales in the election of Governor Ann Richards in Texas and for a number of women in the 1992 congressional races, women who are now positioned to make a real difference in our country's future.

Strategic nurturing, selecting where to put your nurturing energy, helps you to stay conscious of when to give and when to withhold. In my work as a therapist, a job that makes significant demands on this dimension, I've determined that I can see a few clients on a sliding scale and one person for no fee at all. Over the years, I've worked out a loose formula that works for me. When those spaces are full, I don't accept any more clients on a

We need to find a middle ground between withholding and giving too much.

sliding scale. I know what I'm comfortable with and when I start feeling drained. At work, you can choose whom you're going to help and how much. Understanding your limits makes it easier to say no when you need to.

In the past, unbounded nurturance was the expected organizing dimension of women's lives. We perpetually spilled ourselves away. Now we have more choices. As we learn to rely on all of our dimensions, not just the traditionally "feminine" ones, we can nurture knowing that we can also ask for what we want and set firm limits. We can enjoy the richness of this important dimension rather than either freezing it when we walk through the office door or subjecting ourselves to rampant exploitation.

Marion Vittitow, whose creativity has nurtured many women and men, gives us these thoughts:

> The Native American Spider Woman expresses all-pervasive feminine creative energy. A spider can move any way that it wants to, and can do so by creating its own path into that space. It goes after and gets what it needs in terms of nurturance or excitement by putting itself out.
>
> Although Spider woman's energy includes destruction, it's not willful. Disintegration is necessary for integration to emerge. Her energy honors this part of relationship, allowing people to find their own way—even through the dark times—to renewal and regeneration by offering support and encouragement.[3]

This is feminine power. Power with. Renewal rather than power over.

"Honoring relationship . . . allowing people to find their own way . . . by offering support and encouragement. . . . " Marion's words create a roadmap for nurturing on the job. It's about honoring relationships, not caretaking.

Because relationships are reciprocal, it feels good to nurture. We get something back if we have a hand in advancing someone's growth: a warm feeling, a sense of connection, validation of our worth. Even though it's against the unspoken rules in many business environments, we benefit emotionally when we help a colleague, support a new effort, lend a hand. And we change the way it feels to be at work. Here's a story a woman told me about some healthy nurturing she did at her office.

A "re-entry woman," Suzanne began her professional career in her late 40s, after finishing her mid-life college education. And she did it with finesse. She's a success in her industry and continues to flourish with the same commitment and integrity she relied on as a mother and homemaker. Hard work, honesty, and concern for other people are her stock in trade.

In discussing current issues at work, Suzanne shared a great example of appropriate nurturance in what is often a viciously competitive industry. She laughingly acknowledged that she doesn't much like the people at her office in her age group ("mostly men who tend to be old-fashioned chauvinists"), so she hangs out with the younger crowd. Several of them, both women and men, rely on her as a confidante, and she likes the role.

Several of the brighter stars let her know that they were preparing to go to work for a competing company. They didn't really want to go, but they had tried to talk to the chief and he had rebuffed them..

Suzanne listened for a while and offered to talk to the CEO. He had accepted some of her recommendations before "because I'm part of his generation. And he's not used to working with women who talk back to him. He really doesn't know what to do with me."

The crusty, highly-competent, but self-centered CEO wasn't about to listen to a bunch of "kids." But this mature (by now mid-fifties) woman, who had given him some very useful feedback in the past, set him down and told him what he needed to know to save his company from drying up in its own rigidity. He listened to her and became more open to hearing what the younger employees had to say.

Suzanne not only nourished her young colleagues, she "nurtured up." She supported the boss, the "kids," and herself in a typically homey, feminine way. This is a woman who knows what she wants and works to get it. The "mom" stuff is so much a part of her that there's no way to stop it in her relationships at work. And it works for her in a relaxed and natural way. The feminine focus on relationships encourages a free and easy nurturing style for women like Suzanne. But that style doesn't fit everyone. We each need to come to terms with how we express this dimension.

It helps to nurture and support others in ways that will get the work done.

"Nurturance" popped up most quickly and most often when people I interviewed shared their thoughts about femininity at work. Women are expected to be nurturing— that is, caring, open, warm, and giving. But when we're that way in formal business environments, we're seen as naive or unprofessional. On the other hand, when we don't fit this pattern because it just isn't our style—or because we're stressed or focused on something else— we're seen as cold and unfeminine. It's hard for corporate life to relate to femininity, whether we fit our stereotypes or not.

Mothering experience isn't a requirement. Although stereotypes of nurturing often include motherhood, the generous connections that many people make with friends and colleagues at work express this dimension, too. Relationship and social contact form a central part of satisfying work life. Personal support, sharing, and celebrating special occasions are all nurturing ways we connect with each other.

When both women and men can support each other

in this way, it makes work a happier, healthier place to be. Easy contact and sharing are possible if cut-throat competition isn't an issue. Unfortunately, that's not always the case.

If you work in a setting where every move is competitive, nurturing others is likely to be a problem. Take a close look to understand the nature of the competition. Is it necessary? Or is it a way that insecure people protect their turf and make themselves feel better by exerting power over others? Good-natured competition can add interest and excitement to work if mutual respect and trust are part of the process. The cut-throat variety is toxic and destructive, and rarely, if ever, contributes to the overall health of the organization.

Suzanne knows how much money she wants to make, trusts she'll meet her production goals, and isn't driven by greed. She loves making a big sale and gets excited about being the top producer once in a while. But her self-esteem doesn't depend on it and she doesn't go for the jugular to make it happen. And so she can nurture others with no fear of loss to herself. In fact, it makes her happy to do so.

THE SHADOW SIDE

The shadow side of nurturance taints both giver and receiver. Distrust, guilt, and resentment grow in its darkness. Here's where co-dependency comes in.

The cloying, controlling, caretaker who lives through others is a painful example of nurturance's shadow. Generations of women grew up believing they deserved nothing for themselves. Mere survival depended on taking care of a spouse—nurturing grown men bought us a meal ticket. It hasn't been too long since women were treated like chattel, legally and in every other way, and this history's had a profound effect on the way we see ourselves.

In the past, our culture has taken for granted that as women we put the needs of others before our own. The part about taking care of ourselves, too, got left out. Many of us took that message literally for a long time and spent our lives "nurturing" out of guilt and obligation. Others rebelled and refused to nurture anybody. "I don't take care of kids at home; I'm not going to baby sit at work," is the way one manager put it. This approach casts another kind of shadow. It limits the give and take that's central to any personal relationship. Prima donnas are lonely people who wonder why their competence doesn't make them happy.

Modern day misers, women who withhold on general principles, can't give. They're frightened to death of being overwhelmed and of having to give more than they can spare. Or they're fearful that their generosity will be used against them. Miserliness sets an extreme boundary if assertiveness isn't well enough developed. It seems easier to keep the gate completely shut than to have to set a limit when the demands outweigh the resources. So these folks hold on tightly and suffer profound loneliness.

Nurturing is sharing that flows from generosity of spirit. If your resources are limited and you don't feel like sharing, give yourself permission to be *self*-nurturing. All of us have times when we have nothing to give. That's the time to *ask* for nurturance. If you find yourself strategically nurturing in order to accomplish some goal or another, take a second look.

The self-sacrificing martyr whose boundaries are so leaky she keeps nothing for herself fits here too. In order to nurture others, we first have to take care of ourselves. If you habitually give yourself away, rather than taking responsibility for nourishing your own growth, a little self-talk is in order. An excerpt from Carol Lynn Pearson's poem, "Millie's Mother's Red Dress" might help. It captures the pathos of a dying woman's conversation with her daughter as she shines some light into the shadow of nurturance. On an impulse, the mother bought the beautiful red dress for herself, but never wore it:

"And I'm telling you, Millie, if some miracle
Could get me off this bed, you could look
For a different mother, 'cause I would be one.
Oh, I passed up my turn so long
I would hardly know how to take it.
But I'd learn, Millie.
I would learn!"

It hung there in the closet
While she was dying. Mother's red dress.
Like a gash in the row
Of dark, old clothes
She had worn away her life in.

Her last words to me were these:
"Do me the honor, Millie,
Of not following in my footsteps.
Promise me that."

I promised.
She caught her breath.
Then Mother took her turn
In death.

As you explore your shadow in this dimension, pay attention to the rules you've made for yourself about how you're supposed to nurture. Look for those secret trade-offs you make without getting informed consent. If you find yourself being self-critical, your shadow may be trying to teach you a new rule, "If you don't feel it, don't give it."

SELF-REFLECTION

Nurturance is an area of great conflict for many women on the job. Estimate where you fit on the nurturance continuum. Keep in mind that it's your work-related behavior that you're measuring here.

STRENGTH: I find it easy to support others at work. I take care of myself. I often provide training or suggestions for others. Co-workers seek me out when they need support, and I can say yes or no depending on my resources at the time.

SHADOW: I have so much responsibility for the welfare of others at work, I can't focus on my job. I'm the only one who remembers special occasions and instigates a celebration. I'm frequently involved in helping a "wounded bird" at my office. / I expect others to take care of themselves and don't provide support for anyone. It's not my job to nurture.

TIME FOR YOURSELF

What is your nurturing style at work? Is this dimension one you've learned to underplay? Do you feel comfortable supporting others whether they are "above" or "below" you? Are you aware of ways others have nurtured, or failed to nurture you in your growth?

The following tips provide some steps you can take to dive into this dimension of your feminine presence. Choose a few for more exploration.

• NURTURE AT WORK by taking good care of yourself. (Take your lunch break and eat something that's tasty and good for you; stay home when you're sick; make your physical environment as comfortable as possible.)

When you take care of yourself first, you have energy to nurture others genuinely. List some ways you nurture yourself on the job or in relation to your work.

• NAME THE FEELINGS you've had if you've been the object of invasive caretaking at work. Write them in your journal under the heading "How it feels to be suffocated by co-dependent behavior." If you have the feeling that you're always in debt to someone for her or his supportiveness, you may be on the right track. Many women are much more comfortable giving than taking. Caretaking can creep into places where it doesn't belong. The shadow side of the nurturer feels invasive and sticky as uninvited "help" imposed at work. Do you know someone whose behavior I just described? This is co-dependency, not nurturance. How do you feel when you're around this person? Write about these feelings in your journal.

• LEARN TO TALK CLEARLY about your nurturing behavior. "I want to do this for you and I expect nothing in return," might be a good place to start. If you can't honestly say this, determine what you do want and ask for it directly. In the competitive work world, men may interpret your attempts at nurturance as manipulative ploys to "get something" you're not asking for directly. The "good ol' boy" system works on trade-offs, which differs from nurturing. It's a challenge to communicate new ideas about feminine nurturing.

• SUPPORT OTHER WOMEN in nurturing ways. This can be done very simply by kind comments or by creating space for them. If you find that your female colleagues are consistently interrupted by men, or can't get a word in edgewise, you can say things like, "I don't think Janet had a chance to finish her thought," or, "Cindy, what do you think about that idea?"

• INCLUDE OTHERS IN ACTIVITIES that have been assigned to you when that's possible. Everybody benefits. They get training and credit. You get help. Make a list of ways you might do this in the near future.

• WOMEN MAKE A REAL DIFFERENCE in the work environment by attending to birthdays or other special occasions that their masculine counterparts have ignored for years. This is tricky business because it can become a sexist drag. The goal is to make the environment one everyone likes to work in. Little kindnesses can transform a work site. Women may be the mentors here, but men can assume equal responsibility.

- USE YOUR CAPACITY FOR NURTURANCE to understand and appreciate differences in others. List some times this has worked for you.

- THINK ABOUT THE WAYS you take care of others on the job. List five things you've done during the past week that seem like healthy nurturance. Write about what it felt like to do these things.

- IDENTIFY WAYS YOU MAY be "strategically nurturing." Think about your motivation for doing these things. Is your behavior manipulative or co-dependent? If you asked directly for what you want, what would it be? Does something feel too scary for making a direct request? Write about how you learned to relate to people in this way.

- WHEN YOU CHOOSE TO NURTURE, maintain awareness of what you're doing so that you don't move into unconscious co-dependence. Recognize the difference between nurturing and a co-dependent attempt to control. Write about an example of each.

- CLEARLY ACKNOWLEDGE appropriate nurturing tendencies in others, especially men.

Nurturance is a powerful and constructive dimension that women who are in touch with their feminine power can promote in the workplace. But it doesn't usually translate directly from home to work without some conscious thought about what's appropriate and what results in exploitation or uninvited caretaking. Write your thoughts about this dimension in your journal. Think of at least one example where you have expressed it well and one where you wish you had done it differently. Do you like the way you offer nurturance now? If you think some fine tuning is in order, clarify your thoughts by writing them in your journal.

Check the Self-Assessment on page 27 and update your rating.

NURTURANCE GOES TO WORK

In our culture, women are the designated nurturers. As we go to work in masculine environments, we can bring this dimension with us if we haven't abandoned it in ourselves. If you've shelved this dimension as part of surviving and succeeding, now is a good time to take a second look. You have a great opportunity to make a positive difference where you work if you can find ways to share the wealth rather than continuing in your role as primary nurturer.

This means teaching men who have customarily operated in competitive, non-nurturing ways that a different approach has merit. Participative management, team building, and informal communication networks all require nurturing skills. These "new" management skills, which experts see as solutions to our current business crises, require the open give and take of connected relationships. Nurturance is already "in." We need only put into words the importance of this feminine gift at work. Talking about nurturance as a legitimate part of business interaction takes it out of the realm of motherhood and cookie baking. And we can learn to ask for nurturance in return.

This process may begin as "trade-offs," which men understand very well. But nurturance is an emotional connection, not just a mechanical one. It can provide a basis for mutual trust when the give and take is balanced, but when women do all the giving, the old exploitive patterns continue.

For men to feel comfortable nurturing, they have to know they're not going to be asked to give everything up. When asking for support and nurturance, you can say things like, "I'd like your support with _____, but I don't need it with _____."

Or, "Give me a hand with _____ and I can take responsibility for _____."

In order to nurture others, we first have to take care of ourselves.

The teaching mode can be useful at times. You can clue in a male colleague with something like, "So and so is having a tough time with her new assistant. Some coaching from you about how to deal with him could help her out." Giving and receiving nurturance is a legitimate need for both sexes. For women to take most of the responsibility for this process doesn't work at the office any more than it does at home.

As you try to create ways to nurture yourself and find a balance in nurturing others, you're likely to confront two powerful unconscious barriers that are rugged but elusive.

Woman = Mother is the first of these two. The feminine presence grows out of female biology—our child-bearing capacity. Mothers shape our sense of who we are and have a lot to do with how we relate to authority figures. Even though you don't always, or even usually, wear your mother hat to work, you may be seen in a "mother role" by others. Whether you like it or not, if authority is part of your job, people's responses to you are colored by the quality of their relationships with their mothers.

Your feminine presence stirs up feelings in others that are unresolved in their relationships with their mothers—hatred, resentment, and fear on the negative side; yearning, admiration, and love in a more positive vein. And this is before you even *do* anything. No wonder the presence of women prompts agitation and discomfort in some. These feelings bubble around outside awareness and may be expressed as disagreement or resistance to something you say which, if proposed by a male colleague or superior, would be heard and accepted as routine.

"Watch out! The bitch is on the rampage again!" is not a serious response to a female manager's attempts to work with her staff. When you experience automatic resistance to your ideas, especially those involving authority, it is useful to wonder whether "mother issues" are lurking in the listeners. You can help clear up some of the hostility projected onto you in two ways: 1) try to avoid getting hooked by your own anger, and 2) talk plainly about what you're trying to accomplish, providing as much information as possible so that others can share responsibility.

"Dads," male authority figures, certainly create authority issues for co-workers to deal with as well, but they are different. Men are expected to be in charge at work—as women are expected to be in charge at home. For women to be in charge in both places disturbs some men deeply. It helps if they can see you as someone trying to get a job done—not as another mother.

Do	*Don't*
Learn to use authority with comfort and clarity.	Create or add to images that the work group is a "family."
Confront assumptions that you are in charge of nurturing (mothering) at work.	Allude to other women as "mom types."
Be clear in asserting the limits and boundaries of your responsibilities.	Habitually take on "wounded birds" or "ride to their rescue."
Acquire sensitivity to others' fears about you as an authority figure.	Rely on other women to take care of you.
Allow yourself to be as powerful as you are.	Assume that other women are like your mother.

Men Are Powerful—Women Are Silent Caretakers is the second of the nurturance-related barriers. The arrival of a woman on the management team is disturbing at many levels. Do you lower the value of the real estate on this block? What can a man expect? He knows the rules with the guys; will you know how to play?

You probably do, or you wouldn't have made it to this level. But whether you choose to or not is a whole different story. It's at this point that your core strength can serve you best and when you are least likely to hear it or be able to reach in to it. The pressure to act in masculine ways, rather than simply to cooperate with masculine energy, is overwhelming.

Our views are colored by traditions that portray men as powerful and women as obedient—or at least silent—caretakers. What may have started as partnership for survival when most people lived on the land has become lopsided in a way that overloads the masculine and devalues the feminine. This way of looking at the world doesn't take into account individual differences, feelings, values, talents, or needs. It is reflected in an economy in which male high school dropouts make more money than women high school graduates with some college. One percent of women are in the top income bracket that encompasses 20% of white male earners. Even with increased emphasis on equal rights, women's incomes are still significantly below those of men, approximately 62 cents on the dollar. The fact that more single women head households than ever before has had little impact on the American image that men are—or should be—the bread-winners.

The assumption is that men are the powerful, competent ones simply by virtue of their masculinity. Many men believe this and act accordingly. The image is even more potent because women buy into it. We've catered to it by learning to be helpless or by avoiding appearing smarter or more competent than men. Middle-aged women can recall advice like, "If you have a romantic interest in a man, don't let him know when you get the answer before he does," and "Men aren't attracted to women who are smarter than they are." Early this century, satirist Dorothy Parker said it simply: "Men don't make passes at girls who wear glasses!"

Carol Gilligan's research with young women tells us that this process continues as part of our culture. Eleven-year-old girls who were outspoken about their feelings and opinions blur out and become indefinite at sixteen. By junior high, they're sophisticated about seeming less intelligent than they really are.[4]

Growing awareness of the feminine presence in business magnifies the insecure man's fear of losing control. What will happen if this new, different entity becomes powerful? Attempts to prevent this scary possibility show themselves in countless "innocent," seemingly rational ways. To deal with these blocks:

Do	*Don't*
Expect to exercise your authority with confidence.	Collude with the "women serve" mentality.
Confront expectations that you will defer to males who have less authority than you have.	Expect men to be as skilled at personal communication as you are.
Learn to deal with masculine vulnerability to women in authority.	Be manipulated by masculine ineptness at traditionally feminine tasks.
Look at assignments you're given to be sure they're right for your work level.	Take the path of least resistance as a way of avoiding conflict.
Confront unspoken expectations that you'll do the caretaking.	Make the coffee unless everyone shares equally and/or it's your turn.

The feminine urge to do what will stir up the least trouble—to avoid conflict—is a powerful one. (Making coffee is a classic example.) Coupled with masculine expectations that men should be in charge, it contributes to an almost impenetrable barrier at work. If you need to, take an assertiveness training course to learn to confront unspoken expectations that you will defer to males and provide caretaking services. Learning to do this is a skill, not an inborn talent. The more conscious you become of how this barrier slides into place for you, the better you can be at trying to neutralize it. Nurturance doesn't mean staying in second position.

Nurturance does include saying "Hello," in the morning or inquiring about someone's health or family. You have many opportunities during the day to offer support to a co-worker, your boss or others in your organization. You can do this by listening or by "reflecting"—saying in different words—a feeling they've expressed: "I know you're really (stressed, angry, hurt) about that. I'm sorry to hear it."

Your emotional presence is more important than "doing" nurturing things. Learn the difference between "merging" into someone else's space—unconsciously taking on a task or an emotional load that isn't really yours—and connecting in a supportive, intentionally nurturing way. You can be supportive and at the same time communicate to others your confidence that they can manage their own business. When you do this, the interaction between you empowers you both.

Some things to keep in mind as you work with this dimension include these guidelines for nurturing on the job:

- Know where you're going. Suzanne was free to nurture because she knew her goals and how she would reach them. Helping others only added to

her ability to take care of herself.
- Be explicit about what you're giving and what you do or don't expect in return.
- Take the risk of being "had" once in a while. You're not a fool if that happens to you.
- Don't give more than you want to.
- If one of your gifts backfires, try to understand why. Do you need to confront or clarify?
- Take care of yourself before burnout hits.
- Learn to tell the difference between real need and manipulation. One clue is whether you feel good about helping someone out, or whether you feel exploited.

SUMMARY

Nurturance is intricately woven through many aspects of your feminine presence. It's so much a part of feminine behavior that it is taken for granted. As you become more conscious of how you nurture or how you get stuck in your co-dependent shadow, you can learn better ways to take care of yourself. If you're a person who long ago gave up on nurturing as a bad bet, it may be possible for you to revisit some possibilities. Choosing to nurture is easier if you're comfortable setting limits when you've done enough.

Business has much to gain if we can learn to work in ways that are self-nourishing as well as supportive of those around us.

Affinity

Strength is assumed to be a singular thing. Standing alone. Autonomy. The ability to make it on one's own is the standard of success in our male-dominated culture. But competition does violence to connections. You can't compete and cooperate at the same time, and connections are rarely the same when there's been a winner and a loser. Sometimes, it's hard not to be seduced into the fray.

But femininity is about connectedness and relationship—affinity. In her poem, "For strong women," Marge Piercy lays it out very clearly:

> What comforts her is others loving
> her equally for the strength and for the weakness
> from which it issues, lightning from a cloud.
> Lightning stuns. In rain, the clouds disperse.
> Only water of connection remains,
> flowing through us. Strong is what we make
> each other. Until we are all strong together,
> a strong woman is a woman strongly afraid.[1]

For the feminine, strong doesn't mean alone. *Our* strength is in relationship. And this strength grows when others affirm us. When cooperation rather than competition channels the work flow, we can give and receive support and encouragement and feel nourished rather than depleted. At some time or another, everybody seeks the recognition and satisfaction that personal success brings. That success is sweeter when we can hear the applause from friends and colleagues, and know that we didn't sacrifice our personal connections to achieve it.

Janet L. Surrey offers these basic elements as central to the self in women:

1) We're interested in and pay attention to others, which forms the base for emotional connection and the ability to empathize.

2) We expect a mutual process in which *both* people have empathy. The sharing of experience leads to a heightened development of self and others.

3) We expect relationships to be mutually sensitive and responsible. This reciprocity provides the starting point for the growth of empowerment and self-knowledge.

Emphasis on individuality, competing, and getting ahead collides with our needs for connection. At work, we often learn to sacrifice our tendencies toward togetherness and forge on "professionally," regardless of our reticence. And we get ulcers, headaches, and bad temper in the process. If we decide it's not worth the trouble, then we are left to feel isolated. But if we value connection too greatly, we settle for less than we really want so as not to hurt our friends and colleagues on the way up.

As women, we tend to define ourselves in our relationships with others. What we get from and give to each other enriches or threatens our sense of well-being. And so our emotional antennae scan a room to check the climate. Without thinking about it consciously, we sense the emotional vibes—whether others are mad, tense, excited, or open. Comfort, trust, and security rest in the give and take of our relationships.

This isn't weakness or a lesser way of being than the more visible male model that touts autonomy and separateness. It is only different. As we get to know and value this dimension, we can encourage affinity as a contributor to our work life rather than feeling ashamed of its presence in our make-up. Closeness isn't a whim. It's central.

And we need to be assertive that connective values can be valuable in a work environment.

In general, affinity includes these ideas:

• Relationships are important, not just convenient. Interconnection feels good—it's reassuring and valuable. Choices may be based on who's doing something rather than on the task itself. How things turn out for both people makes a difference. It matters that relationships continue, that we live with our actions and their impact on others who are important to us. There is no expedient goal—like profit or promotion—that justifies acts and decisions regardless of their personal consequences.

Closeness isn't

a whim.

It's central.

• Cooperation is comfortable and almost always preferable to competition. The price of winning (often the torn fabric of relationship) leads to fear of abandonment, of disconnection from the defeated one who might be a friend or close associate. It's enjoyable to collaborate even when that means sharing the rewards. Of course, this doesn't mean all the time, or for every woman. Individual work is important and meaningful too.

• Emotions—our own and others'—are an important part of life, including worklife. Empathy, "feeling" someone else's feelings, is an important part of our make-up. In our relationships at work, we acknowledge the emotional aspect as significant rather than pretending we're robots. Even though we need to use judgment about what we choose to express, it's unreal to think that we leave our emotions at the threshold on our way in the office door.

• Children and family life are important. The workplace has responsibility to make it possible to pace one's job or career to produce, nurture, and train the next generation. Even though many men shoulder shared responsibility and commitment to family life, most working women continue to take primary responsibility here. Consequently, work decisions tend to take second place to heartfelt family needs and priorities at times in women's

164

lives. This may be true even when work feels more interesting and rewarding than dealing with the never-ending
responsibilities at home.

This isn't an exhaustive list. And it's not exclusive to
women. But it offers the flavor of affinity in contrast to the
status quo assumptions of autonomy, competition, and
hierarchical order.

Handed down through unending generations of
women who've been excluded from power, the gifts of
affinity have much to offer today's chronically shifting
workplace. Although connection appears to get in the way
of expediency at times, it can make for much more
humane decisions. Personal communication, trust, and
openness where they are warranted weave organizations
together when hierarchies aren't flexible enough to bend
with new complexities.

Decisions that seem simple and logical at the executive level can have far-reaching effects on both personal
and work relationships. In a Sacramento Valley manufacturing company that operates under seasonal pressure, an
executive decision to add an hour to both ends of the
workday would have been handled very differently if
attention had been given to how personal connections
help the company work. The decision was made and
announced two days before the longer work day was to
begin. Apparently, little if any thought was given to the
impact on the workers—on their childcare arrangements,
carpools or other issues related to personal support systems.

In addition to the immediate personal stress and strain
it caused employees, most of whom were women, the
new schedule negatively affected important work relationships. Adding an hour to the end of each day required
rescheduling for management coverage. It wiped out the
brief period during the week when all management personnel could be on site at the same time to meet with

each other. A year's work in team building—a conscious focus on affinity—was undermined overnight. If this had been a response to an emergency and had been announced as such, employees would have taken it in stride. It wasn't. There was plenty of time for input and prior planning by the management teams, and to allow adequate lead time for employees to make the shift.

It wasn't the decision that was bad. Many people were delighted about the possibility of more work. It was the lack of attention to personal impact that was insensitive. When confronted with the morale implications of this move, the executive director had a hard time understanding. "Surely the managers can work this out with their people," he said, "can't they?"

The need for connection has been seen as a problem rather than an asset in traditionally organized businesses, even though among support staff or service providers, affinity clearly makes the office run more smoothly. The office wife/secretary who knows everybody on the floor can get things done through her connections that wouldn't happen otherwise. Research about work shows that social needs are a primary reason that people work, but this factor still doesn't rank high with decisionmakers. The bottom line typically takes precedence over all other factors when organizational decisions are at stake—a very short-sighted view that neglects feminine strengths.

Secretaries have greased organizational skids for years, intuitively operating through affinity. They quietly maneuver organizations with their own cooperative networks to find unorthodox, feminine solutions to all kinds of problems, while bypassing formal power structures. Traditionally, the bosses receive credit for the success and the secretaries end up invisible and underpaid in the support staff ranks.

Since it's contrary to a traditional competitive style, getting things done cooperatively doesn't necessarily gain positive attention in an authoritarian organization. It may even be seen as "weak." When this feminine process blossoms at the management level, people begin to notice and may become critical of unpredictable, non-hierarchical approaches. "I believe in hierarchy!" a female CEO whose style was quite traditional said to me. When her mid-management group attempted to use informal, connective pathways to work through knotty conflicts in her company, their easy way of getting along threatened her sense of order. It was not an acceptable way to do business there, even though the chief was demanding "better communication." That situation was not likely to improve—because the CEO was unable to see her own conflict.

Hierarchy is essential in military organizations and in families where parents need to take care of young children. But in situations that require collective creativity and effort, "flatter" organizational models work better. The art of management is in knowing which model works better for which task. Here again, balance is the key.

Shauna Granger, the first woman promoted into the all-male management ranks of her organization, described her move into a difficult situation. After getting her feet wet, she found herself repeatedly propelled into the role of troubleshooter. She described one particular assignment that had caused the company difficulty for some time. "I knew that those folks weren't going to trust anyone. The only thing I could do was work with them one on one—each in a different way according to their personality, until I could get them to communicate with me. I decided to emphasize training and worked with each person on whatever skills they wanted to develop."

This very personalized, feminine approach, based on sensitivity and excellent communication skills, worked beautifully where less personal, power-oriented approaches had failed. Shauna's affinity and honest concern for the well-being of the employees helped her to move into the situation in ways that other managers hadn't chosen. She was low key and cooperative and relied on her capacity to relate to each individual—which she took the time to do.

Shauna had no need to emphasize that she was the boss. Everybody knew it. Her manner supported the emotional well-being of the workers, mostly women. They had stymied several control-oriented male managers by stonewalling and endless bickering. Because this manager dealt with them individually, they were much more willing to cooperate. Although she spent lots of time and energy working individually with people, the investment paid high dividends in the long run.

Women who are willing to speak out for their feminine needs can be strong agents for change.

Our femininity expresses that part of us that holds and nurtures a deep sense of women as the carriers and protectors of new human life. In the workplace, this can simply mean taking the time and energy to relate to people, taking their emotional well-being seriously. The patriarchal struggle to get to the top of the heap often dams the flow of concern for the importance of the interpersonal connection.

Strong feelings for children and family life feed working women's nightmares as we try to balance home and work. We're torn between our connections at home and our responsibilities there and the demands and challenges at work. We live with impossible schedules and painful emotional stretches that perpetuate a chronic guilt state. We adapt to work patterns that were designed for male workers with stay-at-home wives, although this pattern now fits only a small percentage (I've seen figures that spread from 7% to 20%) of all families. Men's needs have changed, too, without wives at home. The work schedule has to change for them, as well. It's in this area that traditional attitudes toward working people have to shift, but change will happen only if it's pushed.

In the meantime, it helps if we honor our feelings and

talk about them. Responsibility for the well-being of the next generation doesn't belong to you alone. Calling attention to the hardships imposed on family life by company decisions raises awareness of decisionmakers. Even small things, like rules about whether or not it's O.K. to have photos of your children in your workspace—which you might or might not choose to do—communicate an attitude about affinity.

Women who are connected with their inner experience and are willing to speak out for their feminine needs can be strong agents for change. Men who are or have been active parents are excellent allies. Affinity, working cooperatively together to inform employers of the need and suggest solutions, is one way to make a difference.

The Shadow Side

Affinity's shadow hopelessly confuses our loving, loyal connections with feelings of guilt and obligation. When that happens, we disconnect from our centers and live by our efforts to win approval. It becomes second nature to be more in tune with someone else's priorities than our own.

Our needs for connection are so powerful, we sometimes lose track of who we are in attempts to meet them.

Marie's story is a familiar one. She shared this with me in her struggle to return to her own center. The shadow side of affinity had overtaken this competent woman's emotional life. Abuse of her capacity for flexibility permitted her to bend and twist, adapt—and deny herself. She hated the thought of becoming another statistic. She couldn't tolerate subjecting her children to the predictable wounds from the divorce that would end her unhappy marriage.

Marie had organized her life around her husband and

children and tried to will it into being all right. This pattern had moved beyond healthy concern and nurturance. For several years she had negated her deep personal pain, shut down receptivity to her inner feelings. The shadow side of affinity had intruded to the exclusion of her other feelings that were just as valid.

One morning, Marie was abruptly awakened by a phone call. She finished the call and replaced the receiver. Even while she stuck her head under the pillow, images of her sensual mauve and seafoam bedroom, light streaming through the shutters to caress the satin coverlet, wouldn't go away. She and Dan had worked for years to create their beautiful home. It was her pride and joy.

She hoped the phone didn't rouse the kids. She needed a few minutes to contain the wild roar in her brain.

Dan had left for work an hour ago. Now he was coming home.

"I rolled the car. It's totalled," his shaky voice said on the phone.

When she heard Dan's voice, she tried to sound awake, as though she'd stayed up after he left. She replied with whatever people say at times like this. "Oh, honey. How awful! Are you O.K.?"

She had gone back to bed that morning, and nearly every morning for the previous month. She was depressed, not tired. And she couldn't believe her internal response to Dan's accident. She had to admit the truth to herself. She was disappointed that he hadn't been killed. And she was mad at him for wrecking "her" car. She wanted to throw up—to purge herself of her vicious thoughts. She was horrified by her own feelings.

The shock of Dan's accident brought Marie's shadow into the light. Her wish that her husband had been killed oozed from darkness through her denial. She knew she had to do something about her life—to give up pretending that this relationship would work, to admit that her need for connection imprisoned her. Ugly, brutal, terrifying as it was—that revelation was a gift from her shadow. She could not continue to live the lie that if she just worked at it hard enough this marriage could survive.

Affinity casts its shadow at work as well as in our personal lives. Anne loved her job as executive secretary. She had mastered it years ago and from time to time she considered moving on to a management track. In fact, her friends who had done the same encouraged her, brought her announcements of job openings, and one even offered her a job. She knew her boss depended on her. He had been generous with her when she was struggling to make ends meet after her divorce. She didn't ever ask him how he would feel about her leaving, but she felt that would put him in a real bind. When he asked her to move over so he could promote a younger woman to her position she was devastated. She blamed him. It took a long time for her to look at her own part in this bitter tale.

Immobilized in her feelings of appreciation and loyalty for her boss, Anne ignored her own inner promptings. She squelched her needs and didn't risk checking out what her boss had in mind. Even if he had not wanted her to leave, she could have prepared for an exit in such a way that it wouldn't have been abandonment. This relationship wasn't reciprocal, but Anne didn't know it. *Affinity is not servitude.*

At work, when we live on the shadow side of affinity, we find ourselves doing all those stereotyped feminine things that lead to self-hate. We're nice to people we don't like, say "yes" when we mean "no," and bend to things we disagree with in order to avoid conflict.

As we try to move from work situations that are familiar but limiting, this shadow casts a dark obstruction in our way. A friend shared with me recently that she needed to look for new office space to set up her own business but had been fiddling around for several weeks, having a hard time shifting into action. She acknowledged her hesitancy: "I'm afraid to stand on my own in my business where I've always shared office space. It's time to move on, and I'm very reluctant to look for space downtown because I don't know anyone I can share with. It's scary!"

Need for connection is so powerful, we sometimes lose our individuality to it. Chronic self-denial of this sort creates physical symptoms—such as headaches and gastrointestinal distress—as the true self screams for release. Depression is a predictable byproduct too. When affinity's shadow hovers indefinitely, we begin to hate our jobs and everybody there, as well as ourselves.

Affinity is not servitude.

Dealing with people who are in this place is very frustrating because it's impossible to know what they really think or feel. Their niceness or care-taking seems like it should be comforting, but being around them feels more like drowning than being nurtured or supported.

If you find yourself immobilized so that you have a hard time initiating a move or a project on your own, your shadow side is lurking. Relationships are important and we grow by working within them. But we also need to be able to move on our own. If everything you do has to be done in connection, it's worth asking yourself what feels so frightening for you.

The shadow side of affinity is particularly dangerous because it enfolds the feminine stereotype with great comfort. It makes room for timid, indecisive, inexpressive women who are too frightened to look at their own feelings. We can live our whole lives here and never upset anybody.

SELF-REFLECTION

Affinity is a complex dimension affecting several different issues. The main focus includes all those things we feel and do to honor human connections at work. It could be the simple gesture of saying "Hello" in the morning or the complicated process of organizing a childcare center. All flow from the center of femininity and are likely to go against the grain in many work environments.

Where do you fit on this dimension? Use the following suggestions to help you make this self-assessment.

STRENGTH: I'm comfortable with the way I deal with connection at work. I shift without too much stress from home to work and back again. I deal with my emotions well at work and express them when I need to. I can compete as needed and cooperate with others easily.

SHADOW: I'm almost always in conflict between "business-like" ways of relating and how I really feel. I feel like a wooden woman most of the time. / I'm constantly torn between home and work and hate the pain of it. / I can't work independently. I collapse under individual responsibility.

TIME FOR YOURSELF

If you live fully in your womanhood, issues of affinity create constant conflict in work environments that elevate individualistic values. As you understand this more clearly, you can make conscious decisions about how to deal with the chronic stress that results. For one thing, it helps to know that it's not just you. You may not be able to change much of what happens in the work setting, but you can change the expectations you have for yourself about how to manage.

• NOTE IN YOUR JOURNAL the situations at work in which you find yourself in conflict about affinity. (Examples include: Pain about having to confront someone who's a friend; competing with a friend for a promotion; deciding to refuse a promotion to spend more time with the kids; returning to work shortly after giving birth.)

• MAKE A LIST OF DECISIONS you've dealt with that hurt or supported your affinity dimension. List the connected approach on one side and the separatist approach on the other (part-time work so you can be with your kids vs. full-time so you don't get left behind on your career track; honesty about your feelings vs. voicing the party line; involving co-workers in doing a project vs. doing it yourself for all the credit).

• LIST WAYS THAT YOU COLLABORATE rather than compete at work (serve as co-chair rather than chair, include others in important decisionmaking steps even though their job titles might not be equal with yours, job-sharing).

• LIST WAYS YOUR CONNECTIVE NEEDS and feelings support your effectiveness at work (ease of relating to others, capacity for empathy, good communication skills, etc.).

• OBSERVE WHETHER OR NOT men and women in your office behave differently in this dimension. If so, how? Name the feelings that come up for you when you ignore pulls toward affinity because they don't fit your work environment (sadness over loss, feelings of hyprocrisy, emotional numbness).

• DESCRIBE IN YOUR JOURNAL two occasions at work when strong emotions have interfered with your ability to work. How did you handle the situation (cry in the bathroom, leave work, explode, stuff your feelings)? Think about ways you could honor your feelings, support yourself, get support from others. Write some suggestions in your journal.

• IN YOUR JOURNAL, describe as many ways as you can that your shadow side comes to work with you in this dimension. How do you find yourself being compliant rather than dealing with conflict in a work relationship? Are you immobilized in some way because if you make a move you'll hurt someone? Do you give too much value to a relationship that may or may not be reciprocal?

• LIST THREE WAYS you organize your work life to accommodate family needs (career choice, flexible scheduling, delaying a promotion, part-time work). Include in each item a statement that describes how you feel about doing this—both the strong side and the shadow side.

• WRITE YOUR FAVORITE self-support technique for neutralizing work-home conflict stress (assertiveness about sharing childcare responsibility, enough good childcare, acknowledgment that you're a good-enough parent). Ask a co-worker what her favorite self-support technique is. Write it down if you like it, and see if you can add another as well.

• NOTE IN YOUR JOURNAL three things you've learned from someone you know who is able to be effective at work and maintain her relationships in a positive way. If you can, take the opportunity to talk with this person about how she does this and what issues arise for her.

As you work to sort out where you fit in this dimension, give yourself time to reflect on how you really feel about these issues. It's hard to sift through how much is really you and how much has to do with adaptations you've made to get by at work. You may want to come back to this dimension after you've finished all the others. If that's the case, make a note in your journal to remind yourself.

Now that you've explored the affinity dimension, return to page 27 and see if your Self-Assessment needs to be brought up to date.

AFFINITY GOES TO WORK

Most of the organizations in which we work are patterned after the military. Hierarchies and bureaucracies evolved to remove the personal element from tasks—especially to dehumanize the military business of killing or being killed. The feminine presence threatens this leftover, stubborn attempt to sterilize the business environment. If the needs of individuals are taken seriously, the old rules about "disinterest" are no longer adequate guidelines for decisionmaking. Increased participation blurs right and wrong.

Women's ways are different, and that can be a contribution, not a barrier, at work as well as at home. Do what you can to bring the differences out in the open and show how they balance the equally important contributions that men make. The goal is to work in partnership, to benefit from the new energy and creativity that combined resources can generate.

Organizations that welcome and support feminine contributions increase their flexibility and resilience. In doing so, they improve their chances to survive today's chaotic business challenges. Characteristics that such organizations value include:

- Participative management
- Cooperation over competition
- Job-sharing
- Flexible scheduling
- Shared rewards and responsibilities
- Shared decisionmaking
- Personal development
- Concern with family well-being
- Environmental concerns

When you work in an organization that routinely relies on the above strategies, a different basis of support is available for you than when you work in a traditional hierarchical company or agency. In either case, it is to your advantage to develop to their fullest your communication skills and your capacity to work collectively with others. This is a lifetime project, but every little bit helps. Learn to confront supportively, to deal with differences and conflicts in a personal, rather than a rule-based way. Look for, point out, and accept opportunities to work *with* others, to share rewards as well as responsibilities. Initiate suggestions for shared projects or responsibilities.

In response to a barrier that can be called **Women's Ways Are Different (And Therefore Unacceptable)**, here are some guidelines.

Do	*Don't*
Pay attention to your responses to what's happening, even if they don't match the majority's.	Assume that men work the same way you do.
Work at affirming what you want and need.	Jump to closure too quickly just because that's what is expected.
Speak. Talk about what you want and need associated with work style.	Capitulate because linear logic seems so clear that it must be right.
Team with other women.	Be embarrassed because you see and say things differently.
Hold other women in high regard. Support them when you can.	
Acknowledge and suppport men who support women.	

Support others who are trying to work collectively—in job sharing or team approaches. It's especially important to support "new men," those who are willing to risk the rejection of their peers to work in partnership with women. Tell them that you appreciate their trust and openness—that it makes a difference. Sharing increases the complexity of the workplace by doing away with the fantasy of "clear lines of communication." But it humanizes work at the same time.

Support other women. Stay in contact with your own prejudices about bimbos, airheads, and flakes. When your shadow side wants to take over and elevate you or your friend at another woman's expense, take a look at what's motivating you. Find ways to let your gentler aspects connect with women who have hardened themselves as a way to survive the rat race.

Find ways to speak out about "women's issues"— childcare, flexible scheduling, parental leave, and comparable worth. Why are the life-and-death issues about the well-being of the human race and the planet called domestic (women's) issues? Stop acting like children are the special province of women and include fathers more when they're present. Most men have kids. Appeal to them: "Would you want the mother of *your* kids gone ten hours a day?" Read Arlie Hochschild's *The Second Shift: Working Parents and the Revolution at Home* and share it with others, especially your male colleagues. Promote the idea that we're all in this together and that the welfare of our children is of highest importance.

Create a substantial support network for yourself and others at work and outside work.

Alice's way (pages 106-107) of freezing her needs for connectedness was a survival tactic used by many women who broke new ground in the work world a decade or more ago. It hurt her and limited the people she supervised. However, as more women assume more authority at work, the richness of the feminine can pour into our corporate world more freely.

Your interest in closeness, in making connections, brings powerful feminine energy to the place where you work. As you become comfortable and feel strong in these aspects of your femininity, you can master turning them

The goal is to work in partnership, to benefit from the new energy and creativity that combined resources can generate.

into contributions where you work. Your gift for relationship will feel like strength, not weakness or inadequacy or something to be ashamed of. As you understand more about yourself, you can learn to rely on these dimensions for self-soothing and comfort. You can share this part of yourself with others who value the productive energy of relationships at work.

The increasing complexity of today's work scene makes the need for "high touch"—the personal connection—ever more relevant. As you embrace this part of you, you can stay afloat with good support. It will no longer be necessary to submerge the feminine principle.

Summarize Your Inner Work

Each of the dimensions in this "water" section has been outlined individually. As you worked through them, you could see that they are most meaningful in relation to other people. In order to be receptive, someone else must give you something. To nurture, another must receive your care and support. As you continue your exploration of these dimensions, ask other women how they recognize and support these qualities in themselves at work. Heighten your awareness of constructive ways to express this part of your womanhood in your daily work life. Acknowledge others when they flow from this element.

Marge Piercy's image of strong women is that "Only water of connection remains, flowing through us. Strong is what we make each other. . . ." Janet Surrey tells us that ". . . it becomes as important to understand as to be understood, to empower as well as to be empowered."[2] Anne Rudin, Ellen Steele, and Shauna Granger, women whose stories fill this section, know that working through the water of connection is powerful and fulfilling. Getting things done in ways that empower others—rather than tearing the feminine web by violating the connected ways women work—feels much more fulfilling than getting the job done at any cost.

Take some time now to review each of the flowing dimensions in this section and highlight areas for future attention. In your journal, describe how each lives in you—both as strengths and shadows. A brief verbal description or drawing for each of the four dimensions will help you focus your thoughts and feelings.

You're now half-way through the thirteen dimensions. This is a good time to review all the writing you've done in your journal. Take your time. Add notes or drawings where you've gained more understanding. Highlight places where you still have questions or loose ends.

Linger in the water as long as you like. Bathe and soothe your harried soul in the richness of feminine connection. It is a healing element, one to reach for when the intensity of the next fiery section blazes too hotly.

FIRE

PASSION AT WORK

Fire: The Element

olten energy roars beneath all that forms at the surface of the earth. Feminine passion, individually speaking, is just as powerful. With some skill and finesse we can nourish, rather than suffocate, the energy that glows in *Sexuality, Creativity*, and *Aggression*. That way, we neither smother the fire inside us nor reduce ourselves to burnout before our time.

We all know that the potentially destructive power of feminine passion scorches sensitivities at work very easily. In fact, it is so frightening that we've learned to keep it under control—turned down so low we freeze ourselves. Male bosses may be known, and excused, for their rages, or have reputations for being bastards to work for. But they're tolerated, even respected. The same behavior quickly raises hackles and earns a woman outright rejection—as well as the label "bitch," or worse. Feminine fire is so hot to handle that when it flares, it's likely to be quickly doused.

The fiery, passionate feminine doesn't fit neatly into bureaucratic structures or stay quietly within arbitrary boundaries. A woman with drive and commitment to make something happen doesn't do well with restrictive comments like, "This is the way we've always done it."

Containment, peacemaking, and collaboration are part, but not all, of the true nature of the feminine. The fiery side is equally important. Of course we can, and need to, manage our inner fires. But we've over-controlled them for so long that we've nearly extinguished them in attempts to create a safe climate at work. It's time to ask "safe for whom?"

A woman with drive and commitment doesn't do well with restrictive comments like, "This is the way we've always done it."

ANCIENT VIEWS AND MODERN PHYSICS

Fire fascinated our ancestors. Evidence tells us that in prehistoric times fire had god-like status. It danced on altars reflected in admiring eyes. Its mystical value came first; practicality for warmth and cooking occurred later.

This safe and reassuring connection with hearth and home feels warm and comfy. It's O.K. to associate heat with the security of the maternal feminine. The more primitive, more dangerous fascination with the flame is the one we shy away from. But it flickers still, somewhere in each of us.

In *Myths to Live By*, Joseph Campbell portrays some of that power.

> . . . Fire has the property of not being diminished when halved, but increased. Fire is luminous, like the sun and lightning, the only such thing on earth. Also, it is alive: in the warmth of the human body it is life itself, which departs when the body goes cold. It is prodigious in primitive traditions, it has been frequently identified with a demoness of volcanoes, who presides over an afterworld where the dead enjoy an everlasting dance in marvelously dancing volcanic flames.[1]

Wow! We'd better be careful.

Fair enough. It makes sense to be careful. It's not functional for wild demonesses to prance around the office or sexual sirens to run rampant. But it's important for each of us to know how this energy glows as part of our life force. It's unreal to think that the OFF switch is flipped forty hours a week. Where's the balance?

Three conditions permit fire to burn: 1) fuel, 2) high enough temperature to ignite it, and 3) oxygen to feed it. An explosion occurs when rapid burning causes a sudden

increase in the volume of hot air. Spontaneous combustion flares when oxidation occurs in fuel. Not all substances burn in the same manner. Fire is a catalyst that changes one substance to another—sand to glass, iron to steel. Materials are fireproof when they have combined as much oxygen as possible—or when they won't unite with oxygen at ordinary temperatures.

The rules of physics that describe the conditions and properties of fire also apply to our relationships at work. It takes heat to ignite a flame, fuel to keep it going, and air to feed it. Excitement about a project, adequate support, and breathing room for creativity energize work. When inner fires don't have enough space, explosion results. Too much pressure—or not enough time and resources—leads to intense frustration and volatility. Unpleasant though it may be, explosive aggression may serve as a catalyst for change. The explosion may clarify the need for priorities. Or it may destroy the project, the organization, the process. On the other hand, suppressed over time, heat burns us out. Human energy sputters and dies when inner fires burn too fiercely or too long. When we run out of fuel, when the air supply is exhausted, we give up.

The ancients appreciated, even worshipped fire as a core element. It still is. Life is the crucible of the human spirit—and work is a central part of that life. Let's see how we can fan our personal fires—reach a kindling point, find adequate fuel and oxygen—but neither explode nor burn out in the process.

Sexuality

short skirts, long jackets, great legs. Passion, the life force. Excitement, magnetism, flashing eyes, a woman full of herself. A Pandora's box. Along with all our other attributes, we bring our sexuality to the workplace. We are competent and sexual, bright and sexual, responsible and sexual, moral and sexual. Sexuality is part of who we are and of how we are.

Whatever else it is—whatever else might be more convenient or less threatening—feminine sexuality is the most outward indication of the difference we bring to the places where we work. Whether we know it or not, we "think" with our bodies. A woman's sexual presence in the office is the promise of a separate way of seeing things, of solving problems, and of setting priorities. It can promise creativity and a more open agenda than masculine managers and workers may have allowed. Cancelling that sexuality—asking her to deny her curves and her fluidity—is to deny a woman her identity. One woman told me she learned to walk as if she had a steel rod in her spine and steel rods in both legs, just so that she wouldn't be "suggestive." In the context of work, transforming a woman into a configuration of steel rods deprives the office of her comfort and her talents and threatens the workplace with sameness.

> *Sensuality does not wear a watch but she always gets to the essential places on time. She is adventurous, and not particularly quiet. She was reprimanded in grade school because she couldn't sit still all day long. She needs to move. She thinks with her body. . . .*
>
> Ruth Gendler, "Sensuality"

188

Gender difference promises long-needed balance for male-dominated environments that diminish or deny the feminine—but only if we resist defining our sexuality as a liability. We need to understand clearly that sexual approaches, sexist dismissals, and sexual conquests are the most direct ways to maintain patriarchal control and to undermine the promise that we bring to an office.

A woman who is comfortable in her desirability can be confident in her ability, too, and will not be easily sidetracked or intimidated into abandoning her complexity in order to be just a sex object. And the men she works with can grow to respond to that confidence with the desire for proximity, cooperation, and investment in the new work vitality her difference promises.

Only the half-man who lacks confidence in his own sexuality will choose to throw all that away by reducing feminine presence to an opportunity for another meaningless sexual encounter.

Comfort and confidence are part of the same package. But let's not kid ourselves. Comfort with fire takes some doing. Most of us have received negative messages about our sexuality from childhood on, and that can make comfort in our desirability an elusive quality. We must first give ourselves permission to make that comfort a personal goal; then, we just might find that our sexual energy can be the basis for a whole new way of working.

Sensuality, sexual expression, and sexual security are central to our feminine identities, whether or not we choose to believe, as Freud did, that behavior is motivated by sexuality and aggression. How we experience these fiery intensities in our personal lives is private. But if we feel that we have to shut this part of us down, to become gender-neutral, at work, then we lose a major source of energy.

School and work are places where we've learned, sometimes the hard way, to say no to our sexuality. We've been carefully taught that we're responsible, not only for our own sexuality, but also for the sexual responses that men have to us. We've been so injured by images of feminine sexuality as shameful or dirty—and by our treatment by half-men—that healthy, energetic ways to live the promise of our difference elude us. There is something radically wrong with this picture.

Sexual issues always get the biggest response in discussions or workshops on women at work. The idea that sexuality—erotic fire—is a legitimate part of our energy even on the job invites uproar. The power of the patriarchy, the ghosts of our Victorian grandmothers, invariably scream out: "You have to pay attention to what kinds of messages you're sending." "You can't expect men to work if you're wearing a skirt up to your tokus." "You'll never be taken seriously if you're sexy," and the biggest threat of all, "You don't want to be one of those women who uses her sexuality to get ahead."

And we've all had experiences that validate these warnings. Here's an example that's still vivid two decades after it happened to me in my stint as a university counseling center director:

With more involvement than they wanted, the other therapists on the staff offered up pieces of the annual budget, and I assembled the whole. Financial planning was part of my job that I didn't like. My stomach hurt as I worked the calculator and maneuvered staff needs, represented by dollar figures, into artificial categories defined by specific, frequently confusing university regulations.

Strong, mixed feelings zinged through me on the day of the presentation. I was scared to death and felt overwhelmed with responsibility. But I was also a little exhilarated with the anticipation of wheeling and dealing with a campus-wide committee. I believed that campus psychological services—always subject to budget cuts in an academic environment—would lose much needed support if I failed in my efforts. And I couldn't wait to get the whole thing over and done with.

Nearly rigid with performance anxiety, I made it through the presentation. The all-male committee broke for lunch after I finished. They hadn't asked many questions. I had no idea what they thought or felt.

As I walked back toward my office, one of the members caught up with me. "Well, Dr. Krebs, I'll bet you're glad that's over!" he said as he smiled at me.

I was. I was very relieved. He continued, "In case you're wondering why the committee didn't respond very much, it's because we were ogling you while you presented all those boring facts and figures."

"Ogling?" It took a minute for the word to sink in. Needless to say, I was flabbergasted and spent the next few days creating clever retorts. The man thought he offered a compliment. I was appalled and furious. The budget came out O.K., but I felt bad that, at least according to this professor, the committee had discounted my efforts just because they saw me as someone they didn't have to take seriously.

Virtually every working woman can tell stories about her efforts' being ignored or seen as less because she was perceived sexually, to the exclusion of her work abilities. If she's "attractive" that has gotten in the way of her being taken seriously. If she doesn't fit the accepted standards for "looks," she may have been disregarded as unwomanly.

But it doesn't have to be that way. Granted, men have a lot to learn about treatment of women in this department. But we're in charge of our side of the equation. Our comfort with our own sexuality supports us in our ability to be whole women and makes it possible for us to deal with off-balance remarks or behavior.

In the glossary of her book, *The Passion of Being Woman*, Mary Hugh Scott defines sexuality to include "the

A woman who is comfortable in her desirability can be confident in her ability, too.

enjoyment of life moment by moment" and sharing that enjoyment with others. Our fire energy is much more than the narrow interpretation the patriarchal fathers would have us believe. As Scott asserts, it *excludes* "sexual duty in marriage, obsequious behavior, pornography, and obsession with cultural idols."

This chapter is not about being seductive or overtly sexual at the office. Nor is it about exploiting your sexual allure as a promotional strategy. It's about claiming the fire in your sexual energy unashamedly, in a self-supportive way.

Becoming a man clone, or worse yet, a sexless robot, denies a very real part of a woman's identity—and that's certainly no long-term ethical way to respond to sexism. We have to learn, from a centered place, to trust and assert our right to be who we are. And, unfortunately, this includes acquiring the necessary skills to deal with people who choose to isolate this dimension as the only one they want to see.

Although men and women increasingly share power on the job, dealing with the issue of sexuality in a real way is a new frontier. Legislation has been passed in an attempt to protect workers from sexual discrimination and harassment. In fact, the laws have made such a difference that my daughters take for granted opportunities that weren't open to me. But, unfortunately, the laws can only hold the space. They can't begin to deal with the intricate emotional relationships between women and men at work in ways that create respect and safety for the feminine presence to step into the open. As a result, both of my daughters have experienced the kind of harassment that many people think doesn't happen anymore.

Our society, especially the world of work, has changed rapidly, but traditions for relationships between women and men lag behind. Until very recently—the past thirty years—any woman in the workplace who wasn't a nun, a teacher, or a nurse was considered by many men as fair game for sexual exploitation. Customs of equal treatment and regard are still evolving, and men who've had little experience working with women as equals or superiors are still having considerable trouble with the change.

Since we humans are sexual creatures, all our relationships, including those at work, have sexual components, large or small. For the most part, these feelings aren't particularly strong and we ignore them—or perhaps note them and consider them no big deal. We can treat them as we would any other feelings: anger, fear, compassion. We don't have to act on them—but, as with any other intense feelings, we have to have confidence that we can handle them. In terms of our own feelings, the fire can flicker and flare, but we have a choice about whether or not to fan it—whether to use that energy to build a working relationship or a romantic one.

One of the reasons this subject is so volatile is that it has been unacceptable to speak of our sexual reactions. Even if we don't discuss our grief, anger, pain, or joy openly on the job, we can talk about them with our close associates and family. This is not so with sexual feelings; we don't have many outlets for this fiery energy. We feel outrageous or guilty for having them and so we hide them (or act on them impulsively).

Gaining comfort with the idea of yourself as a sexual person increases your options. If you accept your sexuality as part of your normal range of feelings, you can discuss it with a close friend, partner, or therapist without feeling like a bad person. Giving these feelings a voice helps to ground you so that you can appreciate their energy and contain the fire.

Comfort grows from a sense of pride or excitement about your sexual self, rather than embarrassment or shame. How you feel about this has to do with how you've learned about your sexuality. It's a developmental thing. All those growing-up messages and experiences are still saying their piece. If they were positive, you have a solid foundation in this dimension. If they were negative, you face more of a challenge.

Still, it's never too late to learn a different way of thinking and feeling about ourselves. Although we can't change our emotional histories, we can do some significant repair work. When women get together to talk, many share similar stories. Our right to our sexuality—how to be sexual and taken seriously, too—are important topics for these discussions. Talking with others, in women's groups, in therapy, or with friends, can enrich us and clarify ways to be comfortable with this dimension.

Men have a sexual presence at work which is held as their right and isn't neutralized by organizational traditions. Feminine energy is no more or less.

Maintaining a victim's stance gets us nowhere fast. And hiding our femininity is only a last resort. It doesn't work well as an everyday approach, and it doesn't carry the process beyond the status quo.

Many men are the victims of our cultural tradition that exaggerates male sexuality. When they're not in control, they feel personally and economically threatened by women at work. Attempting to maintain their equilibrium, they come on or make off-color jokes or comments aimed at keeping us in our place. They work to prove their importance—or is it their potency?—to female colleagues (and their heterosexuality to other males) by casting a sexual glow on everything.

The old way of looking at things was that a woman was responsible for a man's sexual response to her. Some men (as well as some very adamant women) have had difficulty moving from this point of view into a more personally responsible one. Today, just as in the example from my counseling center days, we work with men who don't quite know how to experience us as work partners. So we need to be clear and comfortable with our sexuality.

If I had been more confident when the "ogling" professor came on to me, I could have said something like,

"Dr. _____, I trust you mean what you're saying as a compliment. If you're really interested in knowing me better, in working with me, I'd be glad to talk with you more about my budget proposal. Your support could make a difference."

Women don't have to be masculine or neutral to succeed in business, though that's basically what we've been asked to do (except in secretarial or other support positions where feminine sexuality is often exploited). But we do need to be sensitive to our sexual presence and have a good working knowledge of our sexual fire. Men have a sexual presence at work which is held as their right and isn't neutralized by organizational traditions. Feminine energy is no more or less. But many men are still ill at ease with that energy in the workplace. We can expect to have to deal with their discomfort and sometimes with the offensive behavior or withdrawal that results from their lack of experience or their wrongful assumption that they are *naturally* in charge. When we feel good about our own sexual presence, we are not thrown off balance by someone who gives us a hard time. And we may have more capacity to reach out in a reassuring way to a man who withdraws.

THE SHADOW SIDE

Sexuality at work offers energetic resources and poses a powerful threat *because it's a reality*. That doesn't mean that everybody at work chooses to be sexual with someone there, but it does mean that sexuality's fire and richness smoke and smolder on the dark side, whether we choose that or not.

Unfortunately, the feminine shadow has often been blamed for the destruction of men—beginning with Eve and carried throughout the Judeo-Christian mythology.

Navajo mythology also provides an unforgettably negative image of feminine sexuality. In her book, *Changing Woman and Her Sisters*, Sheila Moon describes an evil deity named Snapping Vagina. After being manufactured from the marrow of dead persons and Earth Grease, Snapping Vagina mated with other evil forces, producing an array of new monsters.

> All these monsters now began to destroy the people and the Snapping Vagina went her evil way, committing her adulteries, and was the wickedest thing ever seen. . . .

Analyst Moon expresses the depth of the evil evoked by this monster:

> To hear this story . . . in the cadences of Navajo language is to feel a full impact of the negative Feminine. Each of these various monsters issuing from monster matings had its own particularized method of destroying victims. Snapping Vagina's method was to sit down beside and engulf her victim.[1]

No wonder the shadow side of this dimension is so scary. All she has to do is sit down next to her unsuspecting victim and engulf him.

Fantasies of the idealized feminine encourage us to deny our shadow—especially in the sexuality dimension. Eve, the temptress, is a cultural ghost—a long-standing image of woman as evil so potent that we pretend it doesn't exist, especially at work. We don't want negative feminine stereotypes glued to our images.

But this myth is still powerful in the business world. Witch mother, castrating bitch, iron butterfly, and dragon lady are a few of Snapping Vagina's everyday labels that float through corporate hallways on the wings of this mythology. But the deadliest labels have to do with sexuality or sexual practices. These labels attach easily to those of us who don't comply with the "acceptable" feminine stereotypes. They are damaging and dehumanizing—and they turn their target into an object of scorn and rejection. As a way of protecting ourselves against being caught in this negative light, we choose to see ourselves as somehow above sexuality. In doing so, we deny our own shadows. If someone else gets caught in hers, we tend to run away from her rather than reaching out.

In his book, *The Dangerous Sex: The Myth of Feminine Evil*, H. R. Hays weaves an incredible tapestry—the history of the feminine shadow. Awesome power flows from feminine sexuality, from the ability to give birth, nurture, and even destroy life. So great is this power that from ancient times onward, tough taboos and traditions have been designed to keep it under control. And one of the ways has been to interpret feminine sexuality as evil.

On the one hand, all human beings are dependent and fear being left alone. On the other, we have an equally powerful fear of being trapped and suffocated. For men in relation to women, these feelings can get very confusing. In order to deal with their mixed emotions, some men either try to control us or simply disregard us at work—because we're too sexual.

Sexual shadow qualities are perceived by both women and men as so powerful—"the wickedest thing ever seen"—and as containing so much potential to get us rejected that we learn to smother them. With the dread—and reality in experience—that if we're not "good" we'll be alone, we've learned to stuff the shadow: either to avoid its inner heat or to use tremendous energy in denying its presence. At work, this part of our personalities often gets projected onto other women. We see them reflecting our own weakness or power hunger, and we hate them for it.

Sexuality's shadow is particularly troublesome at work

if our style is to seek value as a sex object—to invite sexual attention, mainly for the attention, not for the sex. Men who haven't learned that this is just another smoke screen to cover insecurity reach toward the warmth and get burned. Other women are threatened and put off by this style.

When we use sexuality to control others or to get what we want, we're living in this shadow. From this place, we see men as objects and women as the competition. The workplace becomes a hunting ground and we grow more interested there in proving our power and prowess than in anything else. Work takes second place to our needs for knowing that we're attractive and desirable.

Sexuality at work offers energetic resources and poses a powerful threat because it's a reality.

This is defensive behavior designed to hide real problems with self-esteem. It's a smoky, stuck place that's quite different from the energizing fire of sexuality for a person who's comfortable with herself. And it's a dangerous place with a long history.

We each need to know how Snapping Vagina lives in us—how she seduces us into power trips, addiction, dependency on others for our happiness, or mating with other monsters. The shadow side of feminine sexuality is about control. When we dare to look into the "maw of uncreative possessiveness and thus of destructiveness,"[2] we gain valuable information about ourselves. This part of our shadow reveals hidden power motives that are hard for us to own. As we come to understand what we really want, we can use our strengths, not our sexual shadows, to go after it. And we stand a much better chance of maintaining our gains.

SELF-REFLECTION

Take a moment to estimate your level of comfort with your sexual presence at work. Since this is a very complex subject, you might not arrive at a black-and-white answer. You probably feel differently with different people at different times. Just do the best you can to clarify where you are. Then you'll have a better idea where you might focus your growth efforts.

STRENGTH: I'm comfortable with my sexuality. When men make sexually colored comments to me, I deal with them easily. I enjoy my sexual feelings. I don't flirt at work. I've had a crush on so and so for a long time, but I keep it to myself.

SHADOW: I feel very vulnerable at work because I'm a woman. My boss makes passes at me that embarrass me. / I taunt my female supervisor by flirting with her boss. I get what I want because I'm attractive. / I feel dirty and ashamed much of the time.

Time For Yourself

As with any of the other dimensions, this one provides you with information about your feminine presence at work. In some ways, it is at the center of the difficulty women have had in being accepted in the power structure, and usually it has absolutely nothing to do with how you do your job.

It's an art to appreciate your sexuality. Let it add fire to your activities (including work) and know yourself well enough that you can state limits if and when others invade your boundaries. Here are some ideas to work with toward achieving that goal. Scan through all of them and then select a few to concentrate on.

• THINK OF A WOMAN YOU KNOW, either personally or through the media, who seems comfortable and confident about her sexuality.

Describe her carefully in your journal in writing or drawing. What characteristics lead you to conclude that she is relaxed and confident about her sexuality? How are you similar or different? Write the advice you imagine she might give you about this ever so interesting and sensitive subject.

• KNOW YOUR OWN COMFORT LEVEL with your sexuality and relationships with others on the job. List any areas where you feel insecure, uncertain, or under attack. (For example: I don't know how to deal with my boss's compliments; I'm not sure if my dress style is right for work; I want to go out with so and so, but it could cause problems if it doesn't work; my male co-workers put me down because I'm a woman.)

• LIST FIVE STEPS you can take to make the situation(s) in the previous item better for you. If you have trouble coming up with these steps for yourself, think of someone you can consult and get some help.

• OPEN YOUR JOURNAL so that you have two blank pages available to you. Draw a line horizontally across both pages. Create a time line, from day one of your life to the present, that portrays the creation of your image of yourself as a sexual person. List important events, comments, memories. (First knowledge of yourself as a girl, discovery of the "facts of life," traumatic sexual experiences, first menstruation, times in your life you felt exceptionally good about your sexuality.) Write items that contribute to your positive self-image in red or another fire color. Write items that reflect your negative self-image in shadow tones.

• SELECT AREAS FROM THE TIME LINE to revisit so that you can work with them. Write a strategy for expanding a positive item or confronting a negative one. Strategies might include seeking more information, talking with a friend, joining an incest survivor's group, drawing or writing different endings for scenarios that you create.

• FROM A POSITIVE VIEWPOINT, describe yourself in writing or drawing, or both, as a sexual person. Include comments that clarify your feelings about yourself in this dimension.

* WORK AT COMING TO TERMS with your sexual feelings. Everybody has them—whether they are obvious or hidden. If you fit in the "blatantly present" category, use your sexual fire as energy. That energy can fuel a lot of productivity on the job. If you're more inhibited, get acquainted with how your sexual feelings express themselves indirectly. On a scale of one to ten, with ten being completely relaxed, how comfortable are you with your sexual self at work? Why? Answer this question in your journal.

• DOWN ONE SIDE OF A PAGE in your journal, list sexual innuendos, comments, or behaviors that have hurt you in the past at work. Opposite each one, write a response that you would like to make from a comfortable, confident, centered position.

• PRACTICE MANAGING your sexual feelings. If you have a crush on someone who isn't available for a relationship for whatever reason (including just because you work together), allow yourself to enjoy the fire of your sexual feelings. These feelings are part of the richness of human experience and nothing to be ashamed of. You can enjoy them and keep them to yourself. They will slow down of their own accord as you get to know the real person rather than the fantasy you have created in your imagination.

• EXPLORE YOUR SHADOW. Pay attention to your tendencies to relieve tension by making sexual jokes or innuendoes or by being seductive with male colleagues. Granted, this is one way to break up the office routine. But when you do so you shift the unconscious focus of your co-workers from the business at hand to much more interesting thoughts of primal pleasure. Describe a time when your sexual shadow went after something you wanted. What was the outcome? Write about options you had and a possible different ending.

• LEARN TO DEAL WITH MEN who misinterpret your warmth and openness as a sexual invitation. You can talk with such a person about your intentions in a way that supports him as well as yourself. If someone makes this mistake with you, you can say, "I think that when I offered to help with such and such (or I was interested in your hobby, etc.), you mistook my support for personal interest. I am interested in being supportive to you at work. I'm not interested in a relationship outside work."

• SCHOOL YOURSELF IN WAYS to confront undesired overtures from men who have difficulty respecting your personal boundaries. Three books that deal with this issue in detail are: *Working with Men: Professional Women Talk about Power, Sexuality and Ethics*, by Beth Milwid; *On Your Own Terms: A Woman's Guide to Working with Men*, by Kathryn Stechert; and *Sexuality in Organizations: Romantic and Coercive Behaviors at Work*, edited by Dail Ann Neugarten and Jay M. Shafritz. Know your rights related to sexual discrimination and harassment.

The goal is for you to be comfortable with your sexuality and to integrate its energy as part of your way of working. In order to feel whole and safe at work, it's important to know how to confront effectively when you receive unwanted sexual attention. The more comfortable you are with your sexual energy, the more comfortable others will be with you.

Now that you've explored this dimension in more depth, return to page 27 and change your Self-Assessment Scale if you need to.

FEEL YOUR FIRE

You've explored your personal feelings and concerns in this dimension; now let's get more specific about how to deal with them at work. The true art of the working woman is to find ways to enjoy the energy of passion while maintaining clear boundaries.

Your sexuality, creativity, and aggression fire your ambition and productivity. When your sexual energy is high, get a lot done. Be creative. Have fun with your work—where you can. If it aids your creativity, give yourself permission to be beautiful in your own way. If you wish, push the envelope by wearing clothes and colors that announce your womanhood.

You, your employer, and your colleagues will love the products of your fire if you learn to regulate its heat. Create open agendas. Invite participation. Use your influence to set priorities and solve problems in ways that feel right for you. Discuss differences. Drop the pretense of sameness. Take the opportunity to talk about:
- Feminine connections with life,
- Nature and future generations,
- Capacity for collaboration,
- Brightness of intuition,
- Strength and stamina for getting things done.

Find other women and men of good will who support your efforts and work together.

Of course, as we all know, sexuality invites both barriers and invasion. Of all the barriers that complicate your life at work, the most primitive is **Sexuality Provokes the Raging Beast**. It's unrealistic to ignore the reality that insensitive chauvinists like the "ogling" professor on the budget committee still roam the hallways and byways of working life. But the idea that women at work stimulate raging male hormones and are so distracting that men can't work provides a rationalization for excluding women from shared power positions: "I'm such a virile, horny man, how could I be expected to contain myself—to concentrate—around an attractive female?"

Interestingly, this dynamic doesn't appear to be such an issue if women are in support positions. It's acceptable to be turned on by one's secretary because, in a hierarchical system, she isn't a colleague with whom one must negotiate. She triggers no fear of loss of power. But in professional or management positions, women have been taught that to be taken seriously it is important to avoid looking either feminine (brainless) or sensual (distracting). And so, they have learned to keep their sexuality contained, disguised, covered in tailored suits with high collars and neckwear. Clearly, the issue isn't sexuality but authority.

The delusion that the workplace is a sterile environment free of human emotion is a relic. The feminine presence invites responsibility for a broad range of human emotion, including sexual feelings. The workplace has always been sexual. The difference now is that women are actually present, no longer just the conversational objects of he-man chest beating and imaginary conquest. Now, they have to be dealt with face to face rather than under defenseless scrutiny on the porno pages. This creates real problems for men who are not secure in their masculine identity or who have trouble dealing directly with women.

Do	*Don't*
Identify who the culprits are.	Take it personally.
Talk with other women about your concerns.	Let someone else's immature behavior define you.
Get help if you choose to confront. Any confrontation should be private after you have created your strategy.	Engage in sexual banter as a way of gaining acceptance.
Inform yourself of legal protection against sexual harassment and discrimination. Know the definitions for both.	Mistake sexual attention for admiration of your work.
Make it clear in your own mind that you will not tolerate sexual harassment or discrimination.	Make idle threats about harassment and discrimination. Do give thought and planning to consequences of such action.

A related but more sympathetic barrier is Women Complicate Play at Work. Yes, play! The social aspects of work are where women really mess things up. The presence of women in power positions creates problems with informal office atmosphere and work-related social occasions. The all-male getaway now has to include you. When "the girls" were all in the background, leaving them behind was the logical thing to do. Somebody had to tend the store! And of course "the wife" would stay at home and take care of the kids. Women on a golf weekend completely change the nature of the event.

Stag movies, dirty jokes, sexual language, and pornography are still parts of male social life, business seminars, and meetings. Some women have survived these events by "going along with the guys." They endure humiliation and hold their own. This tactic may succeed in the short run, but it is a real violation of womanhood. Comments or activities intended as put-downs, even as informal talk and play, get in the way. If the prevailing atmosphere is sexist, any attempt to set a limit—such as not laughing at sexist comments—is likely to draw negative attention. Unless you are very self-confident, it feels like the choice is either to go with the flow or to feel even more like an outsider.

Do	*Don't*
Attend recreational functions.	Go along with behavior that degrades women.
Be sensitive to the loss men experience.	Let them get your goat.
Confront sex-role stereotypes.	Take on guilt for being included.
Take care of yourself.	Abuse alcohol.

Do	*Don't*
Team with other women.	Try to be one of the boys.
Regard recreational events as work time even though they're supposed to be fun.	Get into situations where you have no emotional support.
Explore your own capacity to have fun.	

As you gain comfort and confidence in yourself as a sexual person, you will learn to sustain your fire at work and the barriers will be less threatening. You will no longer need to masquerade as a robot or a man to cool the fear your sensual presence stirs in the once masculine management ranks. Your colleagues will feel your power, but they'll know you're not available.

For many of us, this is the most difficult dimension to integrate at work. Either we try to be neutral or we feel extremely vulnerable and threatened. A good middle ground is to know that your sexuality is your business and your energy and that other people's reactions to you don't define you.

"I don't appreciate personal comments about my appearance," is a relatively gentle way to set a boundary for unwanted compliments or suggestive comments.

"I see our relationship as a work relationship, not a personal one," responds to sexual innuendos or invitations.

"Your non-verbal messages suggest that you have a personal interest in me. You need to know that I don't return that interest," provides a way to bring gestures or looks into the open for discussion.

Continued, persistent, unwanted comments or invitations are sexual harassment. When you're confronted with this situation, get help and deal with it. You're not responsible for the unwanted behavior of others.

But if you choose to build a personal relationship with someone where you work, make it a project for your partnership to decide the best way to manage. Decide ahead of time how you will handle work if you break up, and try to be as realistic as you can. Think about the potential impact of your relationship on your colleagues. Will they feel shut out? Are issues of fairness involved?

As you truly grow more comfortable with your sexuality, and your feminine power in general, you can appreciate and contain your sexual energy without acting in seductive ways that confuse your male colleagues. Remember that you are responsible for *your* behavior, not theirs. When you can deal with this highly charged dimension in a self-supportive and constructive way, you offer your male co-workers a new level of security and partnership.

SUMMARY

Feminine sexuality is a fiery topic about which there is a great deal of myth and misunderstanding. The tendency is to blame the victim: "If she hadn't been wearing that outfit, she wouldn't have been raped."

Women will be the ones who change this attitude, but we have to be comfortable with our own sexuality and willing to voice our rights to be *all* of who we are. As more wives and daughters enter the workplace, more men are willing to hear about what really happens there and to take a look at their own ways of relating to women. "Would you want someone to say that to your daughter?" can be a powerful confrontation.

Feminine sexuality has been so dangerous and taboo on the job that working women have cloaked their sexuality by adopting masculine styles or pretending robotism. This makes things safer, but it eliminates vital feminine fire.

If we know ourselves well in this dimension and can own both our strengths and our shadows as sexual creatures, we will be in a position to educate those who misinterpret our warmth or animation as an invitation. At times, it's possible to turn the sexual approach that really says "I want to know you better and to be close to you" into a strong working relationship. It's also important to be skilled at handling sexual approaches that aren't sexual at all, but are power trips designed to disempower their target.

This chapter has only brushed the surface of this most complicated subject. Take as much time as you need to write in your journal about related issues you intend to pursue or resources you will seek. Now is the time!

Creativity

I should have been a great dancer,
but, like my mother before me,
I mopped small spills from freshly waxed
kitchen linoleum

        instead.

I could have been an interior designer,
but, like my mother before me,
I rearranged the musty linen closet one more time.

I might have been a writer of novels,
but, like my mother before me,
I scrawled a note: "please excuse my son's absence . . ."
on the back of last week's grocery list

        Passion fruit

        papaya nectar

        pickle relish (sweet)

I should have been a fashion designer,
but, like my mother before me,
I matched the shoes with the bag
with the hose with the scarf.

Creative juices flow
onto oilcloth,
commingling with the stains
spilled from last night's supper,

      only to be

      absorbed by a green and

yellow sponge; the green side
purposely abrasive, making it
easier to eradicate any stubborn residue.

But I still might be a poet;
Perhaps it's not too late.
I don't know.
My mother is gone, I have
no daughter,
I'm all that's in the way.

Stephanie Ganic Braunstein, "Apology"

irginia Woolf called it "the match burning in the crocus." Feminine creativity—the flash of insight, spark of genius, spirit of play—shapes the raw material of everyday life. At home, we generate meals with ingredients we have on hand, or beautify our surroundings with more talent than money. We substitute, compromise, do what's necessary to feed the multitudes and weave life's fabric in color and beauty for ourselves and for those we love. As workers in our own new businesses, we piece together intricate steps, do what needs to be done. If we're in charge, we're not confined by the limits of other people's standards. We're breaking new ground.

The uncontained feminine kindles the flame. Creativity finds its own way best where expectations are unclear or unknown and a protected space exists.

In everyday life, unfortunately, the stubborn residue of our creativity tends to get eradicated with little notice. We whisk it aside, underplay it. Woven into the fabric of other people's lives—a gift here, a party there, a new way of getting the work done—it rarely results in a major product. We have little time and less belief in ourselves. We sacrifice our dreams and get in our own way. The fire flickers from time to time, but it rarely blazes. And, because we live in a world attuned to the products of masculine creativity, we miss the significance of our own creative work.

Nevertheless, accomplishments emerge bigger than life in those for whom creativity burns fiercely—Georgia O'Keefe, Maya Angelou, Alicia de la Rocca, Barbara McClintock, Martha Graham. These women, with unnumbered less known sisters, indelibly brighten the world with their colors. Boundless energy, daring and dedication, as well as talent, fueled their contributions. Each found her way. But they all stand out as exceptions. Small spills, musty linen closets and notes to the teacher, seemingly tiny interruptions, use up the little fuel there is for more tentative fires. With our efforts divided by relational responsibilities, women rarely find or create the sheltered environment that supports world-class creativity.

We have trouble with what qualifies as "creative" in our own minds. A mistake, a coincidence, an "accident" occurs that opens new possibilities. We get a sense of what we want to do and figure out how to do it. We need to expand our definitions to include marketing design, a teaching unit, software, a therapeutic intervention, running a household adequately on too little money and too little time.

Suzanne, a woman who moved from home to a career in the financial world after age forty, explained to me one day in all seriousness that she really isn't a very creative person.

Surprised, I said, "What are you talking about? Look what you've done! You've translated your ability to do fifteen things at once as a mother and homemaker into a successful career in a dog-eat-dog industry. And you maintain your integrity in the process. You use creativity in your work every day with your clients—not to mention the way you went about getting your education and shaping your career. That in itself was a very creative process."

This is a woman who returned to college while she

managed her household, worked, and mothered three teenagers. After college, she created a niche for herself in an environment that wasn't supportive to women by marketing herself as someone who could relate to older clients—and to divorced women. She finds, or invents, ways to meet her clients' needs, sincerely keeping their best interests at heart. They love her and refer their friends. All this requires more than time management. Suzanne can see the big picture, determine where she fits, and create a unique spin in a highly competitive business.

"I think of creative as the ability to do all those art and craft things that I've never liked," she said. "But I guess I do have to use some original thinking in my work. It makes me feel good to think of that as creativity."

We're used to a male-oriented view of creativity. We look for a product, a creative work. But women are incredibly creative in ways that don't end with a product. The creative feminine is much more likely to be involved in *process*—the way something happens. These contributions are often taken for granted—the kind of thing that doesn't get recognition, but is missed if it's not there.

For many of us, "creative" describes somebody else. But, in all its forms, creativity is *really* the human capacity to see the world through fresh eyes and express what we see in new and different ways. It's not limited to genius-level art or invention. It certainly can't be owned by the feminine. But feminine sensitivity, emotion, and expressiveness can fuel the creative spirit.

Maria Martinez,[1] a Native American of the Tewa tribe, lived her ninety-plus years on the high desert near Santa Fe at San Idelfonso Pueblo in New Mexico. This woman, who at an early age stood out as the best potter in her village, is in many ways the model of the creative feminine. She did produce a product—her wonderful pottery pieces are now in museums and worth tens of thousands of dollars. But, as much as her stunning art, the way she lived

Creativity entails not only fluent and original thought, of which women are very capable, but also the ability to tailor ideas to practical problems.

213

her life was a work of great creativity.

This woman's art is of the earth. The way the fire treated it made it magic. She collected her clay from the New Mexico landscape by hand, painstakingly screened it, and carefully conditioned it for use. She and her artist husband, Julian, discovered that adding cow dung to the kiln fire turned the pottery's natural reddish color to deep black. Tedious hand polishing made it glow.

Maria's pots, decorated by Julian, her daughter-in-law, Santana, and others, were recognized and valued from the 1920s on. But her way was to support other women of the pueblo in their art and their efforts to earn money from it. She taught them how to do the special firing and made no attempt to "patent" the process. She helped other potters sell their wares, sometimes displaying theirs and holding hers back—even signing a friend's pot from time to time in the early days, to help with sales.

Although she was known and respected internationally in the art world, she made decisions about her life from her feminine center. Her choice was to stay at the pueblo, to live in very simple circumstances, in conditions that most would call "primitive" by Twentieth Century urban standards. She and Julian were central to the spiritual life and government of this intimate but complex native community. Later, their sons and their families shared responsibility for supporting and maintaining the Tewa tradition at San Idelfonso. Intellectually brilliant and with an unusual memory for detail, Maria lived her life in the midst of her family. In her 90s she still molded pots extracted from the high desert clay, tempered with just the right amount of water and shaped to a perfect roundness that contrasted with her gnarled but seemingly clairvoyant fingers.

Maria's simple, non-materialistic way has little in common with the rat race that many of us pursue. But her capacity to stay connected to her own process and her loved ones, and to fuel her creative fire, portrays feminine creativity at its richest. She worked closely with the earth as she scanned the color and texture of the soil around her to find just the right clay, patiently waited until it appeared, and then conditioned it for days until it was ready to use. The image of Maria walking the desert sustains me when I think things are difficult or are taking too long.

But the secret was in the fire. The fact that she and her partner found a way to transform shit into art speaks to the practicality of their creative process.

The fire of the creative feminine is key to understanding, nurturing, and supporting feminine power at work. The creativity of everyday life vitalizes any work site where it sparkles. Innovation, bringing a new view from a feminine perspective, adds a real difference. But there are lots of problems associated with getting this dimension out in the open.

Water elements, which are such a central part of the feminine—receptivity, flexibility, nurturance, and affinity—are often the wellsprings of creativity. But unless they flow in a fairly sheltered environment, they drown creativity in two ways: 1) Creative production is often isolated work—relating takes time and energy—and 2) the need to please someone else gets in the way of risk-taking. Fear of hurting or displeasing another invents artificial limits. "I was going to wait until my parents died to paint the pain of our family life," an artist shared with me, "but I'm so full of it, I can't do anything else." We worry about disrupting personal connections by telling the truth, taking the next step.

It's hard to push the limits if financial survival is at stake. Leaving my tenured job at the university to start a private practice took a huge leap of faith. I couldn't know if I could make it work, because I had never done it before. A creative move often has to make it across the chasm in one bound—with little or no safety net. A new product, a new market, or a new way of doing business is, by definition, untested—unproven. The feminine, which seeks comfort in connectedness, may hesitate too long at the brink while old self-doubting messages echo loudly.

Visible support on the other side helps.

The creative feminine is much more likely to be involved in process—the way something happens.

The creative feminine is a tentative commodity on the job where expectations are set and rules are rigid, and it may take longer to gestate than its more masculine counterpart. Harsh conditions smother any quality that's understated or not too well identified. In its fragile, underdeveloped form, it evaporates before it's born. It slips into the mold of existing structures—subtle and too willing to defer. And (it took me a while to figure this out) there are organizations that don't want employees, especially female employees, to be creative. It's just too threatening. So new ideas are actively squelched, or women aren't given credit. How many times have you heard, "I know I can make it work, I just have to get him to think it's his idea"?

New ideas don't always work out. The freedom to fail, security in the face of criticism, is essential. It takes a strong woman or a protective environment to fuel this fire in typical work environments. But when those conditions exist, the results speak for themselves.

Men occupy center stage in the history of art and creative thinking. This lopsidedness speaks to the politics of women's lives, not to any lack of feminine creativity. Creativity entails not only fluent and original thought, of which women are very capable, but also the ability to tailor ideas to practical problems. In the past, the practical problems of women have been home-oriented and mostly invisible, rather than in the public realm. Presently, women who work away from home while taking most of the responsibility for home and childcare have only enough energy left to hear the noisiest of their creative urges. They squeeze the nectar from stolen moments to bring their creations to life.

Some researchers tell us that creative individuals are those who have the capacity to use the feminine side of the self. Here's how Donald MacKinnon stated it in his classic research study:

> The evidence is clear: the more creative a person is, the more he reveals an openness to his own feelings and emotions, a sensitive intellect and understanding self-awareness, and wide ranging interests including many which in the American culture are thought of as feminine. In the realm of sexual identity and interests, our creative subjects appear to give more expression to the feminine side of their nature than do less creative persons. . . . [2]

Michael Dues, a songwriter, makes a similar point: "My friends are the fathers of the songs. I am the mother."[3]

The ultimate feminine creativity carries and delivers new life. Though this process is often life-endangering and warrants endless commitment, it gains neither Nobel Prizes, financial rewards, nor social status. A mother's creative product is somebody else's life. Even if she dedicates most of her energy to nurturing and training this child, her job isn't finished until she can let go—rightfully give credit for growing up to the child, not herself. The maternal analogy fits well for all forms of feminine creativity, regardless of our choices about parenthood.

Fertile feminine mulling is so biological and so ordinary. Its richness and profundity are easily overlooked, by ourselves as well as by those who take us for granted. The creative feminine asks questions, takes on unpopular projects, isn't satisfied with the status quo. But she can quickly begin to feel like the odd-woman out—it's not a comfortable place. Translated to the office, issues that engage the creative feminine—energy for life, concern for its quality and for the well-being of the species—shrink into the background as the daily pressures of business take over. How we learn to support this leading edge of the feminine presence is key to creating feminine balance at work.

THE SHADOW SIDE

The shadow of creativity looms dark and powerful. Rot, decay, and decomposition are necessary aspects of creativity. The old has to disintegrate to make room for the new. That's what makes this dimension so threatening. Light turns to dark turns to light.

And since we're frightened of the dark, we have a hard time seeing it as part of the creative process. In this dimension, maybe more than any other, we have to be willing to dive into our shadow rather than pushing it away.

In her great feminist sourcebook, *The Woman's Encylopedia of Myths and Secrets*, Barbara Walker provides some background for the dark side of creativity. She borrows from mythologist G. M. Neumann to describe Kali, the major goddess of ancient India:

> "Dark Mother," the Hindu triple goddess of creation, preservation and destruction; now most commonly known in her Destroyer aspect, squatting over her dead consort shiva and devouring his entrails, while her yoni sexually devours his lingam (penis). Kali is "The hungry earth, which devours its own children and fattens on their corpses. . . . It is in India that the experience of the Terrible Mother has been given its most grandiose form as Kali. But all this—and it should not be forgotten—is an image not only of the Feminine but particularly

and specifically of the Maternal. For in a profound way life and birth are always bound up with death and destruction."[4]

It's worth noting that this one goddess represents three major feminine (maternal) processes: Creation, preservation and destruction. Kali represents both the light and the dark side of the creative feminine. But the dark side is so scary, it's the one for which she is best known— the dark side of the maternal.

How this darkness forms in our own personal shadow is important information. We eat up our own creative works before they're born. The destruction can be subtle or out in the open. It's the quiet voice that says, "Nobody will like it." Or the loud voice that says, "Who do you think you are? Can't you just do it the way everybody else does?" Unfortunately, work environments often provide real life voices that corroborate these shadowy sentiments, making it doubly hard to avoid getting overwhelmed.

We create socially acceptable diversions of many kinds to avoid facing our creativity straight on. Staying too busy, supporting other people's creativity rather than our own, over-involving ourselves with our children's projects. (How many science projects have you done?)

Writer's block, performance anxiety, test anxiety, and failed confidence in our ideas all speak the shadow's language. Exploring the dark pathways to the roots of these evils helps you untangle the knots that prevent you from expressing yourself. Who says you shouldn't be able to write, perform, excel, create? Diving into these shadows helps you find the permission and self support you need to move forward.

The dark side of creativity, in one of its most identifiable forms, indulges in "retail therapy," overspending on clothes or other things that meet a creative need. "Retail therapy" appears to require less time and energy than doing our own creative work. And we get instant recognition for our efforts. If you look at the vicious cycle of overwork, stress reduction through retail therapy, and more overwork to pay for overspending, you can see the false economy.

Darkness deepens when we generate more ideas than we can use and feel victimized when we can't bring them to life. The creative fire burns out of control—with little capacity to organize well enough to carry projects forward. We get grandiose, believe that we're so creative we shouldn't have to do the mundane work to make the projects happen. Or creativity suffocates, becomes cynicism, fueled by frustration, and a pained anonymity.

Creative tension, thwarted and turned inward, provides just the right conditions for the pseudo relief of substance abuse or assorted sexual addictions. Unreleased creative energy fuels a tension state that burns for expression. An extra glass of wine or mood-shifting chemicals in one form or another seem innocent enough antidotes to bitterness and self-hate. Pursuit of the perfect adoring lover, this week's partner in escape from everyday life, fits here too. If these are your coping strategies, listen to your shadow screaming at you and perhaps you'll find more creative outlets for your life energy. Heed her screams and risk looking for help.

Destruction of the creative work or ideas of others is a vicious aspect of this destroyer mother. Unable to birth her own children, she eats other women's kids. This fits a negative feminine stereotype—that women can't work together. When we operate on the shadow side, often in competition for masculine recognition or rewards, the stereotype fits.

We're likely to smolder when we live on the shadow side of our creativity at work. Nothing is just right. We feel frustrated, blocked. Ideas don't flow. We may blame others or ourselves.

The variable and unpredictable direction of feminine creativity can be threatening to those who prefer straight lines.

When that happens, we need to give ourselves time to get back inside and regenerate. It helps to look at how we have failed to take responsibility for our work situations.

The shadow side of creativity speaks loudly. Hearing her can give you permission to take care of this dimension, which has been so oppressed in the feminine. Dive in. Encounter her darkness and learn from her gold. She'll help you to understand what form your creativity takes. Trust that it exists, whether or not you've recognized it yet. Make some decisions about how, when, and where you'll express it.

SELF-REFLECTION

Contact your creative fire. Is it bright? Barely flickering? Hard to find at all? This dimension exists in all of us and may be more or less intense, depending on current circumstances. When you hardly have time to breathe and stress is at the max, the creative glow fades.

Estimate your place on the continuum for creativity.

STRENGTHS: I trust my creative energies. Often I put things together in ways that haven't occurred to others. I try new things with relative ease. I can tolerate failing when I try something different. I feel good about my efforts even when others reject them.

SHADOW: I see so many options, I can't focus on one. / I get super-frustrated with my routine job. / I'm afraid to try new things. When I fail, I'm devastated. / My talents are irrelevant to my job. / I know I'm not creative.

TIME FOR YOURSELF

Creativity is sandwiched between two other fiery dimensions in this book for a special reason. If those two are suffocated, creativity usually sputters out! As you get better acquainted with your fire dimensions, find ways to support your creativity at work as well as in other parts of your life. Time flies when you can express yourself through your originality and inventiveness—and work becomes a lot more exciting. By taking a risk here and there, you may be able to create a more interesting and rewarding environment for yourself. The following tips provide some ways to help you fire up your own creative process at work. Choose several for deeper exploration.

• IN YOUR MIND, transport yourself to work. List three things you've invented or started up in the past month that help with your work. Think of steps, processes, or relationships you've created that seemed obvious to you, but hadn't been done before. This is your creativity in action. Acknowledge it by writing about it in your journal.

• THINK OF OTHER PEOPLE at work whose innovative approaches flavor their work. List three unpredicted steps or events you've observed within the last month that resulted from co-workers' creativity. How did they establish permission to take those steps? Did they have to deal with resistance and criticism? How did they support themselves or gain support from others? Or did they just "do it?"

• LOOK AT A BLANK PAGE in your journal. Fill it with colors, lines, or shapes—as many or as few as you like—in whatever form seems right for the moment. Don't judge it.

• ON THIS PAGE that you have glorified with color and with line—or on another one—list several words that spark your creative spirit. These may be ideas, objects, people, artworks—whatever inspires you. Add a drawing if you feel like it. Remember that this is just for you. It's not headed for the Museum of Modern Art.

• LIST YOUR CREATIVE STRENGTHS in your journal. What personal qualities spark your creativity? Do you find better ways to do your work or combine activities in unusual ways? Do you challenge the way things have always been done? Do you ask questions that make other people stop and think?

• LIST SEVEN WORDS that describe what support for your creativity has meant to you. Who in your life has supported your creativity? How did she or he encourage you? Write a letter in your journal (or to that person if possible) expressing your thanks.

• LIST THREE EXAMPLES of your own creativity in everyday life outside work. How can you translate the joy of these activities into your work environment? Write about some steps you can take, and then take them.

• IDENTIFY THREE AREAS at work where your creativity could find more expression. What blocks you there? Can you do something about the blocks? List several steps that might help.

• FIND OPPORTUNITIES to be assertive on behalf of others' creative attempts. Creativity needs a safe environment in which to flourish. What can you do to make your workplace supportive to creative efforts?

• WHOM CAN YOU ASK to support you in your efforts? List their names in your journal. Talk with one or more of these people about creative next steps that interest you.

• YOUR CREATIVE EFFORTS at work have to be open to the scrutiny of others in order to thrive and grow. They won't all be successful. Learn to keep the creative fire burning despite the cold water of criticism. Give yourself a little time to recover from the pain. Then see if there is something to be gained from the critique. Sift through what is helpful and use it to your advantage.

- IDENTIFY ONE creative work-related project you would like to pursue in the coming months. For instance, if you're working on your business writing, find a current magazine with a related article. Read it and follow any tips it suggests. Or, if you're trying to increase your client base, read a novel or biography of a woman who is an inspiration to you and see what you can learn from her. Write in your journal when you plan to commit time and how you plan to proceed.

The workplace benefits when the warmth of the creative feminine is fueled. Its fire brings fulfillment and satisfaction to your everyday life. Its shadow darkens the door when the press of business and glamorized images of the creative life make it easy for us to underrate ourselves in this dimension.

Return to your list of creative strengths and underline them in your journal. Write them in neon lights in your awareness. Now, review your Self-Assessment on page 27 and make whatever adjustments are needed. If you've worked through the exercises in this chapter, you probably have expanded your definition of creativity to cover more of you than it did before.

CREATIVITY GOES TO WORK

Learn to support your efforts and those of others who are willing to challenge the system.

This is the way we've always done it, especially if "we" are the masculine molders of the organization, tends to deaden creativity in even the most self-assured employee. This killer phrase stifles everybody's creativity. And the message can be loud and clear even if the words are never spoken. It's especially deadly if the implication is that the traditional masculine way is the right way and that any variation is inferior. The variable and unpredictable direction of feminine creativity can be threatening to those who prefer straight lines.

Many years ago, working in a special reading program, my job was to order several thousand books to be distributed to teachers in fifteen different elementary schools. I pondered this task with great seriousness and, predating the personal computer by a few years, created various systems to limit the potential for unbridled confusion. I settled on an approach that relied on charts and color coding. It made good sense to me. On paper, I grouped the books in color-coded sections and could cross-reference them in the necessary different directions. I knew which school needed which books and, efficiently from my point of view, proceeded to construct the orders. My supervisor, an enormously overworked man who was glad for any help he could get, approved the plan.

But his boss, the superintendent, blew his stack at me. "I don't know what you're trying to do here. This is the silliest thing I've ever seen." Bypassing my creative endeavor, he personally instructed me on how he wanted the orders physically collated, and even stapled in a certain way. It took much longer and added nothing to accuracy or ease of recordkeeping. It was simply his way. Today, I would respond to that kind of pathetic power move by asserting the positive pay-off my method offered. "Yes, this may appear to be a little unusual. But, see, here's what it offers. . . ." At that stage of my career, I was hurt and infuriated. My insecurity and anger scrambled any possibility of an effective, self-supportive response.

This is the way we've always done it, tends to be well entrenched in traditional work sites, and in some non-traditional ones as well. It's a fast-growing virus. Bureaucracies are famous for it. Here are some suggestions for supporting your creative fire in a suffocating environment.

The creative feminine asks questions, takes on unpopular projects, isn't satisfied with the status quo.

Do	*Don't*
Express your ideas tactfully and repeatedly.	Take criticism personally.
	Undermine yourself.
Ask questions.	
	Put down the ideas others express.
Push the limits a little at a time.	
Learn by your mistakes; critique, don't criticize yourself.	Give up because your efforts aren't appreciated.
Reality test with someone you trust about whether you're "off the wall."	Expect to be affirmed for something that threatens to change the way things are.
Make sure support is in place when you try to make big changes.	Lose your sense of humor.
Trust your inner voice.	

Research shows us that, contrary to popular belief, competition curtails creativity.[5] If your eye is on winning, or protecting your backside, your energy slips from the task at hand. You are likely to become more rigid and less able to let your imagination roam freely. In competitive environments, you need to secure the space in which to be creative. Know the areas in which you are safe enough to express your creative energy and those in which you have to be more guarded and self-protective. If you don't expect yourself to be competitive and creative at the same time, you'll be less likely to be self-critical about your limitations.

Barriers to your creativity at work may exist in the

restrictions and limitations of your job or workplace. But they are even more likely to be internal blocks—attitudes *you* cling to, like "This isn't any good—So and so won't like it—It's not that important." Draw a circle around that one and put a line through it.

Maintain contact with your creativity—the creativity of everyday life—at work. Protect some private time and space so that your creative process can form and emerge. "Something's cooking here; I need some time to think about this," can become your theme song. Support your efforts even when they "fail" or don't meet with the approval of others: "That didn't work, but here's what I learned from it. . . ." Support the creativity of others. Stay tuned in to ideas that seem different or new—thoughts that don't slip neatly into the well-worn groove. Don't be afraid to acknowledge a co-worker: "I noticed that you got us hooked into a new resource network. I hadn't thought about using that approach. It will help a lot."

Support your creativity by taking risks. What you perceive as your weirdness may be your unique contribution to the vitality of your workplace. Choose supportive women or men you trust and talk with them about your process for "reaching in." Or let them in on some of your intuitive flashes. Propose an intuitive, non-linear solution for some problem that your work group is struggling with.

Stay in touch with your process—the ways you personally create your job on a daily basis. In even the most structured job you have choices about what you do first or how you choose to approach certain tasks. Use your ingenuity to make your job work for you in as many ways as you can.

If you have a lot of control over your work and how you do it, let your intuition guide you. Move beyond the realm of what's been done before. Bring your individuality and creativity to bear on your work in as many ways as you can.

And for the most fun of all, feminine creativity heats up in group form. If you want to see feminine power at work, get a group of women together who share values and goals and are dedicated to making something happen—a party, a seminar, a political action, or an artistic endeavor.

Photographer Catherine Busch-Johnston[6] spoke of her experience this way:

> I'm producing 8, half-hour shows on older women. I have two women as my crew. They're always doing their best. They assume their responsibility plus a little more. I'm making a video. It's a collaborative effort—very feminine. Everyone depends on everyone's efforts. People on crews usually work together—cover for each other. Everybody helps carry equipment.
>
> The women I'm videotaping are amazing. Nellie Red Owl, an 85-year-old Lakota Sioux Elder; Betty Kazosa, a woman who was in one of this country's concentration camps and has used her experience to enter politics as a catalyst for helping others appreciate the differences in people. I received a Laurence Rockefeller grant and was able to raise matching funds. Four shows are taped—one edited off-line. The vision is there and I can't not do it.

Catherine's creative fire provided her with energy, not only to create and carry forth her vision, but to hustle the resources she needed to make it work. Although working independently at the time I interviewed her, Catherine had spent years in film, TV, and publishing.

"How would corporations be different if women were in charge?" I asked her. We were sitting on a boat dock at a lake near Nevada City, California. She gazed off across the water and let it roll:

Day care, warm environment, paintings, lighting, rugs, layout. An environment creates another way of thinking and feeling—builds trust. If people felt that they were heard—human provisions—they would be happier and more productive. Women would have concern for the well-being of people and provide time to take care of themselves. When workers realize people are spending on them they have incentive to work harder. Flexible hours. When you work with women, you don't have to tell them what to do—don't need a task master, a production manager.

Given time and resources, and the opportunity to work together, the combination of connectedness and creativity can produce stunning results. Create this opportunity for yourself and others at work whenever you can.

And don't take it all too seriously. Your sense of humor is part of this dimension. Creativity and humor have several things in common: 1) the ability to see and appreciate unusual relationships, 2) the ability to combine ideas that don't usually go together, and 3) the intuitive ability to cut through layers of defensiveness to the unconscious truth. Feminine humor, which of course has been around forever as a subversive art, is coming of age. Regina Barreca writes:

We have had to learn to embrace the idea of ourselves as striving for our goals, as aiming for success, as willing to set our sights for the very top. We have learned to love the thought of our own ambition. And we are learning to love our own laughter, to see that our sense of humor makes sense and can help us make sense of the world around us, which means relearning to trust our instincts and to stop

checking whether the guy sitting next to us is laughing before we laugh. If it's funny, we should let ourselves laugh, loud and clear.[7]

Barreca's book, *They Used to Call Me Snow White . . .
But I Drifted: Women's Strategic Use of Humor,* and another
one, *What Mona Lisa Knew: A Woman's Guide to Getting
Ahead in Business by Lightening Up—The Bold New
Strategy for Less Stress and More Success on the Job,* by
Barbara Mackoff, provide fun reading, refreshing insights,
and validation. And, as Barreca points out on her book
jacket, "She who laughs, lasts."

FEMININE CREATIVITY—A PROCESS

Andrea is an administrator, a therapist, and a consultant. She's sensitive, talented, and highly skilled.

She had weathered the stress of early conflict resolu-
tion with the decisionmakers in the software business
where she's an external consultant. She dealt with them in
a centered, confrontive, calming way that moved them forward rather than further into the flames of their strong personal conflicts.

Reorganization of the company demanded restructur-
ing of the technical staff. Women who had worked directly
for one boss since the founding of the company would no
longer be identified with a particular person or job. Two
teams, each supervised by a coordinator, would handle the
heavy work flow. Typical rivalries and personality conflicts
zinged among these women. Solid alliances with previous
bosses made this shift hurtful. It felt like a demotion. The
whole idea was experimental and nobody was particularly
happy about it.

Andrea had worked with the coordinators through
several training sessions. These women were technicians,

not skilled leaders, but the success of this organizational transition depended on their capacity to lead their new "teams." The coordinators and their immediate supervisors were beginning, tentatively, to form a team.

They looked to Andrea for the answers. A two-hour "team building" session was scheduled for each of the groups. It would be the first time the new teams met with their fledgling leaders.

"What would you like from me?" Andrea had asked them.

"Teach us to do what you do. Help us feel secure. Bring your bag of tricks."

Andrea was floored. She'd spent nearly twenty years learning to do what she does. Her work is grounded in solid knowledge of herself gained through years of personal therapy and self-development, plus technical skills gained from three different career paths. The naiveté of their request threw her.

"What can I possibly do in two hours that will make any difference?" she asked herself. And, "We have to start somewhere," she answered.

She had Saturday morning to create her strategy. Optimistically, she tripped upstairs to her home office. She pulled together some books and other materials on team building. Very familiar with this material she mostly stared at the covers while she thought about the contents. She mentally rehearsed a dozen different approaches. None seemed right. Three hours later, she returned downstairs for lunch, not one bit closer to what she'd do than when she started.

She drifted through her heavy weekend schedule distracted—preoccupied. This shouldn't be such a hard problem. She wanted to deal with these women in a real way, not do some canned exercise that might feel good for the moment and make little if any difference later.

Sunday, after dinner, shouldering the bruskness of her

Given time and resources, and the opportunity to work together, the combination of connectedness and creativity can produce stunning results.

231

partner's disbelief, she headed upstairs again. She pulled out her professional bag of tricks—personality inventories, warm-ups, communication-skill-building exercises. "Not enough time. Not right. Too structured." She discarded each.

"These are all women. They're scared, vulnerable. Some are angry and defensive. What if I get them to talk about their strengths and weaknesses as women working together?"

It was all there. She pulled out her sample copy of my Self-Assessment Scale. Her design fell into place. This wasn't going to be a typical team-building process. It was going to be straight from her heart. Either it would work or it wouldn't, but it would be real.

The next morning, as she walked toward the room where the first group was waiting, the office manager approached and said, "Oh, Andrea, I hope you won't mind, but the boss decided to include two more people. Joe will be in this group and Harry in the other."

Andrea blinked. "Fine," she said.

A design focused on the feminine, and now one man would be present in each group. "It's the feminine," she said to herself, "not necessarily women," and she walked on down the hall.

A rack of jitters shivered lightly through her, but, mostly centered, she greeted the waiting group. Each sat as if in her own plexiglas cubicle, separated from the others. Joe looked as if he would rather be anyplace else.

Andrea talked briefly about the purpose of the meeting and the idea of shifting to a team.

She asked them to describe how they felt about this shift. They were honest. The answers boiled down to, "We don't like it."

She asked for their cooperation, just for the two hours. They agreed.

"We know a lot more about being separate than we

know about being together. To work as a team, we have to have some way of connecting with each other. When we're connected, we give energy to each other and we receive energy from each other. Each of us is then more powerful than any of us could be individually."

She invited them to a meditation in which, lightly holding hands, each would visualize his or her heart energy and in turn, with a gentle squeeze, would pass it on to the next person. Not a typical beginning for a corporate team building.

They knew Andrea and they liked her. They'd had enough previous contact with her to trust. Whatever their feelings about their colleagues, they were willing to try what Andrea asked. Following her guided imagery, they opened themselves to meditation. The mood in the room shifted.

More talk about connection.

"We connect better with each other if we know who we are and we know who they are—and if they know who we are." She distributed copies of the Self-Assessment. The next hours flew as each person extracted her (and his) strengths and began to grapple with their shadow patterns. They were honest with themselves and with each other. They were excited. They began to understand more about their problems with each other. And they began to comprehend that their similarities far outweighed their differences.

"You asked me to bring my bag of tricks," Andrea reminded them. She fished a purple silk pouch from her neatly ordered brief case. The chatter quieted. "I tried to think of techniques I could teach you in just a little time. Even the most basic group skills require understanding and practice. We'll work with those along the way. For today, though, here are some things to think about as you work together."

"The turtle symbolizes courage, vulnerability, and persistence for me." A small black onyx fetish sat in her hand. Tiny turquoise, long a symbol of healing in Native American lore, studded each section of the turtle's shell. "She doesn't move fast. She makes decisions about when and how far to stick her neck out. When she does, she can be incredibly vulnerable. She's tough as can be when she retreats into her shell. She gets to where she's going in her own time."

Move beyond the realm of what's been done before.

The foggy glow of a smoky quartz crystal emerged from the bag next. Andrea held it up to the light. "I brought this because, for me, its darkness and lack of clarity represent woundedness. We're all wounded. When we accept that about ourselves we can be much more open to others. We don't have to pretend to be perfect."

Now the soft pink of a rose quartz crystal shimmered as Andrea held a new "trick" up to the light. Its vitality sparkled in amazing contrast to the smoky quartz. "This rose quartz symbolizes healing. The light of life shines through it. Its color communicates hope."

"The green in this tiger's eye marble radiates heart energy—the vitality, courage, essences of life. When we're connected at this level, we have the stamina and flexibility to struggle through our differences. You'll notice a slender rosy thread of color that appears here. For me, its beauty symbolizes femininity—a connection with internal, personal power."

Andrea shifted from linear problem solving—imposing a masculine solution where it just wouldn't fit—to her own feminine connection with the women on the teams. At that point, her creative fire blazed. She gave herself permission to do what made sense to her rather than following the "rules." She created a process that allowed the team members to view working together as a gain rather than a loss.

Summary

Creativity, as with most other subjects researched by psychologists until very recently, has been defined by masculine standards. Research subjects tend to be male, though generalizations are made to cover everybody. When I started looking for material on feminine creativity, it was slim pickings. Research in this area will open up exciting possibilities.

For now, what we need to do, in all phases of our lives, is pay attention to our own creative urges, express them, and value them. We can then appreciate our creativity and validate that of other women. By doing so, we have the capacity to bring a significant shift to the places we work—aesthetically, interpersonally, in the way we do our work, and in the values that underlie the products we produce.

Aggression

How do you feel when you're mad? Or when you're totally committed to pushing toward some goal? Do you see red? Is your body energized? Do you feel solid and strong or shaky and splattered all over the place? What does it take to fire up your aggression?

"*Feminine* and *aggression* are contradictory terms. You can't be aggressive and feminine too." This sentiment, expressed by nearly a third of the people I interviewed— some women, some men—is a fairly common one. Does it fit your experience? In my own life, I feel the hot breath of feminine rage. Occasionally, her blazing eyes glare at me from the face of another. Her fire, energizing or destructive, also flares inside me. I don't always welcome the feelings, but, at times, they crackle with insistence.

Your own slow burn, anger, or rage kindles your feminine aggression. It comes from deep within you. As you read this section, test it. See if you can clearly identify your fire as it flickers or flares. Recognize energy that is different from the masculine-style aggression many of us have adopted as a survival skill.

Well trained to be a nice woman, I've had a hard time getting to know and trust my fire. As with many of us, this dimension was nearly snuffed as I was growing up. And so it tends to erupt as tears, not heat. But it has sustained me at times. I've gloried in achievements won by long slow fights, fueled by outrage and commitment. I've felt the coldness of defeat when my battle failed. I've worked and fought hard to achieve goals that seemed impossible. I've been accused of being ambitious. All that feels like

Feminine aggression isn't usually for territory or position. It's aggression that supports self-sufficiency, not control over someone else.

aggression to me—aggression of a feminine kind.

Most women don't fight to dominate others. Feminine aggression isn't usually for territory or position. It has more to do with personal survival than with power. It's aggression that supports self-sufficiency, not control over someone else.

The raw energy of combative aggression is more masculine than feminine. It's the main way boys' play differs from girls'. Masculine aggression has more to do with taking over, with defeating another. Men appear to enjoy aggressive actions much more than women do. Sports fans admire a bone-jarring hit in a football game. They see combat as a sport—and sport as combat. Women may attend prize fights, but usually as supporters, not fight enthusiasts. Few women experience joy in watching two people knock each other into oblivion or thereabouts.

Feminine aggression lurks in corners—comes out in the open for a cause. Or it presents itself indirectly—in sneaky ways—not for the hearty fun of it. Frank Lawler, a human relations professional in Indianapolis, confessed: "I'd much rather have a man angry with me than a woman. Men are more predictable with their anger. You know where they're coming from. With women, aggression is hidden, malicious—difficult to get a handle on. It's very tricky—a knife behind the back and lots of sideways movement."

Christine Newsom, a rural California physician whose male colleagues outnumber her ten to one, expressed her opinion heatedly: "A hell of a lot of feminine aggression exists in our country—stemming from women's tremendous frustration with their lot. I think more times than not, it's unrecognized. Most women wouldn't come out and say it. Frustration leads to anger and self-hate—which is another form of aggression—self-aggression."

Pure feminine aggression is the energy that harangues until the school crossing is secured, pushes for a defined relationship, organizes a peace march, fights to save the life of a condemned criminal. It's assertion, ambition, and willingness to take on a cause. It forges connections with others, rather than using people as stepping stones to power.

We can handle masculine aggression at work without getting hooked into blowing up or giving in when we're comfortable with our own anger. We can protect our personal boundaries and fight to be taken seriously. We can stand firm to protect opportunities for soft or creative expression.

It's important for us to honor the feminine side of our aggression openly and completely. Here's a story about some consultants who paid dearly for not giving enough attention to their inner fires. They could have made a stronger case, but didn't take the risk.

The woman who told me this story opened by saying, "I don't know whether to laugh or cry!"

Until shortly before she shared this tale of woe, she and another woman had worked many years for a medium-sized manufacturing company.

> For close to a year, we talked with the decision-makers about the importance of reorganizing a particular department, internally as well as the way it served the total organization. We could see that they were headed for trouble. It would have been a major change, requiring big expenditures.
>
> Since our contract ended, the company has hired "Mega Masculine Consulting Firm," for at least four times what they were paying us. The new consulting firm looked at this problem area and saw the administrative failure that we had predicted. The decisionmakers had all but sneered when we called attention to the problem and recommended big changes. Mega Masculine Consulting Firm came up

with recommendations revoltingly similar to those we had made repeatedly. And the decisionmakers went for it.

We were furious. We really wanted to say "I told you so!" It was maddening. We had horrible green-eyed monsters—ferocious images of mayhem and worse.

These women felt their aggression. After the fact. Contained aggression—not acted upon—but aggression, nonetheless, felt too late to do them any good. The same amount of energy firing their early recommendations might have won the decisionmakers' attention.

This event provides a great example of how the feminine presence is exploited in typical work settings. Healing feminine energy was O.K. for keeping the peace and making the organization work better. But when it came to really changing the structure, the way things worked, feminine voices landed on deaf ears. It's O.K. for women to "help," but not to move aggressively into new products or new ways of doing business.

The story might have unfolded differently if these women had taken their own aggressive energy more seriously. They can be angry with the decisionmakers and feel put down, but they can't blame the company executives. Their low-key style was a big part of their defeat. From here, it's easy to see what they *should* have done. More heat and considerably less fear of being seen as pushy— more energy in confronting the way women were treated in that company—would have served them, and their client, well.

Possibly, they could have held the space to move in and do the work that needed to be done. But to do so, the fire had to burn. Their aggression early in the process—in the form of clear, supported assertion and confrontation— could have energized them to fight, to say clearly and directly what needed to happen and why. The consultants hadn't risked fighting hard enough for what they believed—and were put off. The results felt terrible.

Here's a story with a happier conclusion. Although it concerns a single afternoon, not a long process, the principle is the same.

At the time of this event, Peggy worked as a staff assistant to an elected state official.

For some people, it was just another scorching summer afternoon. For Peggy, it was another day of legislative hearings—hours and hours of detailed material that would eventually shape the state law. She hadn't thought there would be a problem with the testimony she had to offer. But as her presentation unfolded, she found herself surrounded by hostile witnesses.

"I find it hard to see this item worth talking about," one staffer bantered.

"I concur," another drawled.

Much to her surprise, the legislative staffers, friends of hers she thought, were belittling the issues at stake. They were playing political games, bantering and exchanging verbal barbs with no apparent commitment to get the work done. A strong but quiet person, Peggy shifted without even thinking about it from routine participation into the energy of her own aggression.

Her voice rose. She fought for eye contact.

"Here's a crucial section . . ." she asserted, and launched into the details.

As the afternoon's dialogue wore on, her agitation grew. The seriousness of the situation hit her. A little panic set in. She was feeling picked on. A slow burn heated her cheeks. She feared tears. "I just can't cry," she thought. "These guys are acting like jerks. I'm not going to let them get to me."

Instantly, she could feel her calm increase and her strength grow. Resolve replaced irritation. This typically soft, gentle woman found that she had abundant fire to counter their smart comments and to squelch the nitpicking that threatened her proposal. She couldn't stop all the damage singlehandedly, but she avoided serious losses. She didn't "win," but she held the space so she could return another day.

The feminine side of life isn't all sweetness and light, but many of us keep this idea going. We douse our internal fires and adopt a smiling face to cover the pain. This smothering process adds to the high frequency of chronic depression among women. As we live in our powerful feminine experience, more of us are better able to care for ourselves in the world. Smiling masks drop and the female depression index slopes downward.

In addition to having it stomped out of us by centuries of male-centered history, we have our own needs to quiet scary aggressive feelings. As the physically weaker sex in terms of mass and muscles, it's dangerous to be aggressive in situations where we're not in control and don't have the power to win. But we duplicate this condition at work, where men hold the organizational power. In typical work situations they still have institutional muscle mass—financial control, decisionmaking power, the right to hire and fire. We need to learn psychological Aikido—the ability to fend off aggression without countering it directly. Our own aggressive energy supports us in knowing we have the right to go after what we want.

On the job, we have to be willing to deal with the defensive and angry reactions that aggression provokes. If we dish it out, we have to be willing to take it. Sometimes it's not worth it.

Most little girls are discouraged when it comes to feeling and exploring aggressive feelings. We learn that these feelings are "bad"—that people won't like us unless we're nice. We find ways to blend with the environment rather than assert our differences. By the time they're in the fifth

As the physically weaker sex, it's dangerous to be aggressive in situations where we're not in control. But we duplicate this condition at work, where men hold the organizational power.

grade, girls have given in to what Catherine Steiner-Adair has dubbed "The tyranny of kind and nice." They've learned to say, "Do you want to know what I think? Or do you want to know what I *really* think?"[1] Since we don't typically accept and explore our own feminine aggressive patterns, we find ourselves tying on boxing gloves that are oversized and weigh too much. We struggle with masculine tactics that don't really fit who we are.

During the 1970s, "assertiveness training" became very popular—a major force that supported women's efforts to get out into the world and get their share. Assertiveness training teaches skills and builds confidence to go for more of what we want and need. When my colleagues and I taught assertiveness skills, we were very careful to accent the difference between "assertive" and "aggressive." To assert was fine—to aggress, a no no. But we need to go further, to understand and express aggression that is an important aspect of our womanhood.

The path is in our most primitive feelings. We need to connect with the energy that fires a mother bear to defend her cubs. We need to reach for Warrior Woman's righteous rage. Individual access to this personal power is a strong, protective force when we know it and can contain it. All humans have primitive feelings. Our choice is to deal with them consciously or lose a vital connection with a prime energy source. Use them to fire assertion, persistence, creativity. In getting to know these very basic feelings, we can honor our feminine aggression, expand our self-understanding, and grapple with who we really are.

Too often, we understand aggression in the ways we see leadership—in masculine ways. They fit us about as well as a jock strap. Because our aggressive feelings have been so unacceptable to us, many of them have been stuffed deep into our shadows. When we have the courage to plumb their depths, the experience is a rich and necessary one—but not a particularly pretty sight. The smiling mask cracks and falls off. We feel exposed.

To copy the masculine style doesn't really do it either. When we learn to play men's games—to go for the jugular or win for the sake of winning—we lose contact with our own feelings. That route leaves us empty and guilty, one more example of acting rather than being. We need to feel our own fire and find ways to channel our hot feminine aggression.

To ignore this part of our existence, though, means that unexpressed aggression simmers and flares in unpredictable ways. It blocks access to our love energy. We can't be mad and loving simultaneously. If we don't know how to get mad and get through it, we just deaden ourselves a little bit. Over time, we feel more numb than anything else. Dealing with anger in close relationships is very hard for most women. It brings up deep fears of loss of connection. But learning how to do this is essential for keeping a real relationship over time—at work or at home.

THE SHADOW SIDE

"Hell hath no fury like a woman scorned." This phrase deals with the shadow side of aggression—pure, raw, unbridled rage—anger spewing with no concern for the consequences. Destruction is the goal, plain and simple.

Aggression comes from the dark. Fiery anger flares in the open. In less obvious ways, carping, cattiness, and mean withholding are also the shadow side of this dimension. When we feel trapped, we splatter our anger, even without intending to do so, on those who are closest and dearest to us. Or we stuff it.

The shadow side of feminine aggression is also familiar as self-hate. It boils when women compete for masculine approval or attention. It appears as getting even, deceitfulness, and cruelty—as destructive explosiveness.

Headaches and depression are often the shadow side of aggression that is too frightening to express directly. Our shadow tries to inform us. When we don't pay attention, or can't, it doesn't just go away.

For some, unexpressed aggression is hungry. Food soothes; eating subsitutes for fighting. Getting fat seems safer than expressing anger toward someone else. The anger is still there, of course, but now self-hate is piled on. You can be mad at yourself. No contest. Anorexia and bulimia are about feminine anger too. They are complex expressions of rage that don't yield to simple solutions but can be successfully treated.

Every working person is familiar with the shadow side of passive feminine aggression—being aggressive without saying anything—at work. We know her tight lips, averted glance, burning eyes. The woman who won't deal with her aggression directly fumes. She isn't fun to be around.

Women in authority have another shadowy option. We can be impossible to satisfy. We use criticism as a weapon, pick on people who don't have the power to fight back, and control others in destructive ways. When we find ourselves in this place, we need to figure out what we're angry about and handle it directly.

One of the most damaging forms this shadowy dimension takes is gossip—"trashing" other people, especially other women, but men get their share, too. We learn to do this as little girls and get even better at it as teenagers. It is a "safe" way to dump aggression, because the target isn't around to fight back.

Smoke, the shadow side of this fiery dimension, is dangerous at work. Flames can burst out at the slightest, irrelevant, provocation. When we find ourselves in a state of chronic low burn—hostile, sarcastic, cynical—it's time to figure out some better ways to take care of ourselves.

Shadowy aggression is not to be ignored, but it is complex to try to understand. We need to be able to sort out the roots of our anger. Are we responding to unrealistic, childish expectations that have been stomped out? Or are we reacting in self-supportive ways to real danger?

By ourselves, we can't do a very good job of sorting out whether our own anger is grounded in present reality or the unresolved past. Outside feedback helps. If trying to manage the shadow side of aggression consumes a major part of your energy, a guide—friend, therapist, or trusted colleague—can be very helpful.

SELF-REFLECTION

Aggression is an important dimension in your feminine power at work. It's your backbone and your fighting spirit. The fire of your aggression protects you in the dark night of exploitation or oppression. But you have to be in charge, not whirling about, out of control, in its smoky heat.

Is your aggression a familiar driving force for you, or can you barely feel it? It's not so much that you should have it in great abundance. It's more that you need to know what to do with it when it arrives. If your fire in this dimension has died or been smothered, other areas are likely to suffer as well.

Now, think about how you see yourself in this dimension. Use these suggestions to guide your assessment.

STRENGTH: I get angry at times and can deal with those feelings. I have a hot temper, but I've learned to contain myself. Sometimes I get so mad I can't see straight, but I can go for a walk and cool down. I don't particularly like to fight, but I won't back down from something that's important to me. I don't let people exploit me.

SHADOW: My rage overwhelms me at times, and I

don't care what I do or say. Sometimes I get physical if I'm really mad. I'll get even, no matter what. / I never get mad. Nothing is worth a fight, as far as I'm concerned. I'm afraid of my anger and never let it out.

TIME FOR YOURSELF

To live in your world with authority, you have to be highly visible at times and take actions that may be unpopular. Expressing your aggression means being ready and able to handle any backlash that comes your way. When you can trust and express your aggressive feelings with confidence and clarity—using good communication skills—your fire energy fuels your inner support system. You know who you are. You know that you're being true to yourself.

It's time to make a place for this frightening dimension of the feminine. Then you will not be so likely to collapse and subject yourself to being used. Here are some ways to practice:

• THINK OF ANY TIME in your life when your aggression has served you well. If you have several examples, you might choose just one to work on for now. Write a few sentences about that time in your journal.

• IF YOU CAME UP WITH no examples in the step above, look for a situation that irritates or offends you in some way. Your aggression may be deeply buried—inaccessible to your conscious search. It is possible that your aggressive fire burns somewhere in that situation. List the ways you might be angry.

• WRITE ABOUT HOW your feminine aggression (fierce, protective, solid, goal-oriented rather than win-oriented) emerged in the incident you described above. Or were you relying more on your masculine style (combative, territorial, need to win)? Neither is right or wrong, good or bad. But it helps to know which is which. If you're relying primarily on masculine-style aggression—fighting to be sure the rules are enforced—you may have more centered fire under that. Aggression that comes from your core, from your own subjective sense of what is right, provides more solid guidance than something you've copied as a survival skill.

• MAKE A LIST of ways you express your healthy feminine aggression. (Push for childcare services where you work; confront inappropriate sexual remarks at work; write letters to the editor.) Think about things you can add.

• DIG OUT YOUR ART SUPPLIES and find some fire-colored pens, crayons, whatever. In your journal, experiment with their brightness. Color a fire if you're so inclined. Or just put the colors on the page. Write words over the colors that name your aggressions.

• THINK OF A TIME AT WORK when your aggressive energy could have energized you to function more effectively. Write about that time. How would you do it differently now?

• DO YOU CRY when you're mad? Next time you have the opportunity, talk through the tears. Concentrate on your fire energy and support yourself with your anger.

• KNOW WHEN AND WHERE you choose to make a stand. Know, too, what you want from the effort. Many of us work in environments that spark aggressive fires on a regular basis. If this is your situation, be selective about which battles you choose to engage in. It makes sense to fight battles you have a chance to win. If there is one brewing now, list steps you might take, supported by your aggression, to make things better.

• PREPARE TO DEAL with the results you don't want that inevitably accompany aggression. Try to estimate the direction and intensity of backlash that any aggressive action entails. Know ahead of time how you plan to handle it. Write about what you predict and how you intend to respond for the example in the previous exercise.

- PAY ATTENTION TO YOUR HUMOR. Much humor is hostile, covering more direct expression of aggression. Think of an incident where you have used hostile humor recently. Write a few lines in your journal about what you think your shadow was trying to say to you.

- KNOW THE DIFFERENCE BETWEEN venting—letting off steam—and making a stand. Pure discharge of feeling is likely to be destructive. It helps if you can say, "I need to let off steam!" When you take a stand, your goal is clearly in mind—something that you have a chance to achieve. Write briefly about one example of venting and one example of fighting for a goal.

- ANGER IS OFTEN A COVER for hurt which neither seething nor venting can heal. Such a hurt needs to be dealt with directly and assertively. If you find that you are chronically hurt, take steps to determine whether you are taking things too personally. If you are being mistreated, make a list of steps you can take to leave what is for you an abusive situation.

- IF YOU HAVE A REALISTIC FEAR of losing control, learn about rage-reduction techniques. People who are fairly inhibited often feel that any show of emotion is loss of control. It's not. On the other hand, if you are explosive and lose contact with how your actions affect others, look at this issue closely. Being able to turn your aggressive heat up or down requires knowing yourself well. List some techniques you can use to contain your anger—keep it under control—so that you can sort out which parts you choose to express directly.

- CHRONIC, OVERWHELMING RAGE that indiscriminately smokes up the environment is a form of feminine aggression that needs special attention. If you're a person whose usual mood state is a low burn subject to ignition by a short fuse, you face a different task from the one this chapter emphasizes. First, you have to learn to integrate and contain your aggression so that explosions don't blow you and your co-workers away. Ultimately, it's important to do some internal fire-fighting. Some places to start include books such as: *The Angry Book*, by Theodore Rubin; *Dance of Anger*, by Harriet Goldhor Lerner, and *The Intimate Enemy*, by George Bach.

• USING THE LAST TIME YOU EXPLODED as an example, write some ways that you could have expressed your anger without losing control. It's important to know the difference between using aggression to energize yourself and dumping it. The latter is destructive to others and to you. List some consequences you have suffered from dumping your aggression—or from being the target of somebody else's dump.

Turn to page 27 and make whatever changes you feel would sharpen your rating on aggression. Use a red pen.

LIVING WITH YOUR AGGRESSION ON THE JOB

Did you ever notice how your boss thinks your fire is wonderful if you're aggressively seeking new clients but not so great if you're angry about something she or he has done? Aggression at work is tricky business. Unless you have the perfect job, more of your aggression is likely to get stirred up than you can express safely. Plan your strategies well. Although your aggressive feeling comes from the depths of your feminine soul, if you dump it thoughtlessly at work the fallout can really hurt you. Be sure that you're centered and able to handle the consequences you trigger.

It's important to learn to stay in touch with your aggression at work. Let it surface and inform you. You don't have to act it out. If you're mad as hell about something, look for the shadow aspects first. What parts of yourself are you trying to reject in the other person or the situation? After you identify these and work with them, figure out what you need to do either to change the situation or to get out. Psychosomatic illnesses—ulcers, some headaches, hypertension—clue you in to the possibility that you're burying your aggression. Listen to your body.

Learn to confront from a centered place when you need to do so. If you haven't already, take an assertiveness training workshop or find one of the many good books on this topic and equip yourself with basic skills in assertive communication.

Whether it's biological or a learned response to crushed feminine aggression, many of us cry when anger flares. If you dissolve into tears when you're mad, it's important to be able to say, "I'm crying because I'm angry. And I want to keep talking about this until we finish the conversation." Your tears aren't a sign of weakness and they don't have to stop you. Let others handle their own discomfort with the situation.

On the other side, any time you push the system, compete, or assert something that threatens the way things are, you're likely to become the *target* of aggression. It's important to know how to protect yourself when aggression is aimed at you. If you do this from a feminine perspective, your stance may be simply to hold the line—without reacting outwardly. Sometimes you "win" if you can stay centered without getting hooked into the fight. Images from Aikido or other martial arts, where the attacker is defeated by his or her own force, are helpful. If you genuinely know your position, you can flex one way or the other so that your antagonist flies right past you. You won't be hurt.

It helps to know, too, if your "opponent's" aggression is based in fear. If that is the case, it may be possible to offer reassurance directly or indirectly to reduce his or her anxiety: "Look. We both have a job to do here, and we're both trying to get ahead. Let's see if we can figure out some ways to work together rather than working at cross purposes. Let's determine exactly where we disagree and see if we can divide up the territory." Remember, the more prickly and nasty a person has to be to protect his or her territory, the more insecure and frightened he or she is inside.

Regardless of how clear you are or how competent

you have become in living with your own strong feelings, there will be times when you have to deal with people who don't play by the rules—when there is no way to "win" fair and square. There are people in the world who have been so psychologically wounded that they have developed no conscience or capacity to care about others. And because of their willingness to hurt or exploit others, many of them are highly "successful" in positions of power. When you have to deal with someone like this, open honest encounters are not effective. Open communication requires some trust. If you're sure this is the kind of person you're dealing with, your choices are to join them in a dirty fight, shut them out, or leave.

If you have the resources to rebound with honor, you may be able to talk about a conflict in a workable way that brings new energy to the job.

Most of your colleagues, though, have their own struggles with aggression and other strong feelings. Wherever people live, work, or play together, conflict is bound to erupt. Trust your resilience and learn to come back and work together or fight another day. Learn to resolve issues through negotiation, neither placating nor dominating. It helps to say things like, "I disagree with you, and I'm angry with you, but I'm willing to work on this until we get it cleared up."

As you speak out against the male-centered tradition of your workplace, the first part of learning to work together may look and feel more like conflict, intimidation, resistance, and explosion. Trust your staying power—your core strength. It is quieter but just as strong as the explosion. Bringing conflict out in the open doesn't have to mean humiliation and defeat. If you have the resources to rebound with honor, you may be able to understand and use your communication skills to talk about the conflict in a workable way that brings new energy to the job.

FEMININE AGGRESSION AT WORK

The huge state department where Ginny worked as a manager directing a statewide project had slashed, cut and squeezed until there was no more give. Budget cuts had become routine, first 10% across the board and then 20%. Now it was just a matter of "how much," not "whether" there would be another. Paranoia was rampant. Managers guarded their territory like starving tigers. Morale sagged.

Ginny stared at the memo in disbelief. She had heard rumors, but didn't think there was a chance it would really happen. With no consultation, the decisionmakers cut the whole category of temporary help from the budget. This way, no permanent people would have to be laid off and no particular programs would be drastically affected. An imperfect, but highly logical solution.

Stunned and furious, Ginny asked around. "How many people does this involve? Who are they? How much does it save? How will it impact programs? What other options are being considered? Nobody really knew the answers to these questions. And it appeared that no one really wanted to know.

Ginny was well aware that her 23-year-old, single-mother secretary, Rosa, fit in this category. She'd hired Rosa after interviewing several candidates for the important, but low-paying clerical job. Rosa's quick wit and dedicated efficiency kept the under-staffed office from bogging down completely. Ginny didn't even want to think about what she would do without her.

Ginny was well aware of political in-fighting among department leaders. As she began to get more information about how their power-brokering was going to affect peoples' lives, she became increasingly outraged. At the top of the department, deputies, directors, and managers, all men, were supported by executive secretaries and office personnel in full-time, permanent positions. When work overload poured in, they hired from a pool of regular employees who were known as permanent part-time, to get the work out the door. These employees worked for specified periods of time and received advance, formal notice when their time was up.

Ginny searched out the information she needed with persistence fueled by her anger. This cut would affect at least forty people. The savings would be hardly noticeable after "exceptions" were made for those managers who successfully protected their "temporary help" from layoff.

Ginny's hunch was right about who would be affected. Newer program managers who didn't have the clout to acquire new positions, mostly women, used temporary help as a resource. Using their creativity and flexibility, they patched together the staff they needed for projects that might last from months to several years. This way, in addition to clerical staff, they could hire people with special skills to do the specific things they needed. Although individuals who took the positions were warned that they were temporary, they took their jobs seriously and depended on them for basic support. In fact, that had been a workable arrangement in the past. Nearly all of the temporary staff were women. Many worked part time around precariously balanced childcare.

Despite her backbreaking workload, Ginny dropped everything and moved into warrior mode. She had never fought for an issue in the open, and she had never taken on something that seemed like a foregone conclusion. But she was so mad at the lack of caring and responsibility involved that she could hardly see. For three days straight, her red-hot aggression fueled her search for information, her creativity in putting together a plan, and her courage to fight hard for an unpopular issue.

She wrote a two-page memo to the decisionmakers: "When budget cuts became a way of life with this department, we agreed that the first priority was our people. Our commitment was to work relentlessly to achieve our main goals and to avoid putting our people out on the street at any cost. I guess we have forgotten that commitment. . . ." Her opening statement set the stage for facts and figures that clearly outlined the impact of the proposal. She finished by urging a reversal of the plan.

The deputies flared.

They were mad at her and she knew it. Not only because she had sent the memo up to the chief, but because they were embarrassed that their insensitivity was showing. This was a first. Sparks had flown in the past, but nothing like this. They didn't quite know how to do battle with this nice woman they'd worked with all these years.

But they couldn't deny the truth she had brought to them. Her willingness to search out the details and provide a clear statement of who was going to be hurt and how little it would really save made the difference. They could no longer eliminate temporary help in the fuzzy haze of ignorance.

The decision was reversed. The decisionmakers found a way to make the shift gracefully enough. Without Ginny's challenge, the initial proposal would have slipped through with no awareness of the sexism involved. Her willingness to bring the issue into the open and fight for it had saved 38 women's and 2 men's jobs against almost certain extinction. Her effort nourished the department's battered morale. She shared a moment of quiet pride when she said, "I'm exhausted and have a lot of work stacked up on my desk. But I feel wonderful about the outcome."

This woman's contained, focused aggression burned to sustain her efforts to help people who couldn't help themselves. It didn't explode all over the place, and she didn't try to smother it. She let it energize her.

Summary

Two of the dimensions in this section on passion, *Sexuality* and *Aggression*, don't fit the ways we have learned to think about feminine behavior at work. But they do provide powerful energy for the woman who knows how to contain and channel them. *Creativity* tends to sit around in the wings, under-appreciated by all concerned. But she's there for you if you invite her into the open.

Spend as long as you like with your journal summarizing how you connect with some of the suggestions in this chapter. If you've identified ways you can appreciate your aggression—or establish more effective methods to manage some of your explosive tendencies—clarify your thoughts by writing them down. Before flying off into Spirit's higher altitudes, use these moments to capture and record any insights or future steps the last three chapters have brought to you.

AIR

SPIRIT: A NEW VISION

Air: The Element

At work, I think about matters of the spirit "simply" in terms of personal integrity—how we stay true to our human spirits.

Big questions, questions about what it means to be a person, waft into our awareness at work as well as in more meditative moments. What's right? What's fair? How do we deal with work challenges to our personal integrity? This section explores *Intuition, Wholistic Thinking,* and *Wisdom and Spirituality,* the dimensions of the feminine that juggle those cosmic questions on the job.

We can connect with our strength and stamina, live in the ups and downs of our relationships, and feel our passion. Air, the invisible element that surrounds us—that we can't do without—symbolizing ethics and personal integrity, is more elusive. It evades our grasp and our sight. Like the wind, we hear its passage sometimes—feel its gentle warmth on our faces or its gritty dust in our eyes. But we have trouble pinning down the issues, because our experience doesn't fit the patriarchal world in which we work.

We breathe in and process this world in a personal, connected way. We get by. But a lot of what we do or how we do it doesn't make sense to us. We need to give ourselves permission to notice our conflicts and think our own thoughts about how we want to manage our inner tugs and pulls. We can still wonder and explore—feel our world with our own hearts and minds.

I can remember, as a kid, lying on my back beneath the sparkling dome of Arizona sky stuffed with blue. I reveled in its unending depth. Supported by the warm earth, covered by that blanket of blue, I felt full and safe—a real sense of what it was to be me.

I thought about the sky, beyond the sky, beyond the sky—tried to pierce its heights with my bare eyes. Explanations for its vibrant color fell short—didn't satisfy me. If the air between you and me is colorless, and the sky is air—why's it blue? I wondered where heaven was in relation to what I could see. And how did the angels stay up there?

Sprawled on the scratchy bermuda grass of my front yard, I could see the San Francisco Peaks, sixty miles away. Lavender against that infinite space that looked blue, their lofty volcanic pinnacles offered a sacred home to the kachinas, legendary Hopi spirit guides. From where I sat, the mountains appeared within easy reach. When the hot pink and purple sunset (this was before "mauve") converted them to silhouettes, it was easy to see that any self-respecting god would call them home.

I'd heard stories of the power and wisdom of the kachinas. Some of the tales of their attitudes toward child development were enough to keep me in line when the off-limits cookie jar called to me. But I was in way over my head when I tried to resolve what I understood about the Native American way I knew at home with what I heard about God at Episcopal Sunday School. To my way of thinking, each view had its plusses and minusses. No way could I reconcile their massive contradictions with each other. I had friends who were Mormon, Catholic, or Baptist—and some who seemed quite nice to me but had no truck with God at all. Their actions all seemed about the same amount of good or bad, right or wrong, based on what was happening—not necessarily on their religious preferences.

When I was twelve or so, Meme died. This woman who had lived in my home from before my birth and had provided major TLC for my sister and me was a Papago who had converted to Catholicism as a child. I was too sad to go to her funeral. But later I overheard my mother telling someone that the service was part Catholic, part Mormon, part Papago. And as their special blessing for her spirit journey, her Hopi friends made offerings of piki bread at the grave site. In its own way, each group expressed love and concern for Meme's earthly departure. I felt a little reassured. Lots of people cared about her. And I understood now that grown-ups had trouble with those choices that always seemed so clear to whoever preached the sermon, but not to me. Somehow Meme, in her spiritual equanimity, had lived them all.

Today, that brilliant Arizona sky that reached forever greys with smog. I'm not sure you can see the home of the kachinas from sixty miles away. And the elms that shaded that scratchy patch of lawn and others along the street that bore their name have long since succumbed to disease and been cut down. The natural haze of the Grand Canyon, its trademark from before time, now binds with impurities that clog the view so that on many days the throngs of tourists no longer see from rim to rim. Pollution particles intensify the sunset, but deaden the daytime sky.

Our environment is in trouble. The human environment of the workplace suffers too. We sabotage the atmosphere on an individual basis. We settle for less than clean air when we lose our connections with our inner selves. More and more of us live in technical, urbanized settings, cut off from our connections with nature. We shutter the authenticity and richness of the human spirit and conform to the expectations that surround us. We focus on survival—play the roles in which we've been cast. We can do terrible damage to our personal air quality and not even know it. There's no immediate visible feedback.

At work, I think about matters of the spirit "simply" in terms of personal integrity—how we stay true to our human spirits. And if we extend the feel of it a little, how we respect, support, and connect with the deep humanity of others on the job. It seems as though this should be fairly simple, but for many reasons the air at work, symbolic or real, can be polluted or in short supply.

We can take more of our blue-sky gazing to work with us than we ever thought possible. In fact, as time goes on, our capacity to stay in touch with and support our own spirituality on the job—to honor who we are at a deep personal level—enriches our lives and keeps us healthy.

Though it provides no answers, each of the following sections offers support for your journey inward, contact with your human spirit as a working woman. The self-discovery that unfolds in these dimensions inspires all the others and can only grow throughout your life.

Intuition

it down to write a letter to a friend. She calls.
Wake up understanding perfectly how to do something
that's been puzzling you for weeks.

Take a different route home from work, only to find
that the regular one was blocked by an accident.

Start concentrating on a project and remember a
phone call you were supposed to make three days ago.

Look at someone you've never seen before and know
what he's going to say before a single word forms.

Greet a customer and know, within a few seconds,
what she's going to buy.

Intuition, the morning breeze of subjective truth,
refreshing and unconventional, vitalizes business when we
know how to hear, respect, and communicate it. Our own
truth, the quick breath of insight, a shifting current within,
alerts us. We get wind of something—without the support
of tangible data. A hunch pushes us to action. We look at
a new situation or problem and know what it's about in a
quick, automatic way. Or we look at an old problem for
the hundredth time and suddenly see a way through it,
without understanding how the solution came together.

As Marilyn Loden has pointed out,

> like other qualities associated more with
> women, intuition in problem-solving was not
> regarded as a skill to be taken very seriously by
> organizations. In fact, evidence suggests that because
> of its association with women, intuition was under-

valued, misunderstood, and regarded as virtually useless in many businesses.[1]

But times are changing. We have to deal with so much complex information in so little time these days that we can't always wait for step-by-step data analysis. In some situations, knotty problems can't be untangled in orderly ways. "Just woman's intuition," is an understatement in serious need of revision. We need ready access to our intuitive processes. And we need to know how to support and express what we find there.

Whether or not women are really more intuitive than men, feminine body energy, receptivity and flexibility are sensitive to intuitive messages in ways that make them useful. In his book, *Intuition in Organizations*, Weston Agor credits Frances Vaughn with "the best-known theoretical treatment of intuition to date." She believes that intuition functions on four distinct levels:

- Physical—bodily sensations that send us messages about people or situations for no apparent reason,
- Emotional—signals transmitted in the form of feelings,
- Mental—recognition of patterns in seemingly unrelated facts, and
- Spiritual—direct, personal perceptions or feelings that reveal the underlying oneness of life.[2]

We are channels for non-linear information from many inner resources.

"I just had a great idea!" precedes an intuitive statement that something new and different is on the way. Fun, colorful, irrational, intuition's unpredictability breezes through us.

In "Five Ways Women Are Smarter than Men about Money," *Money Magazine* writer Gary Belsky says that women do their homework: "Men are much more likely to

Whether or not women are really more intuitive than men, feminine body energy, receptivity and flexibility are sensitive to intuitive messages in ways that make them useful.

act first and think later. Women pay attention to hunches too but then tend to follow with careful research."[3] Not having to know it all, the ability to ask for help, and the persistence to go after needed information are powerful partners for "woman's intuition."

Dreams, fantasies, and shielded memories all expand our view of reality. Intuition invites a shift in our everyday routine. A whirlwind through the rich scramble of the unconscious supplies us with images and information to which no one else has access—our own personal mythology for decoding the world. When current experience connects with this material in a meaningful way, a mini-tornado spins by with insight or information. The form it takes may be visual, incomplete, seemingly unrelated to anything at hand—but its meaning can be expanded if we give it room to breathe.

An inner voice may speak to us in unexpected ways when we are deeply connected with a subject or another person. "I just had a hunch that I should check on Jonathan," a young mother wept with relief as she shared a terrifying experience. She had intercepted her two-year-old just as he tumbled over the edge of the family swimming pool. "Suddenly, I felt uneasy and went to check him," she told me, "When I got up to go outside, I gave myself a bad time for being silly and overprotective. He was playing in a little area we had enclosed for him. I couldn't believe he had opened the childproof gate. I'm glad I acted on my hunch. I saved his life!"

The same process fans our work. Intuition is what we have that computers don't. When we're filled with information and experience, we synthesize and analyze it at a level beneath our awareness. We know, or at least have a good hunch, about what needs to happen even before we step through an item-by-item analysis. We guess what the problem is, what the market's like, what the audience will respond to. Given the overload of information that storms us and the impossibility of dealing with it all, this is a handy asset to have easily available. It makes sense to develop and use it.

At work, an inner riffle to double check my appointment book has saved me from scheduling errors innumerable times. The ability to say "Something just doesn't feel right about this . . . " has opened conversations that led to clearing up conflicts that hadn't yet come to light. Sales people, managers, buyers, psychotherapists, teachers all rely heavily on intuition, whether they identify it as such or not. Scientists, lawyers, inventors, and physicians do to.

Dreams with full-blown problem solutions or sudden ah-ha's come to people who have been working on complex challenges over a period of time. Deena Metzger dreamed the title of her book, *Women Who Sleep with Men to Take the War out of Them*. She also quipped in a talk about feminine spirituality that when she asked her dreams for the rest of the book, she didn't get it.[4]

An early step in all of the organizational analyses that Mary Bolton and I conducted was the "intuitive take." We relied on feelings and hunches to create form where there was none. As we began work with a new organization, we listened very carefully to the workers at many levels. We tried to hear their emotional communication as well as the facts. Often the words didn't match the music. What they said didn't seem to make much sense, or fit too well with the obvious conflicts involved. As we began to collect preliminary information, we would discuss, feel, explore everything we knew about the situation. We walked in a windstorm of mythological ideas, characters from fiction, dreams, and examples, or scraps of previous experience until a graphic "map" would present itself.

Images of Knights Templar, roaring lions, pleasure seekers, and a serving class of indentured women surprised us with their presence in one case. We guessed at how the dynamics of the groups or individuals within each cluster in this medieval scenario might play out. Tentatively, we trusted our guesses as guidelines for next steps. Most of the time, data of a more linear, "reliable" type fell into place to support our intuitive insights—even though initially they seemed absurd or irrelevant.

If you're a person who works intuitively, you'll have other techniques to add to this list. In their research for *Women's Ways of Knowing*, Mary Belenky and her colleagues found that, for women, many of whom rely on subjective experience for knowledge and understanding, truth is an intuitive reaction—not thought out—felt rather than constructed.[5] This truth arrives in many different forms.

What *is* remarkable is the low regard that business and academia hold for subjective experience. Although men can have "gut reactions," it's dangerous for women to admit them. Marilyn Loden and others attribute this to the fact that intuition has been closely associated with the feminine and therefore discounted. In their research, the Belenky group found that women who rely on their own subjective experience as a source of knowledge are at a special disadvantage when they go about learning and working in business and industry. It's the public, rational, analytical voice, not the intuitive, that receives the corporation's attention, respect, and rewards. The product that emerges from intuition's inspiration receives the praise. In "For the young who want to," poet Marge Piercy laments:

> Genius is what they know you
> had after the third volume
> of remarkable poems. Earlier
> they accuse you of withdrawing,
> ask why you don't have a baby,
> call you a bum.

This speaks to the difficulty we have trusting intuition

as a resource. The masculine format of the public culture isn't fond of the feminine "intuitive take." "Logical" or "scientific" approaches may use intuition as a starting point but, until recently, didn't cop to it. This is so much the case that many of us labor under the impression that we're not very intuitive. If indeed we're not, the condition isn't necessarily permanent. Those intuitive zephyrs may be stifled and still, but if you invite them, the air flow will increase.

The blockage didn't start with work. Typical school experiences stamp out intuitive wanderings early and replace them with linear focus. Off-the-wall ideas disrupt classroom conformity and order. We learn to keep our ideas to ourselves if they don't fit in, or if we can't support them with "logic." And so our unique contributions fly out the window as we learn to conform. Of course, this happens to little boys as well as to little girls. Everyone loses.

Intuitive understanding threatens people who relate to the world mostly in terms of what they can see and touch. "How do you know that?" they ask with amazement. It's scary for them if you jump to a correct conclusion without going through the data step by step. And they reject or belittle what they don't understand.

Demands for conformity and "efficiency" in the educational system, bureaucracies, and corporate life dull our intuitive capacities. It's hard to nurture intuitive flashes on a deadline or hear new ideas that don't fit the curriculum guide. We've become very good at ignoring information that doesn't move us toward our goals—goals that, in many cases, have been established without much conscious choice or insight.

Invite intuition to stay in your house and open her gifts. Let her whisk the stale air out of your life. She may not be particularly orderly or predictable, but she is colorful, poetic, and honest. When you listen to her, you hear the music of your soul, sparkling melodies that tune you

What is remarkable is the low regard that business and academia hold for subjective experience.

in to what's important and meaningful for you. Despite her artistic appearance, her high-tech scanning capacities offer you complex information summaries in mere seconds. She can clue you in to the subtleties of your environment. And more than anything, she will advise you about relationships, yours and those you manage. Intuition brings the fresh air of unique personal insight to the mundane strivings of public life. Getting to know her well may bring some painful conflicts into the open, but it's worth it to learn to trust her.

THE SHADOW SIDE

Intuition's shadow harbors dark premonitions and suspicion. You may be afraid of being wrong or afraid of being right. When we've been hurt or abused, we see darkness whether it exists or not. If our internal information is grounded in pain, that pain intuits more than necessary caution and a constant sense of foreboding follows us through our lives. Or our intuition shuts down and we relate only to what we can see or touch. We need proof at every step and can't trust our capacity to "know without knowing." Fright and insecurity rush in when others share their intuitions.

Feeling something strongly but refusing to recognize it expands intuition's shadow. The attempt to resist being who we really are because it's painful or inconvenient blocks receptivity to our intuition. Seeing things we don't want to see may be a disruption from the shadow side of this dimension, and not always welcome, but when we reject these offerings time after time, we deaden ourselves and become less conscious.

Intuition's ability to know things before they happen or predict events with some accuracy can be upsetting if the events are negative. What do you do with "unfounded" information that predicts dire consequences? Is your strong feeling that the plane you're about to step onto will crash intuition, fear of flying, or a death wish? The shadow keeps you stuck here rather than recognizing that each possibility deserves looking into.

Chasing intuitive whirlwinds without other kinds of reality testing can carry you off into impulsive actions that you may regret later. The shadow says, "I'm enough. Act now and check later!" Remember that your intuition is subjective data. Give yourself a chance to see how it fits with the rest of your world so that you're not off tilting at windmills.

Pictures from your intuition don't often come neatly framed. They may be abstract scribbles, blurred and difficult to understand. The shadow whispers, "Ah, that's not worth anything." You can trust, though, that if you look closely enough, you'll find something budding, if not yet quite definable. Stay with it rather than being sidetracked because it feels different.

Similarly, fragmented intuitive information in its raw form may be hard for others to follow. Another kind of shadow reaction, an exaggerated sense of self importance, mistakenly expects to be understood without efforts to order, clarify, and communicate. The shadow says, "Well, if they don't get it, that's their loss." Your intuition is important, but it's just a first step. Bringing it into the open to share with others requires some work.

The unique, self-centered nature of intuition, when not balanced with the ability to test our perceptions, can trap us in an inner whorl filled with distortions and crooked thinking. Bad dreams and other scary images disturb our sense of personal security.

Strong as it is, intuition isn't always "right." We need a way to respect both internal and external input. Sorting out what to pay attention to and what to ignore can be very confusing. It's always worth considering what your

intuition offers. Your process of deciding what to keep
and what to discard is one you develop over time by finding ways to test what works for you.

Even intuition's shadow side—exaggerated subjectiv-
ity—offers rich information. It highlights areas of your
unconscious that are begging for attention. Make the scary
characters in your dreams your allies. Get outside input
from someone you trust about coded messages that are
trying to surface. If you find yourself consistently ignoring
or making light of your intuitive flashes, whether they're
bright inspiration or terrifying nightmares, you're cutting
off a major source of information about your inner life.

SELF-REFLECTION

Your intuition never sleeps. It fills your dreams as well
as your waking hours with information from your unconscious and from the environment around you. As you
learn to give it your conscious attention, you reach toward
yet another powerful internal resource.

Take a few moments to reflect on your intuitive
processes. Where do you tune into the continuum in this
dimension?

STRENGTH: My intuition is alive and well. I recognize
and value flashes of insight or awareness that come to me
at various times. My "off-the-wall" ideas are a valuable
resource to me.

SHADOW: I have no intuition. I hate it when other
people offer silly ideas for consideration. I discard illogical
thoughts that come to me. I want hard data to support
anything I have to suggest.

Time For Yourself

The personal, scrambled, intuitive richness of the feminine offers honesty that brings a new level of human contact to work situations. Whether you decide to talk about intuitive information openly or not depends on how safe you feel. If an off-the-wall idea will get you clobbered, enjoy it in silence or find a safe place to share it. But don't put it down as stupid or silly in your own mind.

Your intuition is an important part of you if you're true to yourself. If it feels weird or meaningless that's likely to reflect the rigidity of the environment, not craziness on your part. If your intuitive channels are open and flowing, you can provide support for others whose feminine power is blocked on this point. If your channels are clogged, some of the exercises that follow may help.

• IN YOUR JOURNAL, make a list of hunches—things you knew without knowing—that you followed and that worked out for you. Do they have anything in common? Write about how much you value and trust your intuition.

• LIST THE FIRST FIVE WORDS that come to you that describe your intuitive process. Don't censor. (For example: quick, bright, funny, morbid, sarcastic. . . .)

• CHOOSE ONE OF THESE WORDS. Mull it over. Think about it in as many ways as you can for about ten seconds. Now write as many related words as you can that positively describe your intuitive style. Use some of these words to write a few lines in support of your intuitive process.

• THINK ABOUT A WORK-RELATED ISSUE that perplexes you at the moment. Write about it in your journal. Choose several words from your list and use them as guides over the next day or so. Just let the perplexing issue float around in the back of your mind without trying to organize it in step-by-step fashion. When ideas or thoughts breeze through, jot them down immediately. Record them in your journal when you have a moment, and then see if a pattern starts to form.

- WRITE ABOUT A WORK EXAMPLE where you intuitively knew something was going to happen and it did. Did you express your concern or excitement? If so, what helped you do so? If not, what got in your way?

- WRITE A BRIEF SUMMARY of a dream you had last night or one you can remember from some other time. Now read it as if it were someone else's story. What parts stand out? Is something asking for attention? What's your best guess about what this dream is saying to you? Write the answer in your journal as something to think about.

- IF YOU GENERALLY ACCEPT intuitive blips that come to you, intensify and expand them. Take them seriously before you decide whether or not to discard them. Listen to them. See if they become a part of you. Tell a friend about an intuition you've had recently.

- IF YOU TEND TO REJECT ideas that come to you—assume others will laugh or make fun of them—try being kind and supportive to yourself instead. Catch the thought before it goes away. Nurture and embellish it. It may not be usable in its present form, but if you work with it, meaning will emerge.

- FIND SOMEONE ELSE at work who is interested in paying more attention to her/his intuition. Share your thoughts and insights. Are you in touch with information that isn't being used or acknowledged? Is it useful to be expressive about your insights? Why or why not?

- FROM A CENTERED PLACE, try sharing your intuitions from time to time as suggestions or ideas to be considered. Don't expect immediate acceptance or appreciation. Differences are threatening to people who don't understand where they're coming from. Over time, as your "off-the-wall" truths are borne out, they will gain more credibility—with yourself and others. If your insights don't always pan out, this is valuable information for you also.

• DRAW THE SHADOW SIDE of your intuition. Is it tiny or huge? Where are its darkest splotches? Write words around the edges of your drawing that describe how your shadow works in this dimension. Does it scare, inhibit, worry, or confine you?

• DESCRIBE A NIGHTMARE or bad dream that you've had recently, or even sometime earlier in your life. If you look at it as a message from the shadow side of your intuition, what do you think it's trying to tell you? Use Ann Farraday's *Dream Power* or another method you know to work with this dream.

• WRITE THREE THINGS you say to yourself to diminish your intuitive flashes. ("It won't work," "It's too weird," etc.) Then write ways to counter each of these internal messages—to test and support your intuition.

• WRITE THREE EXAMPLES of times you've had dark premonitions and what happened to each. Was your "knowing" accurate? Or was the shadow side of your intuition blocking you in some way? Write about what you learned in each of these experiences.

• LOOK FOR EXAMPLES of intuitive thinking by others at work. Do you have a colleague who relies on this dimension extensively? Talk with her or him about how to rely on intuition as an inner guide. Write about what you learn.

• THINK ABOUT HOW YOUR INTUITION and your creativity work together. In the last week or so, what flashes have you had that have led to a creative effort on your part? Describe the moment of insight. How did you expand it to bring it to life?

Take a moment or two to check your initial Self-Assessment on page 28. Was your intuition clear the first time? Make whatever adjustments seem right.

INTUITION GOES TO WORK

Research tells us that women have more connective tissue between the right brain, which is thought to deal with non-verbal input, and the left brain, which seems to organize language. It may be easier for women to translate feelings and hunches from the right-brain into words.[6] To whatever extent this is true, women have more access to right-brain functions, which seem to include non-verbal, non-linear thinking—i.e., intuition. "Woman's intuition" may, in fact, be more than a survival skill developed to cope with living in a one-down situation. There may be biological reasons it is associated more with the feminine than with the masculine. Given this access, it makes sense to become supportive of the gifts intuition has for us on the job, rather than discounting them as unscientific.

Until femininity is more accepted as a legitimate work style, here are some ways to respond to a familiar and intimidating barrier: **Just Woman's Intuition**:

Do	*Don't*
Trust your feelings; they've been right before.	Discount or ignore your hunches.
Risk expressing your ideas.	Let propriety keep you from exploring.
Talk about your idea as data of a different kind.	Be quick to reject someone else's intuitive take.
Try it to see what happens.	Be overwhelmed by "logical" arguments or "scientific" data.

Do	*Don't*
Draw it, dance it, paint it to get it into words if you need to.	Be stopped by the argument "It's never been done before; it won't work."
Check out your hunches.	
	Give up because you have a hard time getting it into words.
See if your dreams are telling you anything about work.	

The first step is to get intimately acquainted with your intuition—with what it contributes as well as the conditions under which it flourishes. If you're an intuitive type, you probably already know these things. If you're not, which is true of about half of us according to the Myers-Briggs researchers,[7] the task is a little tougher. But it's worth pursuing.

Here are some ways your intuition can inform you on the job:

Let it tell you how the inner you connects with what's happening around you. When you can forget the expectations of others or how something is "supposed" to be done, your full concentration can focus on your task. You realize suddenly that something you're struggling with is clear and accessible when you can relax and see it from your own perspective.

You have more information than you can process. Give yourself time to sift and sort—to find the words you need to communicate what you know.

Earlier experiences, things that you may have done in some entirely different context, that you're not currently aware of but that you're processing at a level that's unclear to you, connect with work. The feeling you had when you were in the toughest part of a ten-mile hike may come to you as you grapple with an unwieldy marketing plan.

Now you know how hard it is and you can settle in to work it out step by step.

You may look at the same balance sheet you've been working with for a week and start to think of the color blue, which somehow lets you see where you can make the cuts you need to make.

You may be driving on the freeway and find yourself humming "Ding, Dong, The Witch is Dead" before you realize you have to have a conversation with your boss about how angry you are.

Or, you may realize, seemingly out of nowhere, that "this is like when Mara was cutting teeth—it's just going to be difficult for a while."

When you and your intuition are in trusting dialogue, you have the capacity to project into the future rather than being limited by what's provable. Based on your best guesses, you can create action plans to move in the direction you want to go. Then you can organize to make them work.

You can "reframe" or look at problems in contexts entirely different from the way in which you typically see them. A power struggle with a colleague becomes a challenge to your creativity rather than a measure of your strength or importance.

Intuition tells you whether a place is good for you—whether it "fits" or not. If for no logical reason, an apparently wonderful job possibility doesn't feel right, months later you may find out why. Perhaps the company will prove to be on shaky grounds; perhaps all the new hires will be on the street.

Given a chance, your intuition can tell you a lot about other people. Pay attention to how you feel when you're with them, not necessarily what they're saying about themselves. If you feel intimidated or insecure, they're probably making themselves feel important at your expense. If they're making promises that sound too good to be true, they probably are. You have more to work with than meets the eye when you trust your intuition.

Getting along with others is the area where intuition, knowing without tangible data, serves us best. Even a simple conversation goes on at many levels, most of them unspoken. If more than two people are involved, the situation gets even more complicated. Since it's impossible, for all practical purposes, to understand relationships in a linear way, other ways of knowing are a real asset.

Combining experience, knowledge of human behavior, and the way we feel when we're with someone gives us the information we need to make judgments about relationships. This is true for personnel decisions we make at work, as well as for the more personal decisions we make in our private lives. For most of us, the hard part is developing enough self-discipline to listen to our intuition when it's saying something we don't want to hear.

Since intuition is a subjective experience, not something that anyone else knows just the way you do, it's easy to back down when you're challenged. It helps to be able to restate your idea in several ways and to allow others to have a chance to mull it over. When ideas are new, they often get rejected first but accepted later.

If you happen to be a strongly intuitive person, you may find yourself becoming impatient with people who have a hard time following you. It's not because they're dumb or slow. Different people just have different ways of taking in and expressing information. When you know your intuitive process well, you can listen to it, integrate the information, and translate so that others can understand.

Earlier experiences that you may not be currently aware of but are processing at another level connect with work.

SUMMARY

Intuition has been associated, sometimes negatively, with the feminine. It's a non-scientific, non-linear way of knowing—instantly, without much data—what's happening, what's about to happen, or what could happen. When it works well, it offers insight into complex situations or knotty problems that are unwieldy to study in more orderly ways. Under shadowy conditions it can lead us into dark subjective places that float away from what we know as external reality.

Intuition's reputation as a problem-solver is improving as organizations become more complex. Brainstorming and other techniques that rely on this dimension are commonplace as part of today's management tool kit. By giving more attention and respect to this part of your personality, you learn more about who you are. You also intensify your contact with what's happening around you. You then have more choices about how to initiate action and how to respond, both at work and at home.

Wholistic Thinking

> But there is another kind of seeing that involves
> a letting go. When I see this way I sway transfixed
> and emptied. The difference between the two ways
> of seeing is the difference between walking with and
> without a camera. When I walk with a camera I walk
> from shot to shot, reading the light on a calibrated
> meter. When I walk without a camera, my own shut-
> ter opens, and the moment's light prints on my own
> silver gut. When I see this second way I am above
> all an unscrupulous observer.
>
> Annie Dillard, *Pilgrim At Tinker's Creek*

A friend shared an example that illustrates a difference in
the two views: "My husband fixes coffee every morning
and brings it to me while I'm getting ready for work. I
love him for it. It's a nice way to start my day. When we
run out, he's off to the store to replenish the supply. If I
ask him, he'll bring back whatever I put on a list. It would
never occur to him, though, to look around and notice
that we also need toilet paper, laundry soap and tooth-
paste."

On the other hand, the wholistic* thinker—an
"unscrupulous observer" unrestrained by ideas of right and
wrong or by how things *ought* to be—can take it all in.

---

* For the purposes of this book, Rollo May's concept of *wholistic*—integration of form with passion to make sense out of
life—better describes the archetypal feminine capacity to comprehend and value the complexities and contradictions of the

We embrace big-picture thinking when we become parents. The baby needs to be fed, the toddler needs attention, and the rent has to be paid. It doesn't much matter if it's in the job description or whose job it is. We organize around making it happen. Although immediate needs may limit us to the most basic tending and caretaking, we remain very concerned about the world in which the child will live.

Receiving the world "on my own silver gut" describes the three-dimensional feminine view that includes the emotional impact of information. The "unscrupulous observer" sees it all, unrestricted by anybody's sense of right or wrong, good or bad. A single "snapshot," plucked from its surroundings, doesn't substitute for the truth that only the whole picture can reveal. And it can't work for us to continue to fit ourselves into a work world (or a home life) that is wholly defined by men. We have our own important ways of seeing.

Wholistic thinking blows in from all four directions. This special way of seeing—a broad view that encompasses the many parts of life, unrelated and contradictory though they may seem. Circular and illogical according to traditional "objective" standards, it may treat time and space as irrelevant. It sees with imagination—the opposite of short-term, focused, practical thinking. This dimension, our knowing that the aftereffects are as important as the event, has been sleeping for a long, long time. It's time for us to pay attention to it.

We know that it's not enough to "walk from shot to shot, reading light on a calibrated meter." Psychotherapist Nancy Jungerman says it this way, "In tune with our inner

---

whole scene than *holistic*, which means only that an organic or integrated whole has a reality independent of and greater than the sum of its parts. Rollo May, *The Courage to Create* (New York: Bantam Books, 1976), p. 158.

environment, our monthly cycles, we bring to our work an experience of tidalness. When we can be true to our femininity we ride these cycles in some kind of way—stay connected with the universe."[1] In addition to our technical knowledge and personal sophistication, we're integral parts of a natural whole. As the carriers of new life, we're concerned, not just about our own, but about the well-being of future generations. We need to be in tune with the "big picture." What is safe? What is healthy? What will best preserve the future?

Stephanie Johnson, a corporate executive in an eastern state, talked about wholistic thinking this way: "Women invest more energy in thinking through the full impact of an action—learning to anticipate the next immediate step. Men, including my husband who I love and respect a lot, don't seem to do this—they don't think big picture." This pattern doesn't fit everybody. Some of us are detail-oriented and don't relate to the big picture at all. But at a deeper level, it fits the feminine connection with nature and concern about future generations.

Women tend to see many sides to an issue and take them into consideration in making decisions. While men certainly have the capacity to do the same thing, the traditional masculine approach relies more on rules, the law, or agreed-upon steps to arrive at a solution. If the rules don't seem adequate to getting the job done, women are less likely to stick to them. Balance is important here. As Boston-based creativity consultant Marcia Yudkin pointed out to me, "Certainly a good Supreme Court Justice needs to be able to use both."

Wholistic thinking isn't about creating a great plan and fitting yourself into it any more than it's about fitting into someone else's master plan. It is about taking in the totality of your environment on your own silver gut and holding it there. In time, you digest it, make it your own, and turn it into energy. This energy allows you to express yourself from a centered place based on your view of the world and your place in it.

When I asked Joanne Irene Gabrynowicz[2] what came to mind when she thought of "feminine presence," her first words were, ". . . wholistic—the difference between being the parts of something and the totality that the parts create. The feminine aspect tends to relate to the whole by nature, whereas the masculine relates to the parts of the whole."

Joanne is an attorney who moved from New York City to North Dakota to teach space law and policy in the Space Studies Department at the University of North Dakota. She moved because it seemed right at the time and would do it again, she says. The thoughts she shared with me when I asked her about the feminine touched me deeply. They bring to life the feminine connection with wholistic thinking—how our "silver gut" collects and digests the world around us:

"Many of my students, members of missile and bomber crews, are the people who wait for the President to call. At any given time, one-third of them are on alert—in class in war gear. [Since the time of the interview this ratio has been reduced.] The bomb or missiles are right down the block. I teach on base—see the instruments of war—missiles and bombers.

"The way this first started to emerge in me was that I found myself worrying about my health. Cancer—my mother died of cancer—AIDS, death. I never had done this before. What was happening was that mortality—fear of death—was growing in me. What came fully to consciousness in the face of seeing those symbols—the life force burst forth in me—fear of my own death. Past that, this feminine force said 'life shall be preserved!' To call it maternal is trite. It would be feminine—like Sigourney Weaver in *Aliens*—protecting her baby at all costs. It's important to differentiate—very archetypal. I shared this with my students as well as another experience that affected me deeply.

"We have mammoth bombers here—the newest strategic bombers. If you've ever heard one, you don't forget it. They don't sound like commercial aircraft. One morning lying in bed before the sun came up, I heard one of them flying low toward the air base. As it flew over I started to think—Where did it go? What was its mission? Why did it have to be back by dawn? I told my students. Some of them laughed nervously. After the class some came up and asked if I was O.K. I realized they knew the process I was going through. They live with it.

"These experiences have influenced the content of the classes I teach—policy and law. I have actively begun to teach about the policy of fear. We have many policies based on fear. The driving force behind a lot of Cold War policy decisions was fear. This has to be brought to the surface—recognized for what it is. There may be perfectly reasonable reasons why we should be frightened. We have to know it and say it—recognize the force that it plays in our policies—the role that it plays in our policies. I don't think that many of my male counterparts see it this way. They would say that 'You are a professional, and there is no room for emotions.' My view is that if you are going to be a professional you have to recognize those emotions right up front."

Joanne took in the big picture and told it the way she saw it. She couldn't ignore it or push it away. She listened. She took the truth of her terror seriously—and believed it. Then, in a way very different from her male colleagues', she expressed it. She didn't follow the unwritten rules of silence. Instead, she named the issue—"The driving force behind a lot of policy decisions is fear"—and brought it into the open. Rather than separating her insight as "just an emotional response," she integrated it as a central focus of her teaching.

The feminine takes in, flexes, integrates and compre-
hends in ways that differ from masculine tradition. Our
self-esteem and sense of well-being center in our relationships, so we learn early to understand and care about how
we affect others. In the give and take of relationships, we
learn that self-interest isn't enough. We understand that
what we put into the atmosphere touches us all.

Philosopher Sara Ruddick writes:

> . . . A child's acts are irregular, unpredictable,
> often mysterious. A child herself might be thought of
> as an "open structure," changing, growing, reinter-
> preting what has come before. Neither a child nor,
> therefore, the mother understanding her can sharply
> distinguish reality from fantasy, body from mind, self
> from other. The categories through which a child
> understands the world are modified as the changing
> world is creatively apprehended in ways that make
> sense to the child. If there are comfortably sharp def-
> initions, they are ephemeral. A mother who took one
> day's conclusions to be permanent or invented sharp
> distinctions to describe her child's choices would be
> left foundering.[3]

Not all women are mothers, and Sara Ruddick writes
about "maternal thinking," but her point is a good one. If
we took care of children the way we run our businesses, it
wouldn't work. We can do better by bringing to work
what we know about nurturing kids—the capacity for
melding and molding, for responding and taking things in
context. Why would we follow short-sighted procedures
and planning at the office? How is it that we buy into limiting or destructive practices and products because they
are represented to us as more "professional" or business-
like?

We know, consciously or not, that we can't make decisions about life in small, discrete sections. We all breathe the same air. This is an important asset to bring to the business world, not only for influencing the way work gets done, but also for determining the goals we work toward. Wholistic thinking brings balance to the often misguided attempts at efficiency or profit that artificially chop work into small sections and severely limit connection with the big picture.

The
"unscrupulous
observer" sees
it all,
unrestricted by
anybody's
sense of
right or wrong,
good or bad.

But looking at life wholistically isn't an easy thing to do. In the rush to complete everyday business, wholistic thinking can be quite upsetting. We get so accustomed to tunnel vision we lose sight of how the parts fit with the whole. Taking an overall view, my consulting partner, Mary Bolton, would say impractical things like, "We need to get these guys together (warring factions who did not *speak* to each other) and have them look at how their short-range, instant, profit-focused actions are hurting the long-range well-being of the company." We didn't always necessarily make that intervention; our intuition and judgment balanced our wholistic thinking. But we used the idea to create a step in the direction of healing open wounds.

Long-range, wholistic thinking may work toward the preservation of the species and the planet, but it doesn't fit well with work deadlines. Keeping a focus on priorities— what's important in the never-ending spiral of birth, death, and transformation—makes a weird juxtaposition with deciding what to wear to work or whether or not the sales meeting goes well. The ability to see many contradictory facets—and to value them—rarely slides smoothly into the competitive business mode. It's contrary to the business-style focus on short-term goals that makes it difficult to support or explain the global view. Taking time to evaluate a situation and consider the implications of various courses of action on the future may appear inefficient or unfocused to those who need to get a product out the door today. And yet, wholistic thinking has much to offer today's suffering business and government.

In fact, the long-range view and extra time invested in making decisions can improve the quality of outcome and reduce the time needed to untangle and revise the results of hasty, "logical" decisionmaking.

Wholistic thinking presents a challenge. To meld this gift with more expedient approaches requires yet another balancing act. It's relatively easy to support and justify clear, specific, short-range goals in terms of profit and loss. And it can be overwhelming to look at the long range. The art of problem solving is in knowing when to shift from the feminine overview—holding, mulling, creating—to a more immediate "masculine" focus.

Since wholistic thinking tends to be non-linear, it's often hard to organize and communicate in a way that makes sense to those thinking in a sequential mode. We can feel crazy and confused about our own thoughts and, at the same moment, know they're solid and worthwhile. It's difficult to let yourself think and care about, let alone say, "I know that our new multi-million dollar plant in Korea is state of the art and will reduce our production costs. But it's hard for me to get excited about it when I know that we have high unemployment here and that the company will exploit the Korean workers as much as possible." Your wholistic view is likely to be seen as "disloyal," even though, in addition to your humanistic concerns, you're forseeing your company's difficulties in selling its products in the sliding economy where unemployed workers have reduced purchasing power.

THE SHADOW SIDE

Wholistic thinking gets shady when we become so overwhelmed by the big picture that we're immobilized.

We shut down and can't deal with anything but the most immediate detail. Anxiety rolls in and dancing dust particles obscure the distant view. We stumble blindly, directing our energy toward short-term solutions. When this happens, we need to get help in managing and understanding the anxiety. The shadow is letting us know that we've over-extended and need to pull back and regroup.

An exaggerated sense of self-importance can hide in the shadow of wholistic thinking. We can use this dimension to feel superior and put down those who don't see the world in the same way. Arrogance, or feeling superior because we can't be bothered with the details, alienates those who have to work with us. But sooner or later, if we are tuned in at all, we will get the picture that we can't do it all alone.

Oversight also creeps out of this shadow. When I first learned to drive, I was concentrating so hard on the stop light two blocks away that I ran through one that was right in front of me. That was a scary but potent lesson. We can get so concerned with a long-range goal that we lose touch with present reality. The overall plan is certainly important, but positive, day-to-day contact with customers, clients, or colleagues is what makes work flow smoothly.

The shadow side of wholistic thinking threatens to reduce us to total insignificance. Take any area of needed social change. If we look at the full scope of problems and think about what needs to be done in education, social services, mental health, highway improvement or health care—let alone all of them together—we can feel so small and helpless that any effort we might make seems useless. When this happens we need to get back to home base and find a level where we can make a difference. Very often, that will be in taking care of our own personal business.

The long-range view of our own self-interest also thrives on the shadow side of wholistic thinking. Greed is the shadow side's main component here. In the darker reaches of this dimension, our egocentric blinders slip into place and the big picture fades out of sight. The major push of our culture is to throw ourselves into a money-making or pleasure seeking frenzy and forget about every-thing else. It's no accident that a series of very slick, expensive beverage commercials, many of which subtly equate women with their product, repeat "Why ask why?" on the family television set. It's easy to get stuck here.

SELF-REFLECTION

Where do you fit on the wholistic thinking continuum? Like the other dimensions, this one isn't good and bad. Think about the shadow side, especially your vulnerability to being overwhelmed by too many possibilities, as you work with this dimension. If you get stuck in the big pic-ture, it's hard to focus or know where to start. If the shadow takes over, you can become immobilized or headed in a direction that is not satisfying.

STRENGTH: Typically, I absorb a lot of information that helps me relate one thing to another. I don't have much trouble integrating contradictory information. I like to understand the relationship of one thing to another. Long-range outcomes concern me deeply.

SHADOW: I get impatient with others who are short-sighted. / I get overwhelmed with too many possibilities. I can't focus. If I can't do the whole thing, which is usually the case, I'm immobilized. / I want what I want now and know how to get it.

TIME FOR YOURSELF

This dimension has to do with how you take in and organize information from your environment. Are you aware of how you experience and express this dimension? As you select a few of the following steps to explore in some depth, reflect on ways you use information in a wholistic manner.

• LIST THREE EXAMPLES of times you've seen "the big picture" at work but didn't say anything because you thought others surely must know better.

• THINK OF A TIME you expressed concern about a long-range impact and were laughed at or received some other negative reaction. Who laughed?

• THINK OF A TIME you expressed concern about a long-range impact and your recommendation was accepted. Write about the outcome and how you felt about it.

• LIST SOME OF YOUR CURRENT CONCERNS about decisions at work that may have negative long-range outcomes for your workplace or for the environment. Would your organization be better off if they attended to the things on your list? Do you think they will? If the answer is no, what gets in the way? Write about values conflicts this brings up for you.

• WHEN AN IDEA FORMS or an image emerges, when you have an insight about the big picture, share your thoughts with someone you trust. Allow yourself to feel comfortable talking about your ideas even though you can't support them "logically." Support yourself, no matter what the reaction is. You've made a contribution.

• TUNE IN TO EXPRESSIONS of wholistic thinking by others. Whether you agree with them or not, support their right to their concerns. Be assertive.

Support yourself and others in expressing this dimension of the feminine presence at work. Big-picture thinking by women is threatening to those who are desperately attached to the status quo, and they often deal with this threat by belittling women who express big thoughts.

- Do you know a woman whose wholistic thinking you admire? How does she express this part of her feminine presence so that others understand? Talk to her about this aspect of her feminine power. Write down three steps you learn from her that can help you be more expressive.

- Write four feeling words that describe your emotional state at a time when you have felt overwhelmed by the number and complexity of details you have to manage. List three steps you could take to ground yourself if this happens again.

- Describe your shadow in this dimension. Does it grow and become grandiose so you have no patience for details or the short-sightedness of your colleagues? Or does it intimidate you so that you shrink to insignificance and hang on to the most obvious immediate step you can take? It may do both at different times. As you write your description, exaggerate it a little so that your shadow can stand out even more clearly.

- Think about a time when you focused so hard on the long-range goal that you failed to tend to your immediate business. Write about the lessons your shadow taught you with this experience. What would a more balanced approach have been?

- Draw a picture or diagram that illustrates how your job relates to someone in another country.

Wholistic thinking is nonlinear—not "logical." Through its wide-ranging rambles, the long-term relationships of one thing to another become apparent. It often provides a starting point, a brainstorm, for more practical steps. If you didn't experience strong pulls one way or the other doing these exercises, your thinking style may not fit this model. That doesn't reflect negatively on your intelligence or your femininity.

Did you identify areas where you might want to be more supportive or expensive of yourself at work? Were there some shadow feelings that popped out at you? Write in your journal about the steps you want to take for future work in this dimension.

Wholistic thinking is one of the more difficult dimensions to grasp. Return to your initial Self-Assessment on page 28 and adjust your rating to fit any new understanding you have gained.

WHOLISTIC THINKING GOES TO WORK

The world is shrinking. Multinational corporations are bigger and more powerful than governments. Decisions made by government and industry have life-and-death influence over countless individuals. What we do in our jobs has potential impacts for people on the other side of the globe, as well as in our immediate environment.

Air quality makes a real difference to people on a daily basis in the thriving city where I live in Northern California. Autos by the hundred thousand puff out their toxins as we busily transport ourselves from one end of the city to the other and back again. The Air Pollution Index fits neatly in the newspaper as part of the weather report. Citizens, particularly those with respiratory problems, plan their outdoor activities based on how "good" or "bad" the air is on any given day. Each year it gets more dense.

The newspapers also describe another kind of pollution, a political system clogged with vested interests. That, too, is the focus of this chapter—the deeply personal exploration of the place of a whole person in a whole world.

The state is the single biggest employer in Sacramento. Airtight office buildings where thousands of people spend their days are well-defended against a basic life support that I used to take for granted—fresh air. As city dwellers, we grow accustomed to this deprivation and numb to its consequences. We dull our senses a little to get by, just as we dull our sensitivity to our own feelings and those of others at work. There's no blue sky of any shade inside an office building, no fresh air in a factory, a hotel kitchen, or a warehouse. We survive on the recycled substitute. At work, we have dulled, recycled relationships, too—not too personal, not too real.

The "air quality" in many contemporary organizations is none too good. Demands for short-term profit, productivity, or the basic struggles for financial survival whirl us along like tumbleweeds in a dust storm. As we explore elusive ethical dimensions in the feminine presence, let the symbolism of this murky condition emerge as an image that screams for attention. Self-contact and healthy relationships occupy deep second place in those unnatural environments where we spend most of our waking hours. Concern for the impact on "air quality," symbolic or real, are swept aside by the goals of the existing power structure.

We have to be practical after all. We can't lie on our backs and gaze at the sky and be productive workers—or feed our families, or buy the latest goodies. And who has time to practice four different religions at once?

But we can make room for some other images as well. How would the world be if feminine balance had a voice at work? Can we open the windows, let in the fresh air as we speak out clearly on issues that affect women's ways of working? Can we make our voices heard?

This dimension can make a major difference in how our corporations and governments operate and in the goals they work toward. It's part of us all.

This dimension can make a major difference in how our corporations and governments operate and in the goals they work toward. It's part of us all. But we're so accustomed to fitting in rather than taking our own views seriously that we discount our wholistic view and don't give it an opportunity to grow. In the impersonal atmosphere of the workplace, it's easy to underrate our feminine power and see wholistic thinking as something that other people—those who have real power—do.

The capacity to form an overview and to see how the organization relates to the world at large puts your work in context. Wholistic thinking may be more or less welcome, depending on your company and level of responsibility. But in your own business, it's crucial. You deserve to take your self, including a wholistic view of your life, seriously. Regardless of where you work or your company's philosophy, you are the central creative force in your own life. Looking at your worklife wholistically will help you to keep things in perspective as you manage your own time and energy. No man is an island, and for sure, no woman is.

Step One is to understand fully how work fits into your life—how it is part of the whole. Since work is structured and the demands can be neverending, we find ourselves organizing around work at the expense of everything else. Women tend to blend work and home responsibilities much more than men do. But with constant pressures to deal with work in a masculine way, we can lose ourselves along with our wholistic views, our personal connections with the universe.

Dealing with how work fits into your life, not how your life fits into work, includes looking at how balanced your home responsibilities are. Research and everyday conversations tell us that many women, even though they're working away from home full-time, are still taking most (by far) of the responsibility for home management and childcare. As a result, the depression, burnout, and bitterness rate among working women is out of sight.

If you're single, or a single parent, networking and sharing with others can be important support for you. It can be nearly impossible to keep a full-view perspective when you're burdened with the day-to-day responsibilities of keeping things together. It's unrealistic to think you can do it all. When you can create a good overview for yourself, based on your feelings, intuition, and the practical realities of life, you can make decisions about what's necessary and what's not.

Here's what Joanne Gabrynowicz said when I asked her how she takes care of herself:

"I find other women—in the community. The first year was very difficult. Moving from Wall Street to North Dakota was a shock. In the beginning, I wouldn't have articulated that it was the absence of women that was bothering me. It took a couple of months. In New York, I had a strong spiritual community. I was ripped away from that. I'm a philosophically driven person, and I missed being connected with people who share that. There are men here who are understanding of philosophical and spiritual aspects, but it is not the same.

"The first winter was very hard. If you're not socially established, winter isn't a time you get to know people in North Dakota. It is 40 degrees below zero and people stay home. They don't go for walks.

"When spring came—I made a point of getting out and meeting people—a strong community at the university—very active network of women. It was like a drink of water in the desert.

"The college that I'm in—Aerospace Sciences—is perceived by many in the rest of the university to be a military-oriented institution. This includes the women on campus. It has been interesting to see how they find me. They were receptive when I approached them. I was accepted. They accept me, but I can't talk to them about my institution." Joanne found personal support even though she couldn't share her professional concerns with her women friends.

If you have a partner, figuring out how to look at your responsibilities and make a plan for sharing them is key to honoring this dimension. Working together, you can manage home and work in a balanced way. This includes consciously looking at and determining how much of your life energy each of you chooses to devote to work. Otherwise, traditional feminine responsibilities on top of a job wear you down very quickly.

Step Two is to express your wholistic views at work. Balancing work and home is a lifelong task. As you work toward it, you can contribute at work by growing increasingly assertive about human issues on the job. How does your company manage childcare? Flex-time? Job-sharing? Parental leave for pregnancy, birth, or adoption? Time off for managing family concerns? What are the company's attitudes toward pollution, war, world trade? Your voice on these topics makes a difference.

Many companies today solicit input on company mission and goals, quality of work life, and other core issues from employees at all levels. Quality Circles or other work groups directly seek opinions and ideas from workers. These are ready-made opportunities for you to share your wholistic thinking. The more you have brought it into your awareness, the clearer you can be.

Courage in expressing your wholistic views can make a difference if you work at policymaking levels. Whether or not your ideas are adopted, their expression changes the context. Next time around they will sound more familiar. In positions of less authority, talking about your wholistic views may not change policy but it may start other people thinking and open up new possibilities. If you take yourself seriously, you become credible to others who are willing to open their minds.

Give yourself permission to think and talk about what's best for you and your family, what's best for the company, what's best for the world. These thoughts are part of all of us, but sometimes we lose sight of them or get overwhelmed. Since this isn't the usual way that people at work think about their jobs, it can seem weird to

When you can create a good overview for yourself, you can make decisions about what's necessary and what's not.

talk about the big picture.

A process to work with as you explore wholistic thinking on the job includes these ideas:

- Pay attention to your own cyclical nature.
- Give yourself permission to look at and think about the whole picture.
- See what needs to be done.
- Express what you see.
- Talk about the relationship of your work to the world at large.
- Talk about the importance of balancing personal life with work.
- Find other people who are willing to share their wholistic thinking and talk about issues that require being "unscrupulous observers."

For the past two years, I've been part of a group of professional people who get together once a month or so to talk about emerging feminine energy in our culture, a wholistic topic if ever there was one. Following principles of wholistic thinking, the process stirs the group's energy to explore what comes along with no particular direction in mind. We agreed that, as a group, we wouldn't work on "causes" or support political actions.

Personal, relevant discussion enlivens us each time a topic emerges and develops over the evening. Now something else is beginning to form. Various individual members are undertaking projects—some small, some large—but each something that expresses that person's way of supporting the feminine in our culture. The energy for these activities comes from each individual as group support nurtures her or him.

Shared wholistic thinking allows individuals to support their own efforts. It becomes possible see your work—and your life—in more than its most immediate steps. Look for ways you can provide this kind of support for yourself.

SUMMARY

Wholistic thinking moves us beyond the details of our daily lives. It gives us the perspective we need to guide our most significant decisions. Our materialistic culture has distanced us from this part of the feminine for a long time. And so we easily lose sight of what we know—of the big picture—and get stuck in spending our good energy to meet goals and expectations that we've grabbed because they were obvious or within reach.

Taking this dimension seriously can connect us with our deeper selves and, consequently, with our archetypal feminine presence. As "unscrupulous observers," we can see the world as it really is, not distorted through convenience or what others want us to believe. Learning to live with our wholistic views is a lifelong task that takes trust in yourself and the courage to speak out about what "the moment's light" prints on your "own silver gut."

Wisdom and Spirituality

> . . . here in the skin of our fingertips we see the trail of the wind." And then she made a circular motion to indicate the whirlwind that had left its imprint in the whorls at the tips of the human finger. "It shows where the wind blew life into my ancestors when they were first made. . . . It was in the legend days when these lines happened. It was the legend days when the first people were given the breath of life.
>
> Jamake Highwater, *Kill Hole*

The "trail of the wind" rushes through each of us, connecting us with each other and with the universe—before us and yet to come. We take in the breath of life and let it go.

The idea of "medicine"—spirit, specialness, the uniqueness of each fingerprint—reaches us from ancient times. Each baby is herself alone from day one. If you've had children or experience with tiny infants, you've seen it. She is someone special, similar to others in many ways, but different from everyone else in the world.

Even in this high-tech era, our individual fingerprints, "where the wind blew life into my ancestors," follow us as singular identification throughout our lives. Maybe souls are spiritual fingerprints. Each makes its own mark. This chapter is about treasuring that uniqueness, following the trail of the wind and letting it breathe in you deeply and fully—even at work. A certain amount of wisdom is required for this task, and each of us carries that wisdom—if we can hear it whispering within us.

In her book, *Psychotherapy Grounded in the Feminine Principle*, analyst Barbara Stevens Sullivan writes about feminine wisdom. This treasure is profoundly undervalued in the business world, although each of us harbors it in some way. Sullivan says it is knowledge that comes from experience and is the "product of feminine immersion in life":

> . . . We call this feminine consciousness wisdom . . . the intelligence of the heart, even of the stomach, the wisdom of feeling. It comes with age and maturity . . . only with years of deeply savored and suffered life. It is knowledge of oneself and of the world attuned to one person, to a unique incident. It is never guided by universal, abstract truths.[1]

Feminine wisdom is personal, heartfelt—wisdom of the uterus, of the breast, of the ovaries. It carries on its winds everything we learn from men as well as from other women. Old women have more of it than young women. It grows from life's lessons—losses, joys, pain, progress.

Where are these old women in business and government? Does anyone listen to them any more? How do we learn to hear and value this dimension in ourselves? And speak it with confidence?

Old woman! The crone of times gone by. Like the goddess Hecate at the crossroad, she peers into the future as well as the past—the carrier of life experience that produces wisdom. What a concept. It's so far removed from our youth-oriented way of being that it's almost guaranteed to produce a shudder.

A sign in a department store's personnel office reads: "We do not discriminate against those aged 40 to 70." It doesn't say: "We welcome those whose life experiences contribute to their value as employees."

Our ageist culture rejects old women. We reflect that view when we reject the old woman in ourselves—and her wisdom and accumulated life experiences along with her. We apologize for our age and our life seasoning. Instead, we can look at our own aging faces with love, rather than with horror and dismay. We can embrace and value the crone in each of us who understands that our life experiences count for something. We have learned from them and should trust ourselves with the depth they've given us. And we can use our personal wisdom to guide our work lives.

But wisdom isn't reserved for the old. Each of us is enough if we take the time to honor what we know—and to speak it.

Feminine spirit breathes life into wisdom. It isn't knowledge about a particular thing, but it is knowing. Of the earth, of nature, curled into life's cycles, the spirit wind murmurs through our connections with each other and the universe.

Sherry Ruth Anderson and Patricia Hopkins' book, *The Feminine Face of God: The Unfolding of the Sacred in Women*, discusses feminine spirituality as ordinary, everyday practice. Men go on spiritual quests. Women stay home to find their spiritual practice in their ordinary lives.

The Greek word for soul, mind, or spirit is *psyche*, self. A woman's spirituality includes all those images and feelings around which she organizes her inner life and understands her place in the universe. Whether it's well developed or not, we all have some sense of how we connect with our own life and our own death. As we become more conscious of our feminine heritage, we welcome, seek, and create feminine images that fit our own experience. We no longer have to bend our feelings to fit images we've inherited from our masculine culture.

Wise men have taught us that pursuing our spiritual essence takes hard work and discipline. For those of us who scramble just to manage our worldly responsibilities, such pursuits are what other people do. Although we can enrich ourselves by learning about its history and practices, feminine spirituality isn't something that can be learned separate from our daily struggles. It is just who we are. Wise women learn to honor that feminine spirit of the here and now, the precious quality that feels, lives, and breathes everyday life. We can live in our bodies, do our work and honor our feminine spirit simultaneously. Each of us is enough.

Do you think of your job as a path to spiritual enlightenment? Most of us don't. But things happen sometimes that wake us up. We're expected to do something destructive or dishonest that rubs us the wrong way. We find ourselves lying or cutting corners. Or, on the other side, we breeze along, work flows, and we feel like we're perfectly in tune with the universe.

As we pay attention to our inner experience, we have a basis for thinking about and feeling these conflicts. At times, we're especially tuned in; we know who we are and have a sense of how we fit in the great scheme of things. We trust that what we think and feel has value.

When we don't have this sense of inner direction, we try to fly on automatic pilot—not exactly a feminine concept—at work. At such times, it's hard to pay attention to some of the things we see or feel. So we aim straight ahead with limited sensitivity to our personal values or those of our colleagues. We put on our blinders and drone numbly through whatever turbulence or balmy air surrounds us. We don't take our own flight pattern seriously, because it's just too painful.

Our materialistic culture splits the spirit off into particular days or times—if this untouchable part of our living is acknowledged at all. All we have to do is read the daily paper to see that the feminine spirit is not much of a priority. God has the face of a man we go visit on the week-

Power and strength evaporate when we punch the automatic pilot button and travel along pre-defined directions at work.

end. Except when someone at work dies, or a tragedy of some sort pulls us up short, feminine wisdom and spirituality seem far away. At those exceptional times we find ourselves grasping to understand, comfort, or be comforted.

And yet, if we delve into this dimension, each of us has the choice to walk into work any day as a whole person. We may not always be able to influence what happens, but our inner guides will help us know how we feel about it. And when we do have a chance to say something or decide about an outcome, we can do so in a way that feels solid.

What are we doing to ourselves? How can we stay on the trail of the wind while we work? Can we avoid punching the automatic pilot button? Is it possible to fly with greater attention to the journey?

Feminine spirituality honors the uniqueness and worth of each individual. It breathes with the ongoing circle of life and death. Spirit enlivens woman's connectedness with her inner self at all ages. In ancient times, it was symbolized by the triple goddess—virgin, mother, and crone. Each stage had its own power, with the greatest wisdom living in the crone. How does this trinity apply to today's working woman? Such power and strength evaporate when we punch the automatic pilot button and travel along pre-defined directions at work.

Feminine spirituality has a way of whistling to get our attention if we give it the slightest chance. We have moments when we feel deeply connected with those around us. Or we feel especially in tune with the earth or the sky on a beautiful spring day. A friend points out a truth we've spoken. Or we realize the simplicity of something that's been puzzling us.

When we're just too busy to notice, nighttime delivers unbidden gifts in our dreams and not-quite-conscious wanderings. These momentary glimpses don't substitute for deeper study, but they do provide a starting place.

One of these offerings, a dream, came to me shortly after my 49th birthday. It was different from dreams I commonly remember and so real that I had to pay attention. Here's what I recall:

It was a soft, sunny day. I was outdoors somewhere in the foothills. In the wondrous liquidity of the dreamworld, my movements weren't limited to the conventional. My upturned moccasined toes stretched for sunlight. With my back scrunched on a little wooden chair, I joyously relaxed into an unorthodox upside-down, backwards-reaching posture, feeling open and free.

"It's time for the meeting!" A woman's voice intruded through the warm pleasure of my reverie.

"Do you have the form?" Her tone held accusation.

Irritated, I brought myself to reply, "No, I forgot about it."

"You have to have the form!" she persisted.

"I can finish it when I get there." I was beginning to put it together. One more time I had agreed to attend some gathering that I didn't really want to take time for.

She pushed again. "They won't let you in without it!"

In the dream, my stomach clutched. I noticed that my breath was tight. My shoulders sagged, but I was determined to enjoy myself.

I gathered my energy and said to the woman, "Come on. I'm going anyway. I can't believe the form is so important."

"You can't go looking like that!" she admonished me.

"I'm fine," I insisted, but I didn't really feel fine by this time.

"You have to wear a shirt!"

My confidence slipped, melted into a puddle of ineptitude as I recognized my semi-nudity.

"I'm going like this." If they won't let me in, I'll deal with it when I get there," I insisted.

Her warning echoed many I had heard before. "I'm afraid you'll be sorry."

We followed the bike path over a rise and saw green hills unfolding. The sun felt reassuring.

Music! Women singing. There they were!

Goosebumps jumped onto my arms as the marching troop formed in my vision. Yellow and white serpent-crested flags, standards held formally aloft, flanked the first row. The women inspired images of a medieval throng in their contemporary full-length dresses of green and white print. They looked so strong! I wondered if they were witches. They seemed so sure of themselves.

Old visions of my own unacceptability blipped into my thoughts . . . dirty fingernails at my piano recital . . . slip showing at graduation . . . hair dishevelled.

Awareness dawned. My brain clicked away: "I'm not prepared. I can't get into this group the way I am. I didn't do my homework and I wore the wrong thing.

I would never be part of this group.

The sun rubbed my back as I sat crosslegged on the hill and watched while two women planted the standards. The group appeared to prepare for a ritual. Interesting. I remembered rituals in which I'd participated without belief.

I felt a little sadness . . . I didn't fit in. I watched as the women milled around. An odd scene.

And then slowly, warmly, still in the dream, relief radiated through me. I would hate being part of that. It didn't fit me. That wasn't my group . . . and not the only group.

This dream happens to be mine. But the themes are familiar ones. I hear them all the time from others as they try to fit in, when they think someone else knows the way, and whenever they degrade themselves and their own competence and experience.

Sometimes, I also hear the hope.

Each of us has the choice to walk into work any day as a whole person.

As this healing dream gusted in and out of my awareness, I wondered what it meant to me. I felt inspired to get
off automatic pilot and become more connected to my
own flying patterns. I understood that feminine presence
is different for each of us. Some dimensions fit neither the
cultural stereotypes nor what is commonly seen as a "feminist" point of view. They go beyond traditional views of
femininity and are different from commonly accepted masculine views. We can identify, embrace and own these
dimensions as parts of ourselves that enrich our personal
sense of well-being. They empower us and enhance our
relationships with other women and men.

I decided to begin a project that I had fiddled with in
dim awareness for a long time. I wanted to write a book
about women and spirit and work. I was ready to devote
serious time and effort. I wanted to share what it means to
be a regular, ordinary woman at work—not the woman
with the flying hair—not radical—not subservient—but just
an everyday person trying to do her job and maintain her
sense of personal integrity in the process. I knew it was a
big, hard job. People want to be glamorous, not ordinary.
We want to be "successful" in the eyes of the masculine
world.

I had no idea that it would take years and that I would
do it over and over until it was finished. Nor did I have a
clue about how I would wander and dig or about the
lessons I'd learn along the way.

But I did learn about my own feminine spirit. When I
jotted notes so I could remember my dream, I wanted to
leave out the part about the snakes on the yellow flags.
They seemed so icky to me, a gruesome symbol. Imagine
my surprise to find, as I began exploring feminine mythology, that the serpent represented the Great Goddess of
ancient times and had been a symbol of the feminine way
before it became associated with evil in the Garden of
Eden.

Learning about the feminine beyond my own experience, trying to get a sense about how women could really
live in the feminine presence at work, began to feel like a
search for the Holy Grail. I knew that somehow I would
find a way to work with the idea, but it seemed impossible
to grasp. Whenever I would think, say, or write "search for
the Holy Grail," in my attempts to describe what I was
going through, it felt wrong. But I couldn't quite come up
with the feminine equivalent of the masculine spiritual
search—the hero's journey.

I didn't journey or have epic conquests; I meandered.
Even though I'm a well-organized person, I wasn't going
in a straight line. I'd start out that way and then find
myself wandering. I would look for something, fail to find
it, be frustrated, and find what I wasn't looking for. This
happened over and over. I gathered bits and pieces, and
had small, rich encounters along the way. I suffered
defeats and disappointments, and I kept going.

Naomi Newman helped. As the Jewish mother charac-
ter in her one woman show, *Snake Talk: Urgent Messages
from the Mother*,[2] she explains the whole thing. Here's
what I learned: We dig. We go outside and we dig. We
don't dig in a straight line. We dig here; we dig there. We
take three steps and we fall-down-and-get-up. Fall-down-
and-get-up is one move. And we do it some more. Pretty
soon we find some, not all, of what we're looking for. And
we dig some more. And we each do it in our own way.

I gave up looking for a grand metaphor.

When we invite our spirits to work, we trust the part
that goes outside to dig and fall-down-and-get-up. We
experience a sense of personal power and integrity on the
job. We have a personal basis for making our decisions
rather than just doing what is common practice in the
work environment. We give our inner guides a louder
voice.

THE SHADOW SIDE

The shadow side of wisdom and spirituality harbors some mean women—the cynic, the holier than thou, the know it all. And some sad ones too. If you find them lurking in you, try to discover what fears they're helping you avoid taking a look at.

The cynic, the bitter woman who rejects her feminine presence and everyone else's, makes light of what she can't see or measure. It's hard for her to allow her own feminine wisdom and spirituality much opportunity to grow. She focuses on the material side of life for fulfillment: "she who has the most toys wins."

Another shadow form is the woman who suffers from the holier than thou syndrome. This person has her head in the clouds and has a hard time being present or productive. She may feel intellectually or spiritually superior to others, but this self-deception is a way she avoids confronting her doubts or feelings of insignificance—the scariness her shadow side represents.

She who has found the answer knows it all and has no room for uncertainty or groping lack of clarity. She terrorizes herself when she can't live up to her own unreal expectations about how to be a person. Watch out for her. She'll eat you up. She tries to shut you down when your uncertainties frighten you or your human fallibility disappoints you.

The spiritual junkie moves from one guru or practice to another, drawn to someone else's answers. Last year's solution fades as this year's sparkles brightly, only to dim as it grows apparent one more time that there really are no magic answers. Commitment to the hard work of self-development is hard for her.

Spiritual impoverishment, lack of attention to our inner life, and the absence of soul searching, are major by-products of late Twentieth Century life. We lose ourselves because we don't have time to weigh and consider the values choices we make every day. Emptiness, meaninglessness, a hollow feeling stays with us in what should be our happiest moments.

Wisdom and spirituality are personal matters that each of us encounters and manages in her own way. If we believe we've "found the way" and try to impose it on others, we operate from the shadow. Instead, we need to be expressive without putting others down for their beliefs or lack thereof.

This dimension contains great potential for abuse. What Joseph Campbell called the "institutionalization of mythology," usually in the form of organized religion, is one of the biggest dangers. All groups of people create living myths to explain the unexplainable in their lives. When any group selects part of the myth and consciously tries to foist it off on others as a form of social control, the vitality of the myth, the spirit, is lost and the shadow takes over. In our excitement about our own spiritual discoveries, we can come to expect others to be equally enthusiastic. When they're not, it's important to respect that response. Each of us has to find her own way.

At work, the shadow side of this dimension gets played out in destructive ways. People belonging to one religion or spiritual group feel justified in supporting each other to the exclusion of those who differ. This can affect every part of work life, from hiring and promotion to the way individuals are treated on a daily basis. Since the behavior and decisions are covert, this is a kind of discrimination that's very difficult to confront.

A shadow side of wisdom is activated by people who consider themselves wise just because they've been around a long time or hold high position. Autocratic behavior from a self-appointed "wise man" or "wise woman" leaves little room for negotiation. Lacking the true wisdom to benefit from others' knowledge and experience, such people believe it's their way or no way.

On an individual basis, the shadow side of this dimension deepens when we're so much into our own trip that we don't really hear those around us, or if we assume a sense of personal superiority for one reason or another. The shadow ignores the personal worth of others, and is even more critical and punishing to the imperfect, vulnerable spirit of an ordinary person.

SELF-REFLECTION

Now that you're in this philosophical place, take a moment or two to see where you fit on the Wisdom and Spirituality dimension. Remember, this is not a bigger-than-life kind of thing. None of us does it perfectly. It simply has to do with how you live your authenticity at work—the very human process of being real wherever you are.

STRENGTH: I know my values and have no trouble living them at work. I don't always agree with my co-workers but I respect them for who they are. I try to stay connected with my inner experience while I'm at work. I take time for my spiritual practice.

SHADOW: I associate only with people of my own spiritual persuasion. I know what's best. / I have no patience with people who are off on some mystical trip. All this woo woo stuff has no business at work. / What could a bunch of old women know that would help me get ahead?

TIME FOR YOURSELF

You can reach ever-greater understanding of what's important to you—where you're willing to compromise and where you choose to stand firm. When this wisdom comes from inside you, not from an external authority, you're the same powerful person at home and at work. You're in touch with your feminine spirit, and the gift of self-confidence is yours.

Here are some steps for expanding contact with this dimension at work:

• IN YOUR JOURNAL, list three non-negotiable values, things you really believe in that are deeply important to you. Describe how you live each of these at work.

• WRITE ABOUT WAYS you are asked to compromise your non-negotiable values. What conflict does this cause for you? How do you work it through?

• ARE THERE SOME OLDER WOMEN where you work? Do they hide their wisdom? If you have a relationship with one of these women, have a conversation with her about life's lessons. Write about the feelings that get stirred as you talk with her (fear of getting older, a wish to be taken care of, tenderness, scorn).

• ARE YOU AN OLDER WOMAN? Do people seek your counsel? Do you offer it? Take yourself and your experience seriously. Write in your journal about crone wisdom and how it grows in you.

• MAKE A TIME LINE THAT ILLUSTRATES your spiritual development. Start with early childhood and break it into sections that help you remember— grade school, middle school, jr. high, through to wherever you are now. Or break it into the places you lived, if you have moved around a lot. Or you can organize it around significant people who influenced your spiritual growth. On the time line, write or draw (or both) key events, ideas or people that influenced you.

• FIND WAYS TO MEDITATE or be in touch with your spiritual center or with images related to your spiritual self while you are at work. It was the practice of Mayor Anne Rudin to close her door for a half hour every day to meditate. You owe your employer your time, your energy, your best efforts, *but not your soul.* List five ways you stay connected with this dimension at work.

• MAKE A GOOD CLEAR FINGERPRINT in the middle of a piece of white paper. Using a copier that enlarges, blow the fingerprint up as much as you can. Write a story between the lines that describes your spirit journey following the trail of the winds. Color and decorate the trail story with symbols that are meaningful to you.

• HONOR YOUR CONNECTION with nature. Go for a hike. Go to the park. Look at a tree. Find ways to be in nature whenever possible. Redwoods, mountains, deserts, canyons, ocean waves, and plains put work conflicts in perspective. So does the incredible yellow of a daffodil.

• FIND SOMEONE AT WORK who likes to talk about matters of the spirit, such as the unbroken chain of women since the beginning of time, the idea that your internal state influences whoever stands next to you, the sense that we're all part of a global community. Write down what you learn from these conversations.

• TAKE YOUR OWN SPIRITUAL SEARCH seriously outside work. What are the ways you open up to your feminine wisdom and spirituality? Religious practices, meditation, yoga, reading, art, nature, a woman's group? Take time to draw or write in your journal a brief sketch of this part of your life.

• ON A BLANK PAGE in your journal, color, scribble, or draw your shadow in this dimension. Write ten words that name it (hopelessness, greed, cynicism, judgmentalness, a general tendency to know it all, self-doubt).

- MOVE A LITTLE FURTHER into your shadow. What is it trying to say to you? What fears might you be trying to cover up? Write something that begins, "When I look at my dark side in this dimension, I fear. . . ."

- PAY ATTENTION to what enlivens you at work. Write down three ways your work energizes you and connects with who you are.

- FOR ONE WEEK, briefly summarize any dreams you can remember. Can you find a pattern? Is there something you're trying to tell yourself about who you are and what's important to you?

- READ ABOUT THE EMERGENCE of the feminine and how others are working in this area. Some places to start include: *The Chalice and the Blade: Our History, Our Future*, by Riane Eisler; *The Crone*, by Barbara Walker; *The Song of Eve: An Illustrated Journey into the Myths, Symbols and Rituals of the Goddess*, by Manuela Dunn Mascetti; *When God Was A Woman*, by Merlin Stone; and *The Feminine Face of God*, by Sherry Ruth Anderson and Patricia Hopkins.

Now you have explored all 13 dimensions. Return to page 28 and make any adjustments that seem to fit for wisdom and spirituality.

WISDOM AND SPIRITUALITY AT WORK

Find ways to support your human spirit, your real self, at work. Take seriously the way you respond to things you're expected to do—or decisions you make to get ahead in your own business or career. The way you feel about your connection with the universe and with nature is not something that you drop at the door as you go to work each day. Without having to sit around and contemplate the meaning of life, you can tune in to this dimension in bits and pieces as a rich personal resource.

A very powerful myth about the importance of work exists in our culture. It has two sides. On one side, you give up your identity, your individuality, your soul when you go to work. The company owns you. For women who have felt disempowered in their private lives, this is nothing new.

On the other side is the idea that you *are* your job. This way of identifying with work has been very powerful for men and is now creeping into feminine culture. When men meet, the first question they ask is "What do you do?" You're not so much a human being as a human doing.

This idea fills people up; it provides a sense of self when the inner self hasn't been very well nurtured or developed. But it isn't enough to sustain a real person. It is, in fact, very dangerous. You may have known men who dumped their lives into their jobs or women who "lived through their children" and crashed into emptiness and isolation when they could no longer work or the nest emptied. When you sustain your inner self, your spirit, along with your work life, you live from your center. You can make the daily shift from your personal life to your work life without losing yourself in the process. When your work years come to a close, retirement is a transition, not loss of identity.

As you expand into your feminine presence at work and maintain focus on your emotional presence—your spiritual self—the breeze of your existence brushes those around you. Your presence becomes a threat to a way of life that has been a stronghold for men since the industrial revolution. When you try to progress upward in the organization, **Masculine Identity Is Work** is one of the barriers that comes forward to stop your progress. Here's how:

The deep threat that a man is less than a man if somehow "under" a woman is probably the single strongest barrier to the routine promotion of women to positions of power and responsibility. It's hard for many men to maintain self-esteem if they aren't in control. They may imply that "strong leadership" is needed and that women can't lead. Their fear of loss is hardly ever stated openly. It is more often expressed indirectly by putting down the ability of women to handle power and responsibility. Or by saying that we're unstable or not strong enough.

Some men are supervised by women, but these women may pay a terrible emotional price unless they are unusually centered and secure individuals. Our culture idealizes masculine power in an unrealistic and exaggerated way. Men are under phenomenal pressure to live up to images of potency, strength, and protectiveness. Psychologist/writer Sam Keen and the men's movement are beginning to register protest against these crippling assumptions.[3] Nonetheless, comfortable acceptance of one's ordinary limits and graceful cooperation with a woman in authority don't fit for most American men.

Men too often fight for traditional organizational survival and exclude or diminish their feminine colleague unless she is able to communicate that she is "one of the boys." But when a woman adopts the masculine style, she doesn't do herself any favors. Instead, she distances herself from her core strength and steps into a role rather than enhancing her authentic position. She may be welcomed as a fake man, but not as a real woman who lives and trusts in her feminine power.

Here are some suggestions for dealing with the idea that **Masculine Identity Is Work**.

When we invite our spirits to work, we trust the part that goes outside to dig and fall-down-and-get-up.

Do	*Don't*
Maintain sensitivity to the depth of the threat women bring to work.	Puff up or harden.
	Disparage men directly or indirectly.

Do	*Don't*
Learn to see through bravado and support vulnerability.	Accept statements about "women" as applicable to you.
Describe yourself as another worker, regardless of status.	Go out of your way to show up male co-workers.
Learn to assert your competence to do your work.	Try to be one of the boys.
Articulate the feminine way of doing things as another way, not the right way.	

Support your wisdom and spirituality on the job. Work and identity issues for men have been brewing for a long time. You can be sensitive and supportive, but you can't protect them from their own pain. As you allow yourself to maintain self-contact and be expressive of who you really are at work as well as in the outside world, you provide a model for men who are struggling to do the same thing.

SUMMARY

Wisdom and spirituality form an important feminine power dimension that isn't typically acknowledged as part of the work environment. How you live this dimension is deeply individual and personal. When you can let the spiritual breezes blow through the stuffy air of your workplace, your contact with your deep inner self supports you and makes you strong.

This growing process happens from the inside out—not from "image polishing" or beating men at their own games. It includes working things out directly, interpersonally, rather than relying on rules or tradition to settle conflicts and differences. When you know who you are as a woman and can trust the complexity and power of your feminine self, you are in a good position to offer partnership to your male colleagues.

Feminine values that have been central to our foremothers for centuries—care and responsibility, the importance of life, the well-being of children, respect for emotion—come to work with us. When we take those values seriously, listen to them and believe their worth, we can be true to our connection with our place in the golden chain. As we live this feminine legacy at work, the purity of the air that future generations will breathe is part of our daily thinking. Deep connections with nature, with the phases of the moon, the changing of the seasons, the ebb and flow of our own monthly cycles, become assets that we trust and rely on. We no longer need to treat our femininity as a liability.

Take a few minutes to look at the skin of your fingertips and trace the trail of the wind.

Feminine Power at Work

To say "divine feminine" is redundant.

Rachel Bagby

olding my tired body and flattened spirit into the car one evening after a long day at the office, I turned on the radio. I was just in time to hear former Congresswoman Bella Abzug respond to an NPR reporter's question. The discussion was about women in politics and whether or not the women's movement has had any impact on world leadership. The reporter's question was the proverbial one: "Do you think power will change the nature of women?" Bella's clear strong response brought tears to my eyes and raised goosebumps on my arms. "No," she said, "Women will change the nature of power."

I hope Bella is right. But before that change becomes visible we have some important work to do.

Changing power means knowing who you are, trusting that you're enough, and taking the risk to speak from your heart about things that are important to you. If you're the CEO, your voice affects the lives of many people. If you spend your days at a computer terminal, your colleague who sits next to you hears your voice. It can inspire and energize her to know herself, and you too, in a whole new way.

There's more to breaking the glass ceiling than hard work and legal battles against sex discrimination. For women to reach the heights and live there happily, the feminine—the rich treasure of our inner depths—must reveal itself. We have to know who we are, support ourselves, and be able and willing to talk about our feminine power. Then our voices can affect those who assume that the masculine way is the only way to do business.

Understanding is the first step. Support is the second. Expression and interaction, the final steps, bring your femininity to life in the world.

You've had an opportunity to explore your feminine presence, to mull it over, to think and feel from 26 different directions. With practice, you can contact your core strength, respect your intuition, and dance with your creativity. You know about your shadow and can hear some of what she has to say. Now it's time to put all the pieces together. Are your colors bright and flashy or subdued? Is the coat you've stitched bulky or flowing? Is the texture rough or smooth? Is it reversible so it looks one way in the sun and different on a rainy day?

Review your journal as you read this last chapter. Reflect on how you've learned to value your femininity by understanding more about assets that, until now, have often been defined as liabilities in the business world—nurturance, affinity, wholistic thinking. And think about how you're energized by dimensions you previously thought you had to leave at home—sexuality, aggression, wisdom, and spirituality.

Knowing and trusting your femininity gives you a strong base for understanding and relating to others. Think in terms of your thirteen dimensions. Expand your consciousness about how every one of them lives in you. Polish them like fine jewels so that when you want or need their energy they sparkle for you. Each adds its own light and color. The better you care for it, the more accessible it becomes.

Sexism exists at an unconscious level. By confronting your own negative attitudes toward feminine ways, you're less likely to echo a negative cultural bias toward yourself or other women. By embracing your strengths and accepting your vulnerabilities, you can feel secure. Your relationships with men can be grounded in a sense that you're worthwhile if imperfect, just like they are, and that your ways are valuable.

Self-knowledge—exploring and clarifying the thirteen dimensions—will open new vistas for you at work. As you become more secure in each of them, you can take better care of yourself. When you know where you're coming from and can trust what you feel as valid, it's easier to stay with your impressions and believe in yourself. You can feel comfortable, or at least not scared to death, saying things that differ from traditional masculine views. And you can trust your internal base for expressing values that support the feminine.

Expression and interaction in our male-dominant culture are a challenge. The strong, flowing, passionate, spiritual feminine has been degraded for so long that putting her in plain view feels dangerous, and sometimes it is. Doing so in a way that doesn't simply mirror the masculine isn't easy. Fortunately, you don't have to go on a campaign or do it all at once.

The more you grow into your feminine power, the easier it is to use opportunities to self-define. It will become habitual to say, "My intuition, which I've learned to trust, tells me we need to pay attention to this," or, "I'm receptive to your comments and will get back to you with a response." Ultimately, you can assert, "Let's look at our options. This plan seems highly profitable, but it has a lot of negative side effects. I don't support it."

Remember, paternalism doesn't just affect women. Its constraints and demands shackle men, too. As you become more confident and expressive of your feminine differences, you model for men the possibility that they can be real with no sacrifice to their competence. There's more to life than competing and achieving. As you risk expressing what you really think, some people can hear your truth and then take their own more seriously. When even a few people in a work environment are willing to be honest with each other and dedicate their efforts to taking care of themselves, it changes the feel of the place.

It's important to remember that both feminine and masculine ways are necessary. Part of feminine receptivity and flexibility is knowing when it's time to move from the reflective to the active—from circular to linear logic. In order to make the move in a conscious way, you first need to be grounded in the feminine. Then you contribute to balance rather than abandoning half of all human experience.

Breaking the glass ceiling is a worthy, but not necessarily the only, valuable goal for working women. The quality of your life, at work and off the job, is important. Nobody gets to have it all. The excruciating emptiness of painfully achieved "success" hurts when we abandon our inner selves—our femininity—along the way. The task is to be true to yourself, nurture your relationships, and compete and achieve in the process. It can be done, but only if you're willing to take your own feelings and needs seriously.

Get to know how your dimensions interact with each other, how core strength supports receptivity and flexibility, how aggression fires creativity, how wisdom and spirituality inform nurturance. Your own moving, shifting patterns are familiar to you at an unconscious level. You can use them for firm support by highlighting them in your awareness. When you can trust that creativity will follow anger, you can express your rage without having to act it out. Or, if you know that your core strength moves into place when it's time to set a limit, you can listen with an open mind.

Despite the fact that our culture still views women as objects and defines us as successful only when we meet masculine standards, you can develop new ways of trusting your femininity. As you understand the depth to which your persistence, flexibility, aggression, and wholistic

There's more to breaking the glass ceiling than hard work and legal battles against sex discrimination.

thinking are assets, you value and rely on them more. You're not as vulnerable to manipulation as you might once have been. You can deal with the implication that you're wishy-washy or impractical by asserting clearly the value of your flexibility or your wholistic thinking. Your own self-understanding and confidence will support you.

Winning at any cost isn't an option. As you trust your feminine power, you value your relationships without feeling ashamed or weak. You won't be willing to stab your friend in the back for a promotion or even to ignore her needs or feelings to get ahead. This doesn't mean that you'll become a doormat or abandon your own hopes and dreams. As you feel confident in recognizing the importance of your relationships, you can be honest and assertive with your friends and colleagues. And then you will feel less manipulated by others' need for you to be tough or to "kick ass." When you rely on your feminine strength and stamina, you can be very powerful and caring at the same time.

We live in a high-tech, throw-away society that values image over substance. The fledgling men's movement is starting to question whether the sacrifices of self-abandonment are worth the rewards of material gain. Women who have been "doing it all" talk about burnout, the pain of self-neglect, and what they've missed with their children and other loved ones. It's unreal to think that a back-to-nature movement is the answer. But we do need to come up with some next steps that balance the wonders of our technological gains with our simple basic need for connection with others and the universe.

At least part of the answer is in learning to treasure our ordinariness, to value our human qualities—including the desire for personal connections—and to give voice to the feminine side of life. We don't have to be "special" or masculine to be worthwhile. We need to listen to our personal experience and inner truth and consider it important. And we need to share that truth with each other and with the men in our lives. This will lead us to challenge the basic structures of our culture that talk about valuing the family but finance just about everything else before getting to childcare, parental leave, adequate education, or medical care.

Regardless of where you work in your company, school, or agency, you have only as much power as you give yourself. Women have typically used their energy to support and empower others. We don't think of our efforts to accomplish that as powerful. We're accustomed to thinking about "power" as authority or dominance, concepts that don't fit well with women's ways of working. But there is another way of looking at it.

When you say, "I'm concerned about how this decision will affect our employees' childcare arrangements," that is a powerful statement. "We can produce a better quality product if we use teamwork," has clout too, when you can support it with evidence. "Let's get together for an hour and brainstorm solutions to this mess," empowers others and opens the way to creativity. That's power. It isn't power over anyone, or dominance that makes you look big and important. It's, as Jean Baker Miller defines it, "the capacity to produce a change," the power to get work done. That is feminine power at work. It's persistent, nurturing, aggressive, and wholistic.

Defining power in feminine terms gives you a different way to look at how you're valuable at work. It also calls into question what work is worth doing. If every woman in the United States talked about what needs to happen to make this a better place for the next generation, change would occur. If each of us felt that her perceptions and ideas were worth expressing, our voices would be heard. Power isn't about dominance. It's about feeling whole and substantial—free to talk about and act on how we understand ourselves, the world, and what's important.

Time For Yourself

Take time now to meander back through the thirteen dimensions, smoothing here and reshaping there.

Start by rereading the poem, "Power," in the very first section, "Changing Woman Changing Work." It's time to stitch together the pieces you've been working with to complete at least the most recent version of your feminine power coat. Move around in it. Make sure it fits and will provide you with comfort and warmth, even as you keep remodeling it in the future.

This is a good time to rework dimensions you've left unfinished. Spend more time on those that were hard to deal with on first reading. To review what you've learned about these many aspects of yourself and how they relate to each other takes time and energy. *There's no need to hurry.* Take as much time as you need to hear both sides of each dimension and receive as much as you can.

These final exercises will help you to integrate your new learning with what you already know about yourself. By reviewing the material, you make it yours. Over time, as you work consciously with all thirteen dimensions, you can return to any section and refresh. Add your own insights and exercises.

Look for colorful threads that wind through your journal writing—growing self-acceptance, needs for closeness, a willingness to say what you want, the trust that you will get to be you. Pay attention to the darker hues that define your doubt and vulnerability. What recurring themes travel through several dimensions? Highlight them as important information about your self.

Summarize your understanding one dimension at a time. Treat yourself to the luxury of writing about both sides of each dimension in your journal, if you're so inclined. Or you might simply reflect on each without writing, and select a few for concentrated journal attention. Here's a format to organize your review:

- I trust my (*body energy*) to let me know_____.

- I know I've undermined my (*body energy*) when_____.

- My (*body energy*) shadow takes over when _____.

- (*Body energy*) is most helpful to me when _____.

- (*Body energy*) empowers me at work when _____.

After you finish a section, such as Strength and Stamina, it's worth it to go through and summarize the section as well. For example:

- I trust my (*Strength and Stamina*) to let me know _____.

Avoid temptations to rush through the exercises. If you can allow time and space to let this rich mixture steep, you will become aware of some of the work your unconscious has been doing all the time you've been reading.

Whatever your review process, this is a place of beginning, not ending. Reading this book and working through the exercises are steps in your discovery of the uniqueness and beauty of your feminine presence. Only you can make those discoveries, and this is just one window into that wondrous territory. Look for other books. Talk with your friends. Form or participate in a group to delve into and support your feminine power. Because it comes from your inner truth, your feminine power grows as you explore it, and it spreads to others.

For the past several years, I've spent most of my "free" moments reading, collecting, thinking, and feeling about this material. Now that it's time to say goodbye, my feelings have erupted all over the place. I feel like I'm parting with a dear friend. My deep hope is that I've communicated some ideas that spark your connection with your feminine power and all that means. I've imagined you working as a welder, a secretary, a manager, a drug clerk, a nurse, an executive, or a psychotherapist, like me. As I've worked, I've heard the voices of the people I interviewed. I've thought about Shauna, Ellen, Joyce, Marie, Suzanne, Alice, and the others whose stories brighten these pages.

And through it all, I know that my own meanderings and diggings are just that. I've received much more than I can ever express or acknowledge. Thanks for coming along with me. I keep the coda of the Changing Woman chant taped to my computer cabinet next to a list of words I have a hard time spelling and an inspiring quote from Georgia O'Keefe. It's a small card that says:

> In beauty it is done
> in harmony it is written
> in beauty and harmony it shall so be finished
> Changing Woman said it so.

I hope it will keep you company as you continue your journey.

Thirteen Ways to Live Your Feminine Power at Work

1. Regard your **body energy** as a natural resource and care for yourself accordingly. Dress in ways that are comforting to you. Honor your feminine cycles. Breathe, ground, center, and relax.

2. A journey of a thousand miles begins with one step. Honor and support your **persistence**.

3. Trust your **core strength**. Learn the ways that you are strong and resilient. Develop channels to this inner resource.

4. Listen; take in. Make room for **receptivity**. Allow support and positive energy to enter. Hear your inner voice as she guides you.

5. Honor the **flexibility** with which you go about your daily life. You determine whether you're being flexible or flaky.

6. **Nurture** yourself. Choose when and how much you want to nurture others. Structure your work so that it nurtures you.

7. Assume that your needs for **affinity**—your feelings and values—are valid. Express your concerns about work decisions that affect the quality of human life.

8. Value your **sexuality**. It's yours. Take steps to become comfortable with your sexual feelings. Learn to use your sexual fire as energy at work.

9. Let your **creativity** emerge and unfold. Invite its presence. Don't panic when it hides in the back alleys.

10. Heed the fire of your **aggression**. Listen to its roar before you douse it.

11. Open your inner channels to **intuition** as your guide.

12. Appreciate your capacity for **wholistic thinking**. Enjoy your world view and share it with others.

13. Remember that you're enough. Your **wisdom and spirituality** go to work with you and touch those around you.

Notes

CHANGING WOMAN CHANGING WORK

1. Rianne Eisler, *The Chalice and the Blade: Our History, Our Future* (New York: Harper and Row, 1987).

2. Gerald Hausman, *Meditations with the Navajo*, (Santa Fe: Bear and Company, 1987), p. 13.

3. Cornelia Schulz, Personal interview, Nevada City, CA, June 24, 1988.

4. Carol Gilligan, *In a Different Voice: Psychological Theory and Women's Development* (Cambridge, MA: Harvard University Press, 1982), p. 62.

5. Letty Cottin Pogrebin, "*Ms.* Family Album," *Ms.*, Sept. 1992, p. 48.

6. J. Ruth Gendler, *The Book of Qualities* (San Francisco: HarperCollins, 1988).

7. Susan Faludi, *Backlash: The Undeclared War Against American Women* (New York: Anchor Books, 1991), p. 70.

8. Carl G. Jung, *Collected Works, Volume 7, Two Essays on Analytical Psychology*, Bollingen Series XX (Princeton University Press, 1953), p. 53.

9. Arlie Hochschild, with Anne Machung, *The Second Shift: Working Parents and the Revolution at Home* (New York: Viking, 1989), p. 1.

EARTH—STRENGTH AND STAMINA

1. Anne Campbell, *The Opposite Sex* (Topsfield, MA: Salem House, 1989), p. 190.

2. Hochschild, pp. 3-4.

3. Anne Rudin, Personal interview, Sacramento, CA, May 12, 1991.

4. Susan Griffin, *Woman and Nature: the Roaring Inside Her* (New York: Harper and Row, 1985), p. 219.

BODY ENERGY

1. Nancy Jungerman, personal interview, Davis, CA, July 25, 1988.

2. Lesley Schroeder, M.D., personal interview, Sacramento, CA November 18, 1988.

3. Betty De Shong Meador, "Thesmophoria: A Woman's Fertility Ritual," in *To Be a Woman*, Connie Zweig, ed. (Los Angeles: Jeremy Tarcher, 1990), pp. 173-180.

4. Clarissa Pinkola Estes, *Women Who Run with the Wolves* (New York: Ballantine Books, 1992).

5. Catherine Steiner-Adair, "The Body Politic," in *Making Connections: the Relational Worlds of Adolescent Girls at Emma Willard School*, edited by Carol Gilligan, Nona P. Lyons and Trudy J. Hammer (Cambridge: Harvard University Press, 1990), pp. 162-182.

6. Catherine Steiner-Adair, "Feminine Development and Eating Disorders," workshop, California School of Professional Psychology, Alameda, CA, April 20, 1991.

PERSISTENCE

1. Evelyn Fox Keller, *A Feeling for the Organism: The Life and Work of Barbara McClintock* (New York: W.H. Freeman and Company, 1983).

2. James H. Barker, "Upingarrlainarkta: Always Getting Ready," photography exhibit, Anchorage Museum of History and Art, August 1992.

3. Charles Baroo, Personal interview, New York City, November 19, 1988.

CORE STRENGTH

1. Cathy Luchetti, with Carol Olwell, *Women of the West* (St. George, UT: Antelope Island Press, 1982), page 31.

2. Melissa Lawler, Personal interview, Indianapolis, March 20, 1989.

WATER—THE FLOWING CONNECTION

1. Martina S. Horner, "Toward Understanding the Achievement — Related Conflicts in Women," *The Journal of Social Issues* 28, No. 2, 1972:157-176.

2. Marilyn Loden, *Feminine Leadership, or How to Succeed in Business Without Being One of the Boys* (New York: Times Books, 1985).

3. Joan Konner "Female sensibility starting to influence what's in the media," *Sacramento Bee*, May 18, 1990.

RECEPTIVITY

1. Eleanor Maccoby, "Gender and Relationships: A Developmental Account," *American Psychologist*, April 1990.

FLEXIBILITY

1. Sally Helgesen, *The Female Advantage: Women's Ways of Leadership* (New York: Doubleday/Currency, 1990).

2. Elinore Lenz and Barbara Meyerhoff, *The Feminization of America: How Women's Values are Changing our Public and Private Lives* (Los Angeles: Tarcher, 1985), pp. 34-36.

3. Women's Alliance seminar, *Women's Voices in Troubling Times*, Berkeley, March 1-2, 1991.

NURTURANCE

1. Jean Baker Miller, "Women and Power," in Judith V. Jordan, et al. (eds.), *Women's Growth in Connection: Writings from the Stone Center* (New York: Guilford Press, 1991), page 199.

2. Janet L. Surrey, "Relationship and Empowerment," in Judith V. Jordan et al. (eds.), *Women's Growth in Connections: Writings from the Stone Center* (New York: Guilford Press, 1991), p. 164.

3. Marion Vittitow, personal interview, Seattle, WA, October 1987.

4. Carol Gilligan, Nona P. Lyons, and Trudy J. Hammer, eds., *Making Connections: The Relational Worlds of Adolescent Girls at Emma Willard School* (Cambridge, MA: Harvard University Press, 1990), pp. 10-18.

AFFINITY

1. Marge Piercy, "For Strong Women," *The Moon is Always Female* (New York: Alfred A. Knopf, 1986), p. 57.

2. Janet L. Surrey, "The Self-in-Relation: A Theory of Women's Development," in Judith V. Jordan et al. (eds.), *Women's Growth in Connection: Writings from the Stone Center* (New York: Guilford Press, 1991), p. 59.

FIRE—PASSION AT WORK

1. Joseph Campbell, *Myths to Live By: How We Re-Create Ancient Legends in our Daily Lives to Release Human Potential* (New York: Viking Penguin, 1972), p. 35.

SEXUALITY

1. Sheila Moon, *Changing Woman and Her Sisters* (San Francisco: Guild for Psychological Studies Publishing House, 1984), pp. 92, 93.

2. Moon, p. 102.

CREATIVITY

1. Susan Peterson, *The Living Tradition of Maria Martinez* (Tokyo: Kodansha International, 1977 and 1989).

2. Donald MacKinnon, *In Search of Human Effectiveness: Identifying and Developing Creativity* (Buffalo, NY: Creative Education Foundation, Inc., 1978), p. 61.

3. Michael Dues, Personal conversation with Virginia Kidd, Sacramento, CA, 1989.

4. Barbara Walker, *The Woman's Encyclopedia of Myths and Secrets* (San Francisco: Harper and Row, 1986), p. 488.

5. Catherine A. Martin and Karen L. DeMoss, "The Development of the Woman Child Psychiatry Researcher: A Review," *Journal of the American Academy of Child and Adolescent Psychiatry*, vol. 30, no. 6 (Nov. 1991), pp. 1009-1014.

6. Catherine Busch-Johnston, Personal interview, Nevada City, CA, June 22, 1988.

7. Regina Barreca, T*hey Used to Call Me Snow White . . . But I Drifted: Women's Strategic Use of Humor* (New York: Viking, 1991), pp. 4, 5.

AGGRESSION

1. Catherine Steiner-Adair, "The Body Politic," in Carol Gilligan et al. (eds.), *Making Connections: The Relational World of Adolescent Girls at Emma Willard School* (Cambridge: Harvard University Press, 1990), p. 162-182.

INTUITION

1. Marilyn Loden, *Feminine Leadership, Or How to Succeed in Business without Being One of the Boys* (New York: Times Books 1985), p. 182.

2. Weston Agor, *Intuition In Organizations: Leading and Managing Productively* (Newbury Park, CA: Sage, 1989), pp. 12, 13.

3. Gary Belsky, "Why Women Are Often Smarter than Men about Money," *Money Magazine*, June 1992, pp.76-82.

4. Deena Metzger, "Her Voice, Our Voices," lecture, Women's Alliance Camp, Nevada City, CA, June 1988.

5. Mary Belenky, et al., *Women's Ways of Knowing: The Development of Self, Voice, and Mind* (New York: Basic Books, 1986), p. 69.

6. Anne Campbell, *The Opposite Sex* (Topsfield, MA: Salem House, 1989), p. 224.

7. David Kiersy and Marilyn Bates, *Please Understand Me* (Del Mar, CA: Prometheus Nemesis Book Company, 1978).

WHOLISTIC THINKING

1. Nancy Jungerman, Personal interview, Davis, CA, July 25, 1988.

2. Joanne Irene Gabrynowicz, Phone interview, November 9, 1988, from Grand Forks, ND.

3. Sara Ruddick, *Maternal Thinking: Toward a Politics of Peace* (Boston: Beacon Press, 1989), p. 96.

WISDOM AND SPIRITUALITY

1. Barbara Stevens Sullivan, *Psychotherapy Grounded in the Feminine Principle* (Wilmette, IL: Chiron Publications, 1989), p. 24.

2. Naomi Newman, *Snake Talk: Urgent Messages from the Mother*, Seminar, "Women's Voices in Troubling Times," Women's Alliance, Berkeley, CA, March 2-3, 1991.

3. Sam Keen, *Fire in the Belly: On Being a Man* (New York: Bantam Books, 1991).

Bibliography

Agor, Weston H., ed. *Intuition in Organizations: Leading and Managing Productively.* Newbury Park, CA: Sage, 1989.

Arrien, Angeles. Talk at "Her Voice, Our Voices," Women's Alliance Camp, Nevada City, CA, June 26, 1988.

Astin, Helen S. and Carole Leland. *Women of Influence, Women of Vision: A Cross-Generational Study of Leaders and Social Change.* San Francisco: Jossey-Bass, 1991.

Astrachan, Anthony. *How Men Feel: Their Response to Women's Demands for Equality and Power.* Anchor Press, Doubleday, 1986.

Bagby, Rachel. Campfire comment, "Her Voice, Our Voices," Women's Alliance Camp, Nevada City, CA, June 26, 1988.

Baroo, Chuck. Personal Interview, New York, November 19, 1988.

Barreca, Regina. *They Used to Call Me Snow White . . . But I Drifted: Women's Strategic Use of Humor.* New York: Viking Penguin, 1991.

Belenky, Mary, with Blythe Clinchy, Nancy Goldberger, and Jill Tarule. *Women's Ways of Knowing: The Development of Self, Voice, and Mind.* New York: Basic Books, 1986.

Bennis, Warren. *Why Leaders Can't Lead.* San Francisco: Jossey-Bass, 1989.

Bolen, Jean Shinoda. *Goddesses in Everywoman: A New Psychology of Women.* New York: Harper and Row, 1984.

Bolton, Mary. Personal Interview, Sacramento, CA, July 2, 1991 as well as conversations over fifteen years.

Braunstein, Stephanie Ganic. "Apology," *Poet*, Vol. 1, No. 5.

Broverman, Inge K., et al. "Sex Role Stereotypes: A Current Appraisal." *The Journal of Social Issues* 28, No. 2, 1972: 59-78.

Brownmiller, Susan. *Femininity.* New York: Fawcett Columbine, 1984.

Busch, Catherine. Personal interview, Nevada City, CA, June 22, 1988.

Campbell, Anne. *The Opposite Sex.* Topsfield, MA: Salem House, 1989.

Campbell, Joseph. *Myths to Live By: How We Re-Create Ancient Legends in our Daily Lives to Release Human Potential.* New York: Viking, 1972.

Davis, Karen J. Personal conversations over many years, New York City.

Dillard, Annie. *Pilgrim At Tinker Creek.* New York: Harper and Row, 1974.

Dinnerstein, Dorothy. *The Mermaid and the Minotaur.* New York: Harper, 1976.

Doyle, Michael and David Strauss. *How To Make Meetings Work.* New York: Jove Books, 1976.

Dues, Michael. In personal conversation with Virginia Kidd, Sacramento, CA, 1989.

Eisler, Riane. *The Chalice and the Blade, Our History, Our Future.* New York: Harper and Row, 1987.

Faludi, Susan. *Backlash: The Undeclared War On American Women.* New York: Anchor, 1992.

"Fire, Our Friend and Enemy," *World Book,* Chicago: Field Enterprises Educational Corporation, 1976, Vol. 7, p. 116.

Forbes, Beverly. "Transformational Leadership Model Based on Theory F," publication pending, Seattle, 1990.

Ford, Bonnie L. "Women, Marriage and Divorce in California, 1849-1872," dissertation, Davis, CA: University of California, 1985.

Friedan, Betty. *The Second Stage.* New York: Summit Books, 1981, 1986.

Gabrynowicz, Joanne Irene. Phone interview, Sacramento/Grand Forks, ND, November 9, 1988.

Gendler, J. Ruth. *The Book of Qualities.* San Francisco: HarperCollins, 1988.

Gilligan, Carol. *In a Different Voice: Psychological Theory and Women's Development.* Cambridge: Harvard University Press, 1982.

Gilligan, Carol, Nona P. Lyons and Trudy J. Hammer, eds. *Making Connections: The Relational Worlds of Adolescent Girls at Emma Willard School.* Harvard University Press, 1990.

Goldhor, Harriet Lerner. *The Dance of Anger.* New York: Harper and Row, 1985.

Gray, Barbara. *Collaborating: Finding Common Ground for Multiparty Problems.* San Francisco: Jossey-Bass, 1989.

Griffin, Susan. *Woman and Nature: The Roaring Inside Her.* New York:

Harper and Row, 1978.

Gutek, Barbara A. *Sex and the Workplace: The Impact of Sexual Behavior and Harassment On Women, Men, and Organizations.* San Francisco: Jossey Bass, 1985.

Hancock, Emily. *The Girl Within, Recapture the Childhood Self, The Key to Female Identity.* New York: Dutton, 1989.

Harragan, Betty Lehan. *Games Mother Never Taught You.* New York: Warner Books, 1977.

Hay, Louise. *Love Your Body: A Positive Affirmation Guide for Loving and Appreciating Your Body.* Santa Monica: Hay House, Inc. expanded edition, 1988.

Hays, H. R. *The Dangerous Sex: The Myth of Feminine Evil.* New York: Pocket Books, 1966.

Heider, John. *The Tao of Leadership: Leadership Strategies for a New Age.* Toronto: Bantam New Age, 1985.

Heilbrun, Carolyn G. *Writing a Woman's Life.* New York: W. W. Norton and Company, 1988.

Helgesen, Sally. *The Female Advantage: Women's Ways of Leadership.* New York: Doubleday/Currency, 1990.

Hewlett, Sylvia Ann. *A Lesser Life: The Myth of Women's Liberation in America.* New York: William Morrow and Company, 1986.

Highwater, Jamake. *Kill Hole.* New York: Grove Press, 1992.

Hochschild, Arlie Russell, with Anne Machung. *The Second Shift: Working Parents and the Revolution at Home.* New York: Viking, 1989.

Horner, Matina S. "Toward Understanding the Achievement-Related Conflicts in Women." *The Journal of Social Issues* 28, No. 2, 1972:157-176.

Janeway, Elizabeth. *Powers of the Weak.* New York: Alfred A. Knopf, 980.

Jardine, Alice and Paul Smith, eds. *Men in Feminism.* New York: Methuen, 1987.

Jimenez, Delores. Personal Interview, Sacramento, CA, November 22, 1987.

Johnson, Robert. *Femininity Lost and Regained.* New York: Harper and Row, 1990.

_____. *He: Understanding Masculine Psychology.* New York: Harper and Row, 1974.

_____. *She: Understanding Feminine Psychology.* New York: Harper and Row, 1976.

Jordan, Judith V. et al. *Women's Growth In Connection: Writings From the Stone Center.* New York: Guilford Press, 1991.

Jung, Carl G. *The Practice of Psychotherapy.* (Volume 16 of the Collected Works) Bollingen Series XX. Princeton University Press: 1954, 1966.

_____. *Two Essays on Analytical Psychology,* (Volume 7 of the Collected Works) Bollingen Series XX. Princeton University Press: 1953, 1966.

_____. *The Structure and Dynamics of the Psyche.* (Volume 8 of the Collected Works) Bollingen Series XX. Princeton University Press: 1960.

Jungerman, Nancy. Personal Interview, Davis, CA, July 25, 1988.

Kanter, Rosabeth Moss. *Men and Women of the Corporation.* New York: Basic Books, 1977.

Keller, Evelyn Fox. *A Feeling for the Organism: The Life and Work of Barbara McClintock.* New York: W.H. Freeman and Company, 1983.

Kiersy, David and Marilyn Bates. *Please Understand Me.* Del Mar, CA: Prometheus Nemesis Book Company, 1978.

Krasek, Robert and Tores Theorell. *Healthy Work: Stress Productivity and the Reconstruction of Working Life.* New York: Basic Books, 1990.

LaDuke, Winona. "Indigenous Perspectives on Feminism and the Environment," Women's Alliance Seminar, *Women's Voices in Troubling Times,* Berkeley, CA, March 1-2, 1991.

Lawler, Frank. Personal Interview, Indianapolis, IN, March 19, 1989.

Lawler, Melissa. Personal Interview, Indianapolis, IN, March 20, 1989.

Lenz, Elinore and Barbara Meyerhoff. *The Feminization of America: How Women's Values are Changing our Public and Private Lives.* Los Angeles: Tarcher, 1985.

Lindbergh, Anne Morrow. *Gift from the Sea.* New York: Pantheon, 1955.

Loden, Marilyn. *Feminine Leadership: How to Succeed in Business Without Being One of the Boys.* New York: Times Books, 1985.

Luchetti, Cathy, in collaboration with Carol Olwell. *Women of the West.* St. George, UT: Antelope Island Press, 1982.

Luke, Helen. *Woman: Earth and Spirit, Feminine in Symbol and Myth.* New York: Crossroad, 1984.

Maccoby, Eleanor. "Gender and Relationships, A Developmental Account," *American Psychologist,* April 1990.

MacKinnon, Donald. *In Search of Human Effectiveness: Identifying and Developing Creativity.* Buffalo, NY: Creative Education Foundation, Inc.

1978.

MacLean, Adam. *The Triple Goddess: An Exploration of the Archetypal Feminine*. Grand Rapids, MI: Phanes Press, 1989.

Malloy, John T. *The Woman's Dress for Success Book*. New York: Warner Books, 1977.

May, Rollo. *The Courage to Create*. New York: Bantam Books, 1976.

Meador, Betty De Shong. "Thesmophoria: A Woman's Fertility Ritual," in *To Be a Woman*, Connie Zweig, ed. Los Angeles: Jeremy Tarcher, 1990, pp. 173-180.

Metzger, Deena. Talk at "Her voice, Our Voices," Women's Alliance Camp, Nevada City, CA, June, 1988.

_____. *The Woman Who Slept with Men To Take the War Out of Them* and *Tree*. Berkeley: Wingbow Press, 1983.

Miller, William A. *Your Golden Shadow: Discovering and Fulfilling Your Undeveloped Self*. New York: Harper and Row, 1989.

Moon, Sheila. *Changing Woman and Her Sisters*. San Francisco: Guild for Psychological Studies Publishing House, 1984.

Neugarten, Dail Ann and Jay M. Shafritz, eds. *Sexuality in Organizations: Romantic and Coercive Behaviors at Work*. Oak Park, IL: Moore Publishing Company, Inc., 1980.

Newman, Naomi. *Snake Talk: Urgent Messages From the Mother, Seminar,* "Women's Voices in Troubling Times" Women's Alliance, Berkeley, CA, March 2-3, 1991.

Newsom, Christine. Personal Interview, Nevada City, CA, March 19, 1989.

Owen, Harrison. *Leadership Is*. Potomac, MD: Abbott Publishing, 1990.

Pearson, Caroline. *The Growing Season*. Salt City, UT: Bookcraft, Inc.

Perera, Sylvia Brinton. *Descent to the Goddess: A Way of Initiation for Women*. Toronto: Inner City Books, 1981.

Peterson, Susan. *The Living Tradition of Maria Martinez*. Tokyo: Kodansha International, 1977, 1989.

Piercy, Marge. *The Moon is Always Female*. New York: Alfred A. Knopf, 1986.

Pinkola Estes, Clarissa. *Women Who Run With The Wolves: Myths and Stories of the Wild Woman Archetype*. New York: Ballantine Books, 1992.

Pogrebin, Letty Cottin. "*Ms.* Family Album," Ms., Vol. III, No. 1, Sept. 1992, p. 48.

Rich, Adrienne. *Blood, Bread, and Poetry, Selected Prose, 1979-1985*. New York: W. W. Norton and Company, 1986.

Robbins, Tom. *Even Cowgirls Get the Blues*. New York: Houghton Mifflin, 1976.

Rubin, Theodore Isaac. *The Angry Book*. New York: Macmillan, 1969.

Ruddick, Sara. *Maternal Thinking: Toward a Politics of Peace*. Boston: Beacon Press, 1989.

Rudin, Anne. Personal Interview, Sacramento, CA, May 12, 1991.

Schaff, Anne Wilson. *Women's Reality: An Emerging Female System in a White Male Society*. San Francisco: Harper and Row, 1985.

Schroeder, Lesley, M.D. Personal Interview, Sacramento, CA, November 18, 1988.

Schulz, Cornelia. Personal Interview, Nevada City, CA, June 24, 1988.

Schwartz, Felice. "Management Women and the New Facts of Life," *Harvard Business Review*, January-February 1989, pp. 65-76.

Scott, Mary Hugh. *The Passion of Being Woman: A Love Story From the Past For the Twenty-First Century*. Aspen: MacMurray and Beck Communications, 1991.

Shallcross, Doris J. and Dorothy A. Sisk. *Intuition: An Inner Way of Knowing*. Buffalo, NY: Bearly Limited, 1989.

Starhawk. *Truth or Dare: Encounters with Power, Authority, and Mystery*. New York: Harper and Row, 1987.

Stechert, Kathryn. *On Your Own Terms: A Woman's Guide to Working With Men*. New York: Vintage Books, 1987.

Steinem, Gloria. *Outrageous Acts and Everyday Rebellions*. New York: Holt, Rinehart and Winston, 1983.

Steiner-Adair, Catherine. "The Body Politic," in *Making Connections: the Relational Worlds of Adolescent Girls at Emma Willard School*, edited by Carol Gilligan, Nona P. Lyons and Trudy J. Hammer. Cambridge: Harvard University Press, 1990, pp. 162-182.

Stewart, Felicia, M.D., and Felicia Guest, Gary Stewart, M.D., and Robert Hatcher, M.D. *Understanding Your Body: Every Woman's Guide to Gynecology and Health*. Toronto: Bantam Books, 1987.

Stipek, Deborah and Jacquelyn McCroskey. "Investing in Children, Government and Workplace Policies for Parents," *American Psychologist*, 44:2, February 1989.

Stone, Merlin. *When God Was a Woman*. New York: A Harvest/HBJ Book, 1976.

Suib-Cohen, Sherry. *Tender Power: A Revolutionary Approach to Work and Intimacy*. Addison-Wesley Publishing Company, 1988.

Sullivan, Barbara Stevens. *Psychotherapy Grounded in the Feminine Principle*. Wilmette, Illinois: Chiron Publications, 1989.

Tamson, Ed. Personal Interview, Sacramento, CA, April 1992.

Vaill, Peter B. *Managing as a Performing Art*. San Francisco: Jossey-Bass, 1989.

Vittitow, Marion. Personal Interview, Seattle, WA, October 1987.

Wagner, Jane. *The Search for Signs of Intelligent Life in the Universe*. New York: Harper and Row, 1986.

Walker, Barbara. *The Skeptical Feminist: Discovering the Virgin, Mother and Crone*. New York: Harper and Row, 1987.

_____. *The Woman's Encyclopedia of Myths and Secrets*. New York: Harper and Row, 1983.

Waring, Marilyn. *If Women Counted: A New Feminist Economics*. San Francisco: Harper Colophon, 1988.

"Women Allege Sexist Atmosphere in Offices Constitutes Harassment," *Wall Street Journal*, February 10, 1988.

Woodman, Marion. *The Owl Was A Baker's Daughter: Obesity, Anorexia and the Repressed Feminine*. Toronto: Inner City Books, 1980.

Woodman, Marion, with Kate Dawson, Mary Hamilton, and Rita Greer Allen. *Leaving My Father's House: A Journey to Conscious Femininity*. Boston: Shambhala, 1992.

Yudkin, Marcia. Personal Interview, Taos, NM, July 1992.

Zweig, Connie, ed. *To Be a Woman: The Birth of the Conscious Feminine*. Los Angeles: Tarcher, 1990.

Index

Order Form

(For credit card orders, please call 1-800-233-3792)

Quantity

Changing Woman, Changing Work
by Nina Boyd Krebs, Ed.D.,
ISBN 1-878448-56-0

_____ Hardcover ($22.95 x number of copies) $ _____

For Men Only: How to love a woman without losing our mind
by Joseph Angelo, ISBN 1-878448-53-6

_____ Paperback ($9.95 x number of copies) $ _____

Some Mid-night Thoughts
by Mary Hugh Scott, ISBN 1-878448-52-8

_____ Paperback ($12.95 x number of copies) $ _____

The Passion of Being Woman
by Mary Hugh Scott,

_____ Hardcover ($19.95 x no. of copies), $ _____
1-878448-50-1

_____ Paperback ($12.95 x no. of copies), $ _____
1-878448-51-X

Subtotal $ _____

Shipping ($3.00 for 1st book, $1.00 for $ _____
each additional book to same address)

Colorado residents add 3.3% sales tax $ _____

Total $ _____

Name _____

Address _____

City, State, ZIP _____

Phone_____ (for order clarification only)

Make checks out to MacMurray and Beck and send to:
PO Box 4257, Aspen, CO 81612.